PSYCHOLOGICAL PERSPECTIVES ON THE SELF

Volume 3

PSYCHOLOGICAL PERSPECTIVES ON THE SELF

Volume 3

Edited by
Jerry Suls
*State University of New York
at Albany*

Anthony G. Greenwald
Ohio State University

LEA LAWRENCE ERLBAUM ASSOCIATES, PUBLISHERS
1986   Hillsdale, New Jersey   London

Lawrence Erlbaum Associates, Inc., Publishers
365 Broadway
Hillsdale, New Jersey 07642

Library of Congress Cataloging-in-Publication Data
(Revised for volume 3)
Main entry under title:

Psychological perspectives on the self.

Includes bibliographies and indexes.
1. Self.   2. Self—Social aspects. I. Suls, Jerry M. [DNLM: 1. Self-concept.   2. Ego.
BF697 P974]
BF697.P76   155.2   81-15108
ISBN 0-89859-197-X (v. 1)
ISBN 0-89859-703-X (v. 3)

Printed in the United States of America
10   9   8   7   6   5   4   3   2   1

Contents

List of Contributors

Roy F. Baumeister, *Case Western Reserve University*

Robert Epstein, *University of Massachusetts at Amherst*

Gordon G. Gallup, Jr., *State University of New York at Albany*

Susan Harter, *University of Denver*

Jon Koerner, *University of Minnesota*

Michael Lewis, *University of Medicine and Dentistry of New Jersey, Rutgers Medical School*

John P. Muller, *Austen Riggs Center*

Morris Rosenberg, *University of Maryland*

Susan D. Suarez, *State University of New York at Albany*

Dianne M. Tice, *Case Western Reserve University*

Preface

The study of the self by psychologists dates from the beginnings of psychology as a distinct discipline, but in the last decade questions about the self-concept, self-esteem and self-evaluation have received increased scrutiny. This volume, and its predecessors, present some of the most important efforts undertaken by psychologists on this subject. Volume 1 concentrated on conceptual and empirical work of social psychologists. Volume 2 extended the scope to include the perspective of researchers in personality. This volume emphasizes developmental perspectives from infancy through adolescence. Hence, the spotlight in Volume 3 is on questions of how the self develops.

The book is divided into two major sections. Part I concerns self-recognition and self-awareness, an area of theory and research active for more than a decade. Although self-awareness is considered by many to be the defining human characteristic, is it so? How does one determine that animals are capable or incapable of self-awareness? One contention is that if an organism can recognize itself in a mirror, rather than reacting to the reflected image as if it were a stranger, then the animal is capable of self-awareness. In a series of studies, Gordon Gallup showed that two species of primates are capable of recognizing their mirror images. All other species fail to recognize themselves, regardless of how long they are exposed to their own images. In the first year of life, humans are also unable to recognize their own reflections, but by 15-18 months, they do recognize themselves. It therefore appears that self-awareness is a developmental phenomenon that is restricted to homo sapiens and two species of great apes (chimpanzees and orangutans).

In chapter 1, Gallup and Susan Suarez review their work on mirror recognition in primates and its implications for the development of self-awareness.

Not all psychologists agree that mirror self-recognition is a test of self-awareness. Behaviorists B. F. Skinner and Robert Epstein have contended that self-awareness is an epiphenomenon; what appears to be self-awareness is merely a byproduct of environmental contingencies. In chapter 2, Epstein and Jon Koerner review their recent Columban (pigeon) simulations, which seek to provide an alternative interpretation of the findings of Gallup and others on self-recognition.

Michael Lewis and his colleague, Janet Brooks-Gunn, have had an active program of research on the developmental course of self-recognition in human infants. In chapter 3, Lewis describes this research program, discusses its implications for the existential (process) self and phenomenal (content) self, and considers the extent of individual differences. Lewis has some especially intriguing findings about how early social deprivation may actually accelerate self-awareness.

In the final chapter (4) of Part I, John Muller writes about the Lacanian perspective on the self. Jacques Lacan, the French psychoanalyst, is an important figure in psychiatry in Europe and has a growing influence among American psychiatrists. Discussion of Lacan in the present context is entirely appropriate because of the prominent role the mirror and self-consciousness plays in Lacan's theory of self (or ego). Muller presents an outline of Lacan's theory, discusses the role of self-consciousness in modern psychoanalytic theory, and notes those points where Lacanian theory converges and diverges from contemporary psychological research and theory.

Part II of this volume is concerned with self-development from middle childhood to late adolescence. In the first chapter (5) of this section, Morris Rosenberg reviews his and others' research on the development of global self-esteem from middle childhood through adolescence. Rosenberg is one of the pioneers of study of adolescent self-esteem and his discussion charts the findings of two decades of empirical work. One of the major themes in the chapter concerns how children shift from thinking of themselves in external terms to increasing reliance upon internal representations. Another important theme concerns the vicissitudes of self-esteem as a function of age and gender.

In chapter 6, Susan Harter considers whether self-esteem should be considered as a single score or as a set of domain-specific judgments. Her research assesses the relative contributions of self-appraisal versus the appraisal of significant others on self-esteem of children. She also discusses the self-concept in special groups of children such as the mentally retarded and the learning disabled. Finally, Harter raises questions about the function of a global sense of self-worth for motivation, affect, and behavior. This wide-ranging chapter introduces some recent empirical data to address a variety of classic questions about the self.

Chapter 7 takes a socio-cultural perspective to the adolescent period. Adolescence is commonly viewed as that period of development when the individual undergoes a crisis in the process of developing a strong sense of identity. Roy Baumeister and Dianne Tice argue, however, that adolescence is not a universal phase of "storm and stress"; in other societies and in past centuries, the teens were not distinguished from adulthood. Moreover, concern with one's identity is not a universal preoccupation. In chapter 7, Baumeister and Tice discuss social and literary evidence for the contention that adolescence is a relatively recent cultural construction. In the latter part of the chapter, they consider the implications for current study of the self.

This volume is not intended as a comprehensive survey of recent work on the development of the self. Rather, it is a representative collection of state-of-the-art thinking on the development of self-awareness and self-esteem. As such, the present contributions complement and supplement the efforts presented in the preceding volumes.

The editors extend their thanks and appreciation to Larry Erlbaum and Jack Burton for their support of this project.

Jerry Suls
Anthony Greenwald

SELF-AWARENESS AND MIRROR RECOGNITION

1 Self-Awareness and the Emergence of Mind in Humans and Other Primates

Gordon G. Gallup, Jr. and Susan D. Suarez
State University of New York at Albany

Self-awareness, as defined by the capacity to become the object of one's own attention (Gallup, in press), has been the subject of increased interest in recent years. Particularly as applied to nonhumans, there are many diverse points of view. For instance, Griffin (1981) claims that self-awareness is a widespread phenomenon shared by many if not most species. Echoing Griffin's rather diffuse and intuitive approach, Solomon (1982) has recently gone so far as to claim that even barnacles are self-aware. At the opposite extreme, others argue that self-awareness is simply not amenable to objective analysis in animals (e.g., Dawkins, 1981), and, not surprisingly, there are those who hold that humans are unique in their capacity for self-conception (Buss, 1973; Kinget, 1975). Some philosophers maintain that self-awareness is a logical impossibility (e.g., Ryle, 1970), and there are still psychologists who feel that self-awareness does not exist and that instances of what might appear to be self-aware behavior are a mere byproduct of environmental contingencies (Epstein, Lanza, & Skinner, 1981).

In this chapter we show that self-awareness does exist, that it can be objectively studied in animals, and that rather than being widespread, the number of self-aware species may be very limited. We also attempt to detail the cognitive consequences of self-awareness and examine the emergence of this capacity in children.

MIRRORED INFORMATION ABOUT THE SELF

The ability to decipher mirrored information about the self can be used as an objective means of inferring self-awareness. In front of a mirror any visu-

3

ally capable animal is, in principle, an audience to its own behavior and an object of its own attention. Mirrors enable organisms to see themselves as they are seen by others. However, unlike humans, most animals react to themselves in mirrors as if they were seeing other animals and even after periods of extended exposure they persist in showing social behavior directed toward the image. Because of their inability to recognize their own reflection, most species seem to lack a cognitive category for processing mirrored information about themselves, and the nature of this deficit may be related to the absence of a sufficiently well integrated concept of self (Gallup, 1977). One of the unique features of mirrors is that the observer's identity and reflection in a mirror are one and the same. Thus, the ability to infer correctly the identity of the reflection requires an identity on the part of the organism making that inference. If you do not know who you are, how can you possibly know who it is you are seeing when confronted with your own reflection in a mirror?

Although the logic of this approach seems straightforward, others have argued that simply because organisms cannot recognize themselves in mirrors does not mean they are incapable of self-awareness (e.g., Eglash & Snowdon, 1982; Fox, 1982; Ristau, 1983). In this chapter we describe a means of cross-validating instances of self-recognition based on a species' ability to use its experience to infer the experience of others. But first we need to examine the means by which one can conduct a compelling and unobtrusive test of self-recognition.

SELF-RECOGNITION IN NONHUMAN PRIMATES

In the initial experiment designed to assess whether animals might be capable of recognizing themselves in mirrors (Gallup, 1970), a number of preadolescent chimpanzees were given individual exposure to themselves in a full-length mirror for a period of 10 days. Their first reaction to the reflection was to act as if they were seeing another chimpanzee (e.g., bobbing, threatening, vocalizing). After a few days, however, rather than persist in responding to the mirror as such, they began to use it to respond to themselves. That is, they used the mirror to gain visual access to parts of their bodies they had not seen before and began experimenting with the image (e.g., making faces, inspecting the inside of the mouth, looking at their anal-genital regions, etc.).

To demonstrate that the chimpanzees had succeeded in resolving the dualism that is otherwise implicit in mirrors and had correctly inferred the identity of the image, the following test was conducted. After the last day of mirror exposure, each animal was anesthetized and removed from its cage. While it was unconscious, a bright red, odorless, nonirritating, alcohol-soluble dye was carefully applied to the upper half of an eyebrow ridge and the top half of the opposite ear. The subject was then returned to its cage and allowed to recover in the absence of the mirror. The rationale for this procedure is based on the following considerations: Because the red marks were applied while the animals were under deep anesthesia, they would have no information about the application procedure. Second, the dye was selected because it was free from any residual tactile or olfactory cues. And, finally, the marks were strategically placed at predetermined points on facial features that could not be seen without a mirror.

Once the animals had fully recovered, the mirror was replaced as a test of self-recognition. Upon seeing themselves with red marks on their faces, they all proceeded to touch and inspect the marks while watching the reflection. Several comparable chimpanzees without prior mirror experience were also anesthetized and marked. However, when they saw themselves in the mirror, the dye was completely ignored and they acted as if they had been confronted with another chimpanzee.

These findings have been replicated with chimpanzees a number of times (e.g., Calhoun, 1983; Gallup, McClure, Hill, & Bundy, 1971; Hill, Bundy, Gallup, & McClure, 1970; Lethmate & Dücker, 1973; Suarez & Gallup, 1981). Orangutans also show signs of self-recognition after a few days of mirror exposure and can use mirrors to locate marks on the face (Lethmate & Dücker, 1973; Suarez & Gallup, 1981). However, with the exception of chimpanzees and orangutans, all other nonhuman primates have failed to show compelling evidence of self-recognition. As many as 20 other species, including gorillas, have been tested, but none have shown any indication that they realize that their behavior is the source of the behavior depicted in the mirror (see reviews by Anderson, 1984a; Gallup, in press). In several instances monkeys have been given extended exposure to mirrors, but to no avail. For instance, we have a pair of rhesus monkeys that have been housed together in our laboratory in front of a mirror since 1978, and even now they occasionally threaten their own image. In stark contrast, chimpanzees and orangutans often begin to exhibit self-directed patterns of mirror-mediated behavior after as few as 2 or 3 days (Gallup, 1970; Suarez & Gallup, 1981). Moreover, once chimpanzees have learned to decipher mirrored information about themselves, the effect is surprisingly durable. Calhoun (1983) recently reported that following an initial test, chimpanzees still recognize their own reflections after as long as 1 year without any intervening mirror experience.

The Mark Test

There are some logical flaws inherent in several recent attempts to show self-recognition in such diverse species as pygmy marmosets, pigeons, and dogs (e.g., Eglash & Snowdon, 1982; Epstein, Lanza, & Skinner, 1981; Fox, 1982), and it is important to emphasize that the mark test serves only as a means of confirming impressions based on seeing animals use mirrors to spontaneously inspect and manipulate themselves. For instance, within several days, chimpanzees begin to use mirrors to investigate the inside of their mouths, anal-genital areas, top of the head, back, bottom of the feet, and so on. They also can be seen to use the mirror to "experiment" with unique facial gestures and body postures. In the absence of explicit training (a point to which we return later), no one has ever reported a reliable instance of mirror-mediated, mark-directed behavior prior to the emergence of such self-directed responding.

In their zeal to show that cognitive processes can be subsumed by more parsimonious analyses, some investigators have apparently misconstrued the rationale for or the significance of the mark test as a means of inferring self-awareness. For instance, Epstein et al. (1981) produced, in pigeons, the behavior of pecking at a blue dot on themselves that was visible only in a mirror. In one sense, the demonstration by Epstein et al. merely testifies to the fact that reinforcement works. They have no evidence that pigeons can recognize themselves in mirrors (see subsequent section). The mark test is a compelling means of validating impressions that arise out of seeing animals make a variety of unprompted, self-directed responses to mirrors. But if an organism shows mark-directed behavior in the absence of other collateral instances of self-directed responding to mirrored information about itself, the results are simply uninterpretable.

THE COLUMBAN SIMULATIONS

As exemplified by the work of Epstein et al. (1981), many operant psychologists feel that cognitive concepts are unnecessary and may even obscure the search for controlling variables. But the converse may be true. Operant psychology, if it prevails, could obscure the search for cognitive phenomena! In an explicit attempt to model different results in other species which are often attributed to cognitive processes, Epstein and his co-workers have developed with pigeons a number of operant analogues known as the *Columban simulations.* The essence of this approach is to produce in pigeons behavior that resembles the criterion (e.g., language), and then argue that reinforcement provides a plausible account of the analogous phenomenon.

As applied to self-recognition, Epstein, Lanza, and Skinner (1981) produced, in pigeons, a behavior that they describe as "using a mirror to locate an object on its body which it cannot see directly" (p. 696). The procedures involved three mirror-naive pigeons that were given 10 days of training of up to 2 hours per day. As depicted in Table 1.1, training consisted of four phases. In the first phase, using food reinforcement, they taught pigeons, which were maintained at 80% body weight, to peck directly at blue stick-on dots

TABLE 1.1
Paradigm Used by Epstein et al. (1981)

TRAINING	
Phase 1	Birds were initially shaped to peck at blue dots positioned on different parts of the body.
Phase 2	With the mirror exposed birds were taught to peck at blue spots on the wall of the test chamber.
Phase 3	Dots were presented briefly and birds were reinforced for pecking at the spot on the wall where the dot had been.
Phase 4	Dots were flashed only when they could be seen in the mirror and birds were rewarded for turning and pecking where the dot had been.
TESTING	
	Birds were fitted with bibs and a blue dot was placed on the breast so that if the bird lowered its head the bib would cover the dot. With reward no longer available, they recorded the number of times the bird would lower its head in front of the mirror and peck at the position on the bib that corresponded to the dot.

positioned on different parts of their bodies. Next, with the mirror exposed, birds were conditioned to peck at blue dots on the wall of the test chamber. In the third phase, blue dots were projected briefly and the pigeons were reinforced for pecking the spot on the wall where the dots had been. Finally, dots were flashed only when the pigeons could see them in a mirror, and birds were reinforced for turning and pecking the place where the dot had been.

On the test trial, pigeons were fitted with bibs and a blue dot was placed on the breast, so that if a bird lowered its head the bib would cover the dot. When placed in front of a mirror, the number of "dot directed responses" (p. 696) was scored by judges from videotapes.

Aside from possible problems of evidence (as indicated by one report of a failure to replicate the Epstein et al. study — Gelhard, Wohlman, & Thompson, 1982), the training procedure contains some potentially serious methodological problems. First, inasmuch as none of the pigeons ever received mirror exposure prior to training, there must have been considerable social behavior occurring in the test chamber throughout training and testing, as birds are notorious for reacting to themselves in mirrors as if they were seeing other birds (see Gallup, 1968 for a review). It is curious that any mention of such behavior is completely omitted from the Epstein et al. report. It is as if, having picked a criterion response, they ignored all other behavior.

Secondly, because reinforcement was omitted during testing, the test phase was essentially an extinction session. Pigeons reliably show aggressive behaviors under conditions in which food reward is withheld, and, bobbing and pecking being the dependent variables, the situation could have been confounded by extinction-induced aggressive tendencies. Pigeons reliably show aggressive behavior toward mirrors during periods in which food reinforcement is not forthcoming (e.g., Cohen & Looney, 1973; Dove, 1976).

Epstein et al.'s (1981) report indicates that bobbing could be scored along with pecking as a criterion response. It is not clear, however, what bearing such behavior has on the pigeon's ability (or lack thereof) to respond to mirrored information about itself. During training, birds were taught to peck at blue dots, not bob.

In the last analysis, what is obtained from a conditioning regime often represents little more than what was programmed into it. Any time an animal requires extensive training to perform a task, it can be difficult to disentangle the achievements of the subject from those of the people who designed the conditioning procedure (Gallup, 1977). Such tactics, in other words, entail the hazard of cognitive and procedural masking. Having taught a pigeon to peck on itself at blue dots that can be seen only in a mirror, are we to conclude that the pigeon recognizes itself, or that it is simply doing what it has been reinforced for doing and is oblivious to the significance of what it sees in the mirror? For instance, no one has shown that a pigeon is capable of differentiating between its own reflection in a mirror and that of another pigeon.

The central issue posed by an operant analysis of cognitive processes has to do with arguments by analogy based on modeling. Epstein and his colleagues (1981) imply that if the behavior of one species can be modeled by reinforcing a series of successive approximations of what looks like the same routine in another species, then reinforcement will suffice to explain such behavior. But does that mean that the behavior of the former species arose in the same way? Not necessarily. Indeed, if teaching pigeons to peck at blue dots on themselves constitutes a viable analysis of self-recognition, then as a byproduct of such training the pigeons ought to show a variety of other spontaneous instances of mirror-mediated self-referenced behaviors. They do not.

In regard to the logic of this approach, consider the following examples. If I were to teach a pigeon to peck a sequence of keys reading "two plus two equals four," would that provide a plausible account of how humans acquire mathematical skills? If a pigeon were taught to peck the appropriate responses on an answer sheet to the Graduate Record Examination and it achieved a combined verbal and quantitative score of 1500, would that provide a reasonable account of the performance of college students taking this test? Are these hypothetical simulations fundamentally different from what Epstein et al. (1981) did with pigeons and mirrors? Just what does a simulation accomplish?

Plausibility proves nothing. Plausibility is in the eye of the beholder. If the point is to show that reinforcement provides a plausible account of the behavior of chimpanzees in front of mirrors, then why is it that other primates fail to show self-recognition after years of exposure to mirrors? Epstein et al. (1981) argue that the reason humans and chimpanzees show self-recognition in the absence of explicit training is because we are more sensitive to such contingencies. This amounts to a tautology. Differences in sensitivity do not explain the results, they merely describe them. How can reinforcement theory be used to explain the behavior of one species, and at the same time explain away the absence of such behavior in another? In this context operant psychology comes dangerously close to taking on many of the properties of Freudian theory. When it comes to cognitive phenomena, operant psychology often provides little more than a post hoc account of behavior in the absence of any direct evidence.

Species differences in learning ability are matters of degree, not kind. Whereas chimpanzees form learning sets more rapidly than do rhesus monkeys, if the latter are given extended training they can eventually reach the same level of performance (Rumbaugh & McCormack, 1967). Why is it, then, that with extended exposure to mirrors rhesus monkeys never learn to decipher mirrored information about themselves? Contrary to what an operant analysis would predict, species differences in learning ability simply do not predict performance on tests of self-recognition. The performance of gorillas on all traditional tests of learning and problem-solving ability is indistinguishable from that of chimpanzees (see Suarez & Gallup, 1981 for a review), yet gorillas fail to show any evidence that they realize that their behavior is the source of the behavior depicted in a mirror.

In defense of their use of shaping procedures, Epstein et al. (1981) argue that pigeons do not normally respond to marks on themselves in mirrors because they lack the necessary response repertoire. But, instead of teaching pigeons the prerequisite responses and conducting a test of self-recognition using the established form of the mark test, they taught pigeons the criterion response (i.e., pecking at a blue dot on themselves). By analogy, being taught the correct answers to the questions on an IQ test might increase a person's IQ, but it is doubtful that it would improve intellectual ability. The logic of Epsetin et al.'s appeal to response repertoires is further rendered questionable by two additional considerations. The elaborate preening behavior of birds demonstrates a basic capacity for self-referenced behavior that should obviate the need for any shaping. Moreover, monkeys and chimpanzees have widely overlapping response repertoires. What then is it about the monkey response repertoire that is lacking? For an operant analysis of cognitive phenomena to be viable it must provide specific answers to such questions rather than appeal to post hoc generalizations.

Epstein et al. also argue that the failures to find self-recognition in other primates (notably macaques) may be a consequence of their greater activity levels that create "fewer opportunities to come under the control of contingencies governing mirror use" (p. 696). By this criterion, however, gorillas should show clear evidence of self-recognition because, in captivity, they are far less active than chimpanzees. But they do not (see section on gorillas).

It is interesting to note that Savage-Rumbaugh (1984) has recently concluded that the analysis of language initially advocated by Skinner (1957)
provides a compelling account of the language performance of the chimpanzees, Sherman and Austin (e.g., Savage-Rumbaugh, Rumbaugh, & Boysen,
1978). Yet in spite of her pro operant stance, she concludes that the Columban simulation of Sherman and Austin's performance (Epstein, Lanza, &
Skinner, 1980), amounts only to satirical simulation, with little or no bearing
on the question of language. The Columban simulation of self-recognition is
similarly problematic.

CAN MARMOSETS RECOGNIZE THEMSELVES
IN MIRRORS?

The absence of self-recognition in nonhuman primates, other than chimpanzees and orangutans, has not been received by many behavioral scientists
with unbridled enthusiasm. Eglash and Snowdon (1982) typify the resistance
to these findings by claiming that self-recognition is like most other behavioral phenomena in displaying a gradation between animals that have it and
those which do not. They argue that although marmosets may not be capable
of mark-directed behavior on a test of self-recognition, they do show behaviors that represent precursors to self-recognition and claim that pygmy marmosets may have the same capacity for self-recognition as chimpanzees. If
this is true, it is an extraordinary finding and one that will require some radi-
cal rethinking of the previous failures to find self-recognition in other
primates.

Eglash and Snowdon gave 12 pygmy marmosets 4 weeks of exposure to a
mirror. Animals were housed in pairs, and a wooden board the same size as
the mirror was used as a control stimulus. Animals were observed for 20 mins
each day and the data were clustered into three categories: threat responses,
novel responses (e.g., piloerection), and mirror responses (e.g., looking at
the mirror). At the end of this period, eight of the animals were given the opportunity to view other unfamiliar marmosets in adjacent cages that could
only be seen in the mirror.

Data in the threat and mirror response categories showed, not surprisingly,
that marmosets could tell the difference between the mirror and the board.
As noted earlier, many species react to mirrors as though they were seeing
other animals (Gallup, 1968). But Eglash and Snowdon (1982) argue that
their results show that marmosets display some aspects of self-recognition
for the following reasons: Threat responses to the mirror extinguished after
the first day; several marmosets were observed to play peek-a-boo with the
mirror; and animals differentiated between the reflections of strange conspecifics and their own reflections. Eglash and Snowdon (1982) admit that by

the criterion of grooming an otherwise unseen spot, pygmy marmosets fail the test of self-recognition. Undaunted in their commitment to salvage the conceptual integrity of monkeys, they explain this failure on the grounds that marmosets do not engage in self-grooming behavior, and therefore the mark test is rendered inapplicable.

However, chimpanzees do not actually groom the facial marks when tested for self-recognition. Rather, they use the mirror to locate the marks, touch the marks, attempt to rub off the marks, and occasionally smell or look at their fingers after the marks have been contacted. Certainly marmosets engage in self-touching behavior. To determine whether the mark test is a valid assessment procedure for marmosets, all one would have to do is mark a portion of the animals' body that they could see directly, and note how they respond. If they touched visible marks, then their failure to use mirrored information to locate marks elsewhere on the body would be a telling blow to those who espouse notions of behavioral continuity among primates. The mark test is not the sine qua non of self-recognition as construed by Epstein and others. Rather, it simply represents an objective means of validating impressions arising out of seeing animals use mirrors for various forms of self-inspection. Much like Epstein in the case of pigeons, Eglash and Snowdon (1982) report no evidence of self-directed behavior by marmosets at any point during the entire period of mirror exposure. How can they then cling to the notion that marmosets may have the same capacity for self-recognition as chimpanzees?

Again, reminiscent of the Epstein et al. (1981) report, a careful reading of the Eglash and Snowdon (1982) paper reveals their conceptual preferences. For instance, although they claim that threat behavior directed toward the mirror extinguished after the first day, their results can be interpreted otherwise. In fact, threat responses were relatively high on the first day and dropped to a low rate — between one and two per daily observations thereafter. However, because observations were restricted to 20 mins each day, there was still a fairly high level of threat behavior being directed toward the mirror. The reduction in threat responses to the image after the first day is likely a consequence of the fact that with extended exposure the image becomes more familiar and threat behavior habituates. Contrary to the claims of some (e.g., Fox, 1982), lack of interest in or habituation to a mirror can hardly be used to make an incontrovertible case for self-recognition.

The occasional instance of playing peek-a-boo with the mirror that Eglash and Snowdon (1982) report further suggests an overinterpretation of the actual data. They define peek-a-boo by instances in which marmosets appeared to hide behind an object in front of the mirror and (or?) look around the object at the mirror. The obvious first question is: How often does such behavior occur among conspecifics in the absence of mirrors? Eglash and Snowdon provide no data on this issue. The term *peek-a-boo* also carries connotations that are less than self-evident in the description of such behavior by marmosets. How are we to know that the marmosets were actually hiding behind such objects, let alone playing? But, even, if we grant marmosets the benefit of the doubt, playing peek-a-boo with the reflection does not constitute a rigorous test of self-recognition. Indeed, among humans the game is played with others, not with oneself, suggesting that this may be another instance of treating the reflection as if it were another marmoset and not an image of the self.

Finally, what about the claim that marmosets can use a mirror to locate other marmosets and respond differentially to their own reflections? This can be just an instance of individual recognition, not self-recognition. In all probability, the differential responsiveness is simply a consequence of the fact that after 4 weeks of mirror exposure their own image is no longer unfamiliar and when confronted with the reflection of strangers they respond differentially. In short, there is nothing contained in the Eglash and Snowdon report that cannot be explained in terms that are much more straightforward than an appeal to precursors to self-recognition.

ARE GORILLAS A COGNITIVE EXCEPTION?

To most people the most surprising exception to self-recognition involves gorillas. In addition to chimpanzees and orangutans, which can recognize themselves in mirrors, gorillas are the only other primates classified as great apes. Biochemical and genetic studies (e.g., Yunis & Prakash, 1982) show that all the great apes and humans are closely related. Humans and chimpanzees are the most similar, followed closely by gorillas. Orangutans were the first to diverge from the protohominoid line and are biochemically most different from humans. Yet humans, chimpanzees, and orangutans can recognize their own reflection in mirrors, and gorillas cannot.

Patterson (1978) claims that the gorilla Koko can recognize herself, but as yet she has offered no experimental evidence in support of that assertion. Lethmate (1974, and personal communication, September, 1981) has tested as many as 12 gorillas using the same procedures as have been applied to chimpanzees and orangutans but finds no convincing evidence of mirror-mediated, self-referenced behavior or mark-directed behavior on the test of self-recognition. Ledbetter and Basen (1982) also failed to find self-recognition in a pair of captive gorillas that were given hundreds of hours of mirror exposure extending over several months.

In the only comparative study of self-recognition involving all three species of great apes, we attempted a more rigorous assessment (Suarez & Gallup, 1981). Because it remained a remote possibility that the gorillas' failure to recognize themselves might simply be a consequence of a general lack of interest in themselves and/or lack of motivation to touch and inspect superimposed body marks, we used an accessible marking procedure that included facial marks and marks on the wrist as a control. After recovery from anesthesia all the gorillas showed an avid interest in the marks on their wrists, which they repeatedly touched and inspected, but none of the gorillas used the mirror to respond to comparable marks on the face. As added evidence that gorillas are oblivious to mirrored information about themselves, they failed to show any change in viewing time on the test of self-recognition. Chimpanzees, on the other hand, typically show a dramatic increase in visual attention to the reflection when they see themselves with marks on their faces (e.g., Gallup, 1970; Gallup et al., 1971; Suarez & Gallup, 1981).

In spite of these findings, however, Ristau (1983) has recently concluded that gorillas may still be capable of recognizing themselves, but that motivational deficits and/or motor coordination difficulties may preclude positive results on the mark test. Ristau also argues that although self-recognition is informative, the absence of appropriate behavior on this task is not.

It is important to respond to both of these points in turn. First, the use of visually accessible control marks provides an explicit means of addressing the question of motivational deficits, and the comparative literature shows that on a variety of other motor and problem solving tasks gorillas show performance that is indistinguishable from that of the other great apes (see Suarez & Gallup, 1981). It is important to re-emphasize that the mark test is but one of several ways of inferring self-recognition. Not only do gorillas fail the mark test, but, of equal importance, they have never been observed to engage in mirror-mediated, self-referenced activities even after hundreds of hours of mirror exposure. Furthermore, as is elaborated later, Ristau's (1983) claim concerning the uninterpretability of negative results on the mirror test is unfounded. The inability to recognize oneself in a mirror should be associated with the absence of a variety of subtle, but complex attributional processes (which ought to translate into substantial differences between gorillas and the other great apes in terms of social strategies). As we hope to demonstrate, evidence of an inability to use one's own experience to model the experience of others can be used to cross validate deficits in mirror self-recognition.

In one sense, the gorilla's inability to recognize itself in a mirror is a cause for concern only to the extent that one conceives of evolution as a progressive process. Although we are closely related, humans did not, as many people think, evolve from chimpanzees. We and the rest of the great apes are related by virtue of sharing a common ancestor. When it comes to the study of psychological phenomena there is a very real danger in letting ourselves become intellectually shackled by taxonomic categories that have been developed on the basis of gross morphology (Gallup, 1982). Psychologists are notorious for misconstruing evolutionary relations (e.g., Hodos & Campbell, 1969). Misconceptions of evolution abound among behavioral scientists and are a major impediment to clear thinking about several issues. Evolution does not occur by design but is a byproduct of selection, and the raw materials for such selection are genetic accidents called mutations. Life represents little more than a vast array of self-perpetuating accidents. Similarly, recent evidence shows that evolution may not have always occurred in a gradual or continuous fashion (e.g., Eldredge & Gould, 1972; Stanley, 1979). Based on a detailed analysis of the fossil record, there is now evidence that evolutionary changes have often been sporadic and sudden, interspersed by periods of relative equilibrium. Even different species, as defined by nonoverlapping gene pools, represent discontinuous distinctions, and few, if any, contemporary species are ancestral to one another. Therefore, the existence of a few behavioral discontinuities might, in fact, be consistent with rather than at odds with what we now know about the nature of evolutionary change.

It is also important to note that there may be neurological differences between gorillas and the rest of the great apes. LeMay and Geschwind (1975) have found that the gorilla brain is structurally the least lateralized of all great ape brains.

Cognitive Consequences of Self-Awareness

Whereas the concept of self has been the focus of much discussion, debate, and research in such areas as clinical psychology, personality, social psychology, and child development, the importance of self-awareness has been assumed primarily on intuitive grounds. As yet, no one has been able to specify in concrete terms the advantage of being self-aware. In this section we outline a conceptual framework and methodology that demonstrates how self-awareness participates in both intellectual functioning and cognitive development. As implied previously, this framework can also be used as a means of cross validating inferences of self-awareness based on self-recognition.

The essence of the theory (Gallup, 1982, 1983) is that, because self-aware organisms can become the object of their own attention, they are aware of being aware. An organism that is aware of its own experience is in the intellectually unique position of being able to use its experience to model the experience of others. Therefore, knowledge of self provides a means of achieving an inferential knowledge of others. For instance, when we see people in situations that are similar to those we have encountered, we tend to assume that their experience is similar to our own. Although it is probably true that no two people experience the same event in exactly the same way, there is enough commonality among members of the same species in terms of receptor function and neurological structure that there is bound to be some overlap. Therefore, not only can I use my experience to infer your experience with some degree of accuracy, but given a knowledge of my own mental states and their relation to external events I can achieve an intuitive knowledge of yours.

This opens up some extraordinary possibilities. By using my experience as a means of mapping yours, not only can I begin to anticipate what you might do, I might even be able to influence your behavior. Deception is a case in point. By withholding information or providing misinformation in a deliberate attempt to mislead you, to be effective I would have to be able accurately to gauge your probable perception of and reaction to such information. Instances of intentional deception all involve making a variety of attributions and inferences about the experience of others. Humans not only attribute purpose, intent, and various other mental states to one another on a moment-to-moment basis, but there is a tendency to generalize such attributions to other species (e.g., The dog is angry, The cat is hungry, The baby monkey is sad and lonely). Clearly, the tendency to impute a mental state to another organism (be it a member of your own species or not) presupposes a subjective awareness of such states on the part of the individual making those inferences. Anthropomorphism, according to this view, is a byproduct of self-awareness.

As a consequence of their inability to become the object of their own attention, species that lack self-awareness should fail to evidence intentional instances of sympathy, empathy, sorrow, gratitude, grudging, deception, and attribution. The absence of such traits has not been more obvious because of several factors. First, because of our predisposition to anthropomorphize, we tend to assume that such traits are present despite evidence to the contrary. Second, as detailed on several occasions (Gallup, 1982, 1983), most species have been selected during the course of evolution to act as if they were capable of using their experience to infer the experience of others, but in fact such instances can be shown to be devoid of a deliberate or conscious component.

As a case in point, take the behavior of dogs. Because of having been domesticated for thousands of years, dogs have probably been selected to show a variety of human traits. Moreover, as a result of being reared by humans dogs often treat people as they would other dogs and they treat their owners as kin. But in spite of the everyday impressions that may be created, there is no hard evidence that dogs are aware of their own existence or that they can become the object of their own attention.

Consider the following hypothetical example: Imagine being confronted by your dog, which has returned from the woods with his nose full of porcupine quills. You could use a pair of pliers and attempt to extract those quills. But for you or me that would be an excruciating ordeal. It is not that we would experience any pain as a consequence, but it would be difficult to refrain from imagining just how painful that must be for the dog. Because we know what pain is like and can reflect on our own unpleasant experiences, it would be difficult not to empathize with what we assume to be going on as we tear those quills out of the dog's nose and watch his reaction. But, would another dog watching this transaction be similarly affected? It depends. If it was a puppy and the other dog was its mother, I doubt the mother would remain passive. The mothers of most mammalian species have probably been selected during the course of evolution to respond to signs of distress on the part of offspring. But what if the other dog was unrelated to the victim? What if a dog were to watch you extract porcupine quills from the trunk of an elephant? For you or me it would not make much difference whether the victim was a dog, elephant, rabbit, or horse, it still would be a source of mental anguish. But if the witness was a dog, I doubt it would be similarly affected. To the extent that the dog responds at all, it should be proportional to the number of genes shared in common with the victim and as a consequence is a byproduct of evolutionary predispositions, not conscious processes.

A particularly vivid illustration of what it would be like to be unaware of being aware is a phenomenon called *blindsight* (Weiskrantz, Warrington, Sanders, & Marshall, 1974). This is a condition in which destruction of major areas of the visual cortex causes people to think they are blind. It was commonly assumed that they were blind, until Weiskrantz et al. probed the apparent inability to see in several patients with occipital lobe damage. To everyone's surprise, they discovered that, if the patients could be persuaded to guess about the location of objects in visual space, they showed a high degree of accuracy. In fact, such people can even correctly guess the form of objects (e.g., coffee cup vs. book). These patients, therefore, are still capable of processing visual information, but they are not aware of it. In effect they have been rendered mindless in the visual modality. Vision in such instances has been reduced to an unconscious sensation.

As evidence that chimpanzees are aware of being aware and as a consequence can use their experience to infer the experience of others, consider the following examples (for more details see Gallup, 1983): Premack and Woodruff (1978) have shown that chimpanzees are capable of making surprisingly accurate attributions and inferences about mental states in humans. If shown a videotape that depicts a person shivering, the chimpanzee will choose from a sample of different photographs the one that shows the person activating a familiar heater. Similarly, if shown an actor trying to get out of a locked cage, play a familiar phonograph that is not plugged in, or attempting to wash down a floor with a hose that is not attached to the faucet, the chimpanzee will pick photographs that provide correct solutions to each problem. Premack and Woodruff also report that choices are apparently influenced by how the chimpanzee feels about the actor. Rather than identifying correct solutions for a person the chimpanzee did not like, the animal often picked pictures depicting the actor involved in untoward outcomes (e.g., falling over a box).

Menzel (1973, 1975), in an elegant illustration of the cognitive consequences of being self-aware, has shown that chimpanzees can convey complex information to one another about the direction, probable location, and relative desirability of hidden objects that only one has been allowed to see. After brief exposure to this kind of problem in a large outdoor enclosure, the uninformed chimpanzees began to extrapolate the location of hidden food based on the leader's initial movements and would often run ahead in an attempt to get there first. When highly prized items were involved, informed chimpanzees were observed apparently to mislead others by moving initially in directions unrelated to the location of the incentive. In time, the followers reacted by abandoning an extrapolation strategy and reverting to keeping the leader under continuous surveillance.

As a further illustration of the development of sophisticated social strategies derived from the ability to model the experience of others based on your own, de Waal (1982) provides numerous examples among chimpanzees of reciprocal altruism, cheating, grudging, deception, concealment, pretending, reconciliation, and feigning good intentions in order to create an opportunity to retaliate for a prior transgression (which can be displaced in both time and space from the original incident).

Emergence of Mind in Children

Since 1970 many studies have been conducted to determine the age at which human infants recognize themselves in a mirror. The typical procedure involves applying red rouge to the child's nose and observing its reaction when placed in front of a mirror. Approximately 70% of babies aged 18 to 24 months respond by touching their marked noses (Amsterdam, 1972; Johnson, 1982, 1983; Lewis & Brooks-Gunn, 1979; Schulman & Kaplowitz, 1977).

Unfortunately, these studies contain a number of methodological and procedural problems. Inasmuch as the nose is one part of the face that can easily be seen without a mirror, it is unclear why this area has been targeted for marking rather than the forehead, chin, or ear, which cannot be seen without a mirror. Furthermore, most studies do not use a baseline period to determine if the marked nose is touched prior to the introduction of the mirror, nor do any studies provide an additional control mark on a visually accessible body part (such as the hand) to negate the possibility that failure on the mark test may simply be an artifact of lack of interest in touching marked body areas. Not only is rouge applied while the child is awake, it also typically has olfactory and tactile cues that may lead to false positives, unlike the dyes specifically chosen for use in nonhuman primate studies of self-recognition (see Anderson, 1984b; Gallup, 1979 for further criticisms).

In addition, some studies (e.g., Amsterdam, 1972; Bertenthal & Fischer, 1978; Lewis & Brooks-Gunn, 1979) have focused on the use of the child's own name or "me" as evidence of self-recognition when a child sees its reflection. A child held in front of a mirror by its parents and told its name over and over might learn to associate that name with the image, but that would not mean it had learned to recognize itself. Labeling the reflection is merely a measure of associative learning, which itself can be unreliable. For instance, it has been shown that even babies who can recognize themselves use their own names or "me" with the same frequency regardless of whether they see their own or another baby's image on a video monitor (Bigelow, 1981; Johnson, 1983).

The available data show that self-recognition in children is both maturationally and experientially dependent and relies, in part, on the development of other perceptual/motor abilities. Yet, with few exceptions, there have not been many attempts to relate self-recognition to such precursor capacities. The most obvious requirement seems to be the coordination needed to reach up and touch one's nose. Although no studies bearing directly on this issue have been conducted, an alternative method has been devised that suggests that motor coordination may play a role. Lewis and Brooks-Gunn (1979) presented babies with three variations of videotapes. In the first condition, subjects were shown a live presentation of themselves on the video screen (contingent self); the second condition consisted of a tape of the subject made at an earlier time (noncontingent self); the final version involved a tape of another child. All conditions used a probe of a person entering the televised field from behind the image on the screen. Self-recognition was indexed by whether the subject turned around to see the person only in the contingent self-condition. In this procedure, some babies as young as 1 year were able to respond appropriately.

It also seems that children must attain certain levels of perceptual functioning in order to integrate information arising from an image of themselves. Infants attain person permanence (the ability to retain a mental image of another person) by about 12 months (Bell, 1970) and object permanence between 15 and 18 months (see Bower, 1982). Significant positive correlations have been reported between self-recognition and performance on object permanence tasks in infants (Bertenthal & Fischer, 1978; Lewis & Brooks-Gunn, 1979). The ability to make inferences about the cause of an event also appears necessary for self-recognition. When a baby sees its reflection in a mirror, it must infer that, if it is the only person present and the person in the mirror does everything it does, then they must be one and the same. Although no data speak directly to this issue, it is known that by 17 months babies can infer that an unfamiliar name must apply to an unfamilar object (Kagan, 1981).

Although it was originally developed from data on nonhuman primates, the theory expounded in this chapter suggests that children should begin to use their experience to model the experience of others once they evidence self-recognition. To assess this we conducted a review of the literature on morality and prosocial behavior, these being most closely analogous to the types of behavior seen in chimpanzees. Until the last decade, empirical studies of very young children usually concentrated either on sensory and perceptual abilities of those under 1 year of age or on the development of language in children between 1 and 3 (see Kagan, 1981). Although considerable effort had been spent studying the development of moral behavior, prevailing views generally excluded the possibility of moral reasoning in younger children (Piaget, 1965; Kohlberg, 1969). Thus, it is not uncommon to find books devoted to the topic that are almost entirely restricted to studies of verbally capable children with a minimum age of 4 years (e.g., Rosen, 1980; Siegel, 1982).

Most behaviors that can be classified as moral or prosocial (such as empathy, sympathy, altruism, and guilt) are predicated on the ability to put oneself in another's place in the sense of adopting the other's point of view. When one attains a self-concept, one eventually confronts others who have perspectives, thoughts, emotions, and such that differ from one's own. The self-aware child should, therefore, become accomplished in role taking. Contrary to the belief that children can not successfully perform visual role-taking tasks until 7 or 8 years of age (Piaget & Inhelder, 1967), it has been found that 2-year-olds can take into account another person's visual perspective (Fishbein, Lewis, & Keiffer, 1972). Other data indicate that children in their second year can infer another's visual experience based on their own. Novey (1975) gave 15-, 27-, and 36-month-old children either a pair of opaque or clear goggles to play with; on the next day the children watched their mothers put on opaque goggles. In comparison with children who had played with transparent goggles, those in the two older age groups who had experience with the opaque goggles behaved as if their mothers could not see. They tried to remove her goggles, asked mother to remove them, and made fewer gestures to her. However, the 15-month-olds did not differentiate based on their own prior experience with such goggles. In another study (Lempers, Flavell, & Flavell, 1977), 12-month-old babies readily complied with mother's request to show her an object even when her eyes were closed or covered by her hands. In contrast, 24-month-olds indicated their awareness that mother could not see by making attempts first to uncover her eyes. A similar incident has been reported for a chimpanzee. Premack and Premack (1983) described how a young chimpanzee removed a blindfold from her trainer's eyes in order to lead him to a box of food that she could not open herself. As evidence that the chimpanzee was inferring something about the person's visual ability, she attempted to remove the blindfold only if it covered the trainer's eyes; no attempt at removal was made if the cloth was placed over the person's mouth or hair.

By the age of 3, children are also accomplished role takers in terms of cognitive perception, in that they make inferences about what others think, their attitudes, and preferences (Zahn-Waxler, Radke-Yarrow, & Brady-Smith, 1977). For example, if given an array of items to choose from, they can select appropriate gifts for parents and peers and can select correct food items for others based on prior observations of a person's likes and dislikes. Zahn-Waxler et al. (1977) also gave subjects seven pictures portraying a dog chasing a frightened boy and asked them to tell the story. Three pictures were then removed, leaving a friendly dog and a boy playing. When asked to tell the story as someone would who had not seen all of the pictures, the children responded correctly. Thus, it is now well established that by the end of their second year, children can infer the mental states of others (Hoffman, 1982).

Once a child can impute mental states to others, the way is paved for a variety of moralistic and prosocial acts. Although very young children are not amenable to interview techniques, such as those typically used to study these behaviors (e.g., Kohlberg, 1969), investigators highly trained in naturalistic observation have provided interesting data on very young children. Some of the most widely observed behaviors that can be used to support our model are empathy and sympathy, which involve imputing a (usually negative) mental state in another and responding to it with positive affect. Closely coupled with these is prosocial behavior (often referred to as altruism), in which one attempts to aid another in order to alleviate a negative circumstance or affective state. The following cases illustrate these points.

Hoffman (1975) reports an incident in which a 15-month-old boy (A) and his friend (B) were fighting over a toy and B began to cry. A let go of the toy but B still cried. A brought B his own teddy bear, but to no avail. Then A went into B's bedroom and brought out B's security blanket, which succeeded in quieting him. The interpretation is that A reasoned by analogy that B would be comforted by something he was attached to in the same way that A was to his bear. In other words, A was capable of using his experience to model the experience of another.

Borke (1972) reports a similar exchange involving a child in his second year of age. One boy accidentally knocked down another while the two were playing. When the victim began to cry his playmate hugged him, tried to pick him up, and, finally, located the other's bottle and handed it to him, at which time he stopped crying. In another report a 1 ½-year-old girl stroked another (unrelated) baby's hair, offered him cookies, patted him, and then brought her mother over to him to pick him up while he cried (Zahn-Waxler & Radke-Yarrow, 1982).

As an illustration of sympathy, Hoffman (1975) describes the case of a 20-month-old boy who had a friend visiting. The friend started crying when it was time to leave, complaining that her parents were not at home. (Her caretakers explained that the girl's parents were out of town for 2 weeks.) The little boy's immediate reaction was to look sad, and then he offered the girl his teddy bear to take home. His parents reminded him that he would miss it if he gave it away, but he insisted.

After observing scores of such reactions in young children investigators have identified a developmental sequence that involves significant changes in reactions to another's distress from 10 to 24 months of age (see Bales, 1984; Hoffman, 1982; Radke-Yarrow, Zahn-Waxler, & Chapman, 1983; Zahn-Waxler & Radke-Yarrow, 1982; Zahn-Waxler, Radke-Yarrow, & King, 1979). At 10–12 months, in response to someone's being hurt or in distress, the baby typically will stare at the victim, will appear agitated, and may seek comfort itself. At 15 months the baby makes tentative approaches to the victim and attempts to comfort it, but will still cry and be agitated itself. At about 18 months, in what has been termed an "explosion of prosocial behavior" (Bales, 1984, p. 20), children will help, protect, defend, comfort, and console a victim, and give simple advice on ways to set things right. By 2 years of age children are adept at trying alternative interventions when one attempt fails and freely offer verbal sympathy. From the middle to the end of the 2nd year of life they also show evidence of guilt, by trying to make appropriate reparations for their own transgressions against others.

In addition to anticipating others' reactions based on their own past experience for prosocial means, children in their second year can also use this ability to accomplish antisocial ends. Hoffman (1975), in the following account, describes a clear case of intentional deception. A 20-month-old girl asked her older sister if she could play with one of her toys. When the request was denied, the baby immediately walked over to her sister's favorite rocking horse (which no one was allowed to touch), climbed up on it, and began shouting "Nice horsey!" while continually watching her sister. Her sister angrily dashed over to the horse, whereupon the infant ran directly to the toy she originally wanted and snatched it up.

A standard paradigm for gauging social development involves observing an infant's reaction to reunion after a brief separation from the mother. Babies who avoid their mothers, push them away, or appear angry or passive are categorized as "anxiously attached," while those who seek contact and smile when reunited are "securely attached" (Ainsworth, Blehar, Waters, & Wall, 1978). Lewis, Brooks-Gunn, and Jaskir (1983; see also Lewis, this volume) recently examined the relationship between self-recognition and such attachments. Surprisingly, infants who appeared to be insecurely or anxiously attached showed self-recognition earlier than those classified as securely attached. Although these data were opposite to what Lewis et al. had predicted, they are quite compatible with our formulation. Infants who expressed their insecurity by anger or passivity could well have been making attributions about having been abandoned. Thus, rather than showing insecurity, they may have been evidencing grudging. That these babies showed an early ability to recognize themselves follows from the notion that the use of attributions presupposes self-awareness.

It is also interesting to note that by the time children are 3 years old they can make attributions of intentionality and judge a child in a hypothetical story as being naughtier if damage the child caused was intentional rather than accidental (Imamoglu, 1975). Furthermore, infants first show evidence of intentionality at 18–24 months of age, when they can mentally combine means and ends before acting (Frye, 1981). For instance, a toddler who is about to try to hit a peg into a slot with a toy screwdriver may stop in midswing to exchange the tool for a hammer.

Lastly, anthropomorphism, or the attribution of human-like mental states to nonhumans, is believed to occur first at about 18 months of age (Piaget, 1929; Sharefkin & Ruchlis, 1974). Collectively, such marked changes, which correspond almost exactly with the development of self-recognition, provide intriguing evidence in support of the hypothesis that self-awareness opens the door to the development of a variety of sophisticated and complex, intro-spectively based social strategies. In terms of possible neurological corre-lates, it is also interesting to note that there are a number of substantial changes in human neural development between 1 and 2 years of age and that the frontal cortex, in particular, grows more between 15 and 24 months of age than does any other part of the cortex (see Milner, 1967).

Implications for Awareness

If a species fails to behave in ways that suggest it is aware of its own exist-ence, why should we assume it is aware of what it is doing? Either one is aware of being aware or unaware of being aware, and the latter is tantamount to being unconscious. The sleepwalker is sufficiently aware to avoid colliding with obstacles but is unaware of being aware. Blindsight patients are still ca-pable of processing certain kinds of visual information and even responding appropriately, but they are unaware of being aware in the visual modality. The extent to which other species have experiences similar to our own de-pends in large measure on whether they are self-aware.

As evidence that awareness, as you and I know it, presupposes self-awareness, consider *infant amnesia* (e.g., Child, 1940). Prior to about 2 years of age apparently no one has experiences that can be consciously recalled in later life. There are people who claim to remember earlier events, but it usu-ally turns out that they were told about them and come to believe they re-member them. It follows from the thesis of this chapter that the point at which infant amnesia stops corresponds precisely with that period at which children begin to recognize themselves in mirrors.

Prior to the emergence of self-awareness we may all have been uncon-scious.

REFERENCES

Ainsworth, M. D. S., Blehar, M., Waters, E., & Wall, S. (1978). *Patterns of attachment.* Hillsdale, NJ: Lawrence Erlbaum Associates.

Amsterdam, B. (1972). Mirror image reactions before age two. *Developmental Psychobiology, 5,* 297–305.

Anderson, J. R. (1984a). Monkeys with mirrors: Some questions for primate psychology. *International Journal of Primatology, 5,* 81–98.

Anderson, J. R. (1984b). The development of self-recognition: A review. *Developmental Psychobiology, 17,* 35–49.

Bales, J. (1984). Research traces altruism in children. *APA Monitor, 15*(1), 20–22.

Bell, S. M. (1970). The development of the concept of the object as related to infant–mother attachment. *Child Development, 41,* 291–311.

Bertenthal, B. I., & Fisher, K. W. (1978). Development of self-recognition in the infant. *Developmental Psychology, 14,* 44–50.

Bigelow, A. E. (1981). The correspondence between self and image movement as a cue to self-recognition for young children. *Journal of Genetic Psychology, 139,* 11–26.

Borke, H. (1972). Chandler and Greenspan's "Ersatz Egocentrism": A rejoinder. *Developmental Psychology, 7,* 107–109.

Bower, T. G. R. (1982). *Development in infancy* (2nd ed.). San Francisco: Freeman.

Buss, A. (1973). *Psychology — Man in perspective.* New York: Wiley.

Calhoun, S. (1983). *The question of contingent image self recognition in apes and monkeys.* Unpublished doctoral dissertation, Hunter College.

Child, I. L. (1940). The relation between measures of infantile amnesia and of neuroticism. *Journal of Abnormal and Social Psychology, 35,* 453–456.

Cohen, P. S., & Looney, T. A. (1973). Schedule-induced mirror responding in the pigeon. *Journal of the Experimental Analysis of Behavior, 19,* 395–408.

Dawkins, M. S. (1981). General discussion–7th July. In D. G. M. Wood-Gush, M. Dawkins, & R. Ewbank (Eds.), *Self-awareness in domesticated animals.* Hertfordshire, England: The Universities Federation for Animal Welfare.

Dove, D. L. (1976). Relation between level of food deprivation and rate of schedule-induced attack. *Journal of the Experimental Analysis of Behavior, 25,* 63–68.

Eglash, A. R., & Snowdon, C. T. (1982, November). *Mirror-image responses in pygmy marmosets.* Paper presented at the meeting of the Psychonomic Society, Minneapolis, MN.

Eldredge, N., & Gould, S. J. (1972). Punctuated equilibria: An alternative to phyletic gradualism. In J. M. Schopf (Ed.), *Models in paleobiology.* San Francisco, CA: Freeman & Cooper.

Epstein, R., Lanza, R. P., & Skinner, B. F. (1980). Symbolic communication between two pigeons (*Columba livia domestica*). *Science, 207,* 543–545.

Epstein, R., Lanza, R. P., & Skinner, B. F. (1981). "Self-awareness" in the pigeon. *Science, 212,* 695–696.

Fishbein, H. D., Lewis, S., & Keiffer, K. (1972). Children's understanding of spatial relations. *Developmental Psychology, 7,* 21–33.

Fox, M. W. (1982). Are most animals "mindless automatons"?: A reply to Gordon G. Gallup, Jr. *American Journal of Primatology, 3,* 341–343.

Frye, D. (1981). Developmental changes in strategies of social interaction. In M. E. Lamb & L. R. Sherrod (Eds.), *Infant social cognition: Empirical and theoretical considerations.* Hillsdale, NJ: Lawrence Erlbaum Associates.

Gallup, G. G., Jr. (1968). Mirror-image stimulation. *Psychological Bulletin, 70,* 782–793.

Gallup, G. G., Jr. (1970). Chimpanzees: Self-recognition. *Science, 167,* 86–87.

Gallup, G. G., Jr. (1977). Self-recognition in primates: A comparative approach to the bidirectional properties of consciousness. *American Psychologist, 32,* 329–338.

Gallup, G. G., Jr. (1979). Self-recognition in chimpanzees and man: A developmental and comparative perspective. In M. Lewis & L. Rosenblum (Eds.), *Genesis of behavior: Vol. 2. The child and its family.* New York: Plenum.

Gallup, G. G., Jr. (1982). Self-awareness and the emergence of mind in primates. *American Journal of Primatology, 2,* 237–248.

Gallup, G. G., Jr. (1983). Toward a comparative psychology of mind. In R. L. Mellgren (Ed.) *Animal cognition and behavior.* Amsterdam: North Holland Press.

Gallup, G. G., Jr. (in press). Self-awareness in primates: Current status and future prospects. In G. Mitchell (Ed.), *Comparative primate biology: Vol. 2.* New York: Alan R. Liss.

Gallup, G. G., Jr., McClure, M. K., Hill, S. D., & Bundy, R. A. (1971). Capacity for self-recognition in differentially reared chimpanzees. *The Psychological Record, 21,* 69–74.

Gelhard, B., Wohlman, S., & Thompson, R. K. R. (1982). *Self-awareness in pigeons: A second look.* Paper presented at the Northeastern Regional Meeting of the Animal Behavior Society, Boston, MA.

Griffin, D. R. (1981). *The question of animal awareness* (rev. ed.) Los Altos, CA: William Kaufmann.

Hill, S. D., Bundy, R. A., Gallup, G. G., Jr., & McClure, M. K. (1970). Responsiveness of young nursery reared chimpanzees to mirrors. *Proceedings of the Louisiana Academy of Sciences, 33,* 77–82.

Hodos, W., & Campbell, C. B. G. (1969). *Scala naturae:* Why there is no theory in comparative psychology. *Psychological Review, 76,* 337–350.

Hoffman, M. L. (1975). Developmental synthesis of affect and cognition and its implications for altruistic motivation. *Developmental Psychology, 11,* 607–622.

Hoffman, M. L. (1982). Development of prosocial motivation: Empathy and guilt. In N. Eisenberg (Ed.), *The development of prosocial behavior.* New York: Academic Press.

Imamoglu, E. O. (1975). Children's awareness and usage of intention cues. *Child Development, 46,* 39–45.

Johnson, D. B. (1982). Altruistic behavior and the development of the self in infants. *Merrill-Palmer Quarterly, 28,* 379–388.

Johnson, D. B. (1983). Self-recognition in infants. *Infant Behavior and Development, 6,* 211–222.

Kagan, J. (1981). *The second year.* Cambridge, MA: Harvard University Press.

Kinget, G. M. (1975). *On being human.* New York: Harcourt Brace Jovanovich.

Kohlberg, L. (1969). Stage and sequence: The cognitive-developmental approach to socialization. In D. A. Goslin (Ed.), *Handbook of socialization theory and research.* New York: Rand McNally.

Ledbetter, D. H., & Basen, J. A. (1982). Failure to demonstrate self-recognition in gorillas. *American Journal of Primatology, 2,* 307–310.

LeMay, M., & Geschwind, N. (1975). Hemispheric differences in the brains of great apes. *Brain Behavior and Evolution, 11,* 48–52.

Lempers, J. D., Flavell, E. R., & Flavell, J. H. (1977). The development in very young children of tacit knowledge concerning visual perception. *Genetic Psychology Monographs, 95,* 3–53.

Lethmate, J. (1974). Selbst-kenntis bei menschenaffen. *Umschau, 15,* 486–487.

Lethmate, J., & Dücker, G. (1973). Untersuchungen zum selbsterkennen im spiegel bei orangutans und einigen anderen affenarten. *Zietschrift für Tierpsychologie, 33,* 248–269.

Lewis, M., & Brooks-Gunn, J. (1979). *Social cognition and the acquisition of self.* New York: Plenum.

Lewis, M., Brooks-Gunn, J., & Jaskir, J. (1983). *Individual differences in visual self-recognition.* Unpublished manuscript, Rutgers University, New Brunswick, NJ.

Menzel, E. W., Jr. (1973). Chimpanzee spatial memory organization. *Science, 182,* 943–945.
Menzel, E. W., Jr. (1975). Natural language of young chimpanzees. *New Scientist,* 127–130.
Milner, E. (1967). *Human neural and behavioral development.* Springfield, IL: Charles C. Thomas.
Novey, M. S. (1975). *The development of knowledge of others' ability to see.* Unpublished doctoral dissertation, Harvard University.
Patterson, F. (1978). Conversations with a gorilla. *National Geographic Magazine, 154,* 438–465.
Piaget, J. (1929). *The child's conception of the world.* London: Routledge & Kegan Paul.
Piaget, J. (1965). *The moral judgment of the child,* (rev. ed.) Glencoe, IL: Free Press. (Original work published 1932).
Piaget, J., & Inhelder, B. (1967). *The child's conception of space* (J. F. Langden & J. L. Lunzer, Trans.). New York: Norton.
Premack, D., & Premack, A. J. (1983). *The mind of an ape.* New York: W. W. Norton.
Premack, D., & Woodruff, G. (1978). Does the chimpanzee have a theory of mind? *The Behavioral and Brain Sciences, 4,* 515–526.
Radke-Yarrow, M., Zahn-Waxler, C., & Chapman, M. (1983). Children's prosocial dispositions and behavior. In H. M. Hetherington (Ed.), *Handbook of child psychology: Vol. 4. Socialization, personality, social development.* New York: Wiley.
Ristau, C. A. (1983). Symbols and indication in apes and other species? Comment on Savage-Rumbaugh et al. *Journal of Experimental Psychology: General, 112,* 498–507.
Rosen, H. (1980). *The development of sociomoral knowledge.* New York: Columbia University Press.
Rumbaugh, D. M., & McCormack, C. (1967). The learning skills of primates: A comparative study of apes and monkeys. In D. Stark, R. Schneider, & H. J. Kuhn (Eds.), *Progress in primatology.* Stuttgart: Fischer.
Ryle, G. (1970). Self-knowledge. In H. Morick (Ed.), *Introduction to the philosophy of mind.* Glenview, IL: Scott & Foresman.
Savage-Rumbaugh, E. S. (1984). Verbal behavior at a procedural level in the chimpanzee. *Journal of the Experimental Analysis of Behavior, 41,* 223–250.
Savage-Rumbaugh, E. S., Rumbaugh, D. M., & Boysen, S. (1978). Symbolic communication between two chimpanzees (*Pan troglodytes*). *Science, 201,* 641–644.
Schulman, A. H., & Kaplowitz, C. (1977). Mirror-image response during the first two years of life. *Developmental Psychobiology, 10,* 133–142.
Sharefkin, B. D., & Ruchlis, H. (1974). Anthropomorphism in the lower grades. *Science and Children, 11,* 37–40.
Siegel, M. (1982). *Fairness in children: A social–cognitive approach to the study of moral development.* New York: Academic Press.
Skinner, B. F. (1957). *Verbal behavior.* New York: Appleton-Century-Crofts.
Solomon, R. C. (1982). *Animal minds, animal selves, animal rights.* Paper presented at a symposium sponsored by The Institute for the Study of Animal Problems, Danvers, MA.
Stanley, S. M. (1979). *Macroevolution: Patterns and process.* San Francisco: W. H. Freeman.
Suarez, S. D., & Gallup, G. G., Jr. (1981). Self-recognition in chimpanzees and orangutans, but not gorillas. *Journal of Human Evolution, 10,* 175–188.
de Waal, F. B. M. (1982). *Chimpanzee politics.* London: Jonathan Cape.
Weiskrantz, L., Warrington, E. K., Sanders, M. D., & Marshall, J. (1974). Visual capacity in the hemianopic field following a restricted occipital ablation. *Brain, 97,* 709–728.
Yunis, J. J., & Prakash, O. (1982). The origin of man: A chromosomal pictorial legacy. *Science, 215,* 1525–1530.
Zahn-Waxler, C., & Radke-Yarrow, M. (1982). The development of altruism: Alternative research strategies. In N. Eisenberg (Ed.), *The development of prosocial behavior.* New York:

Academic Press.

Zahn-Waxler, C., Radke-Yarrow, M., & Brady-Smith, J. (1977). Perspective-taking and prosocial behavior. *Developmental Psychology, 13,* 87–88.

Zahn-Waxler, C., Radke-Yarrow, M., & King, R. A. (1979). Child rearing and children's prosocial initiations toward victims of distress. *Child Development, 50,* 319–330.

2 The Self-Concept and Other Daemons

Robert Epstein
*University of Massachusetts at Amherst and
Cambridge Center for Behavioral Studies*

Jon Koerner
University of Minnesota

> *But wouldst thou bid the daemons fly,*
> *Like mist before the dawning sky.*
>
> —Sir Walter Scott

The concept of a self-concept is part of a legacy. People have always classified, labeled, and explained their behavior. For lack of facts they have often resorted to verbal devices: They have invented inner agents, mental processes, traits, and cognitive structures which — grammatically, anyway — seem to explain things. The self-concept and its close relatives, self-knowledge, and self-awareness, are a subset of the many inventions of this sort which have been handed down to modern psychology.

Phrenologists explained behavior by measuring bumps on the head. In some respects modern psychologists have moved backwards, for the explanatory fictions they promote do not even have physical status. The Devil has given way to short-term memory, associations, the ego, mental images, personality traits, expectations, attitudes, intelligence, semantic networks, schemes and schemas, rule structures, processing units, and mental software. It is no surprise that the promoters claim that the new explanatory fictions are better than the old — but they are fictions nonetheless.

There are alternatives. We are organisms, and the behavior of organisms, both covert and overt, can be studied using not only the methods but the most stringent criteria of explanation employed in the natural sciences. Facts about anatomy, physiology, genes, and ontogenic and phylogenic histories are preferable to verbal inventions. Admittedly, progress has been slow — in part, because of the promotion of explanatory fictions — but there is no reason to believe that even the most complex human behavior cannot someday be accounted for with such facts.

In this chapter we examine a portion of the extensive experimental literature on the self-concept which has proliferated in recent years, and we offer what we hope is a constructive and parsimonious interpretation of major findings. We first offer some general comments on the very concept of a self-concept.

THE SELF-CONCEPT

Reification

The term "self-concept" is often treated as if it refers to a thing, which it does not. Philosophers have called this kind of error "reification" or "hypostatization" or "the substantialization of abstracta." A boy is observed to behave in certain ways — for example, he stares at a photograph of himself longer than at photographs of other children — and from that a psychologist infers that he possesses a "cognitive entity" called the "self-concept." The self or self-concept has been variously referred to as "an *object* to be known" (Wicklund, 1979), "*parts* of the phenomenal field" (Snygg & Combs, 1949), "an *object* of conscious inspection" (Gallup, 1979), "*regions* of our life" (Allport, 1955), and "an interpersonal *entity*" (Cooley, 1902). It has been said to have a "*structure*" and "*components*" (James, 1890) and, *like an embryo,* to "grow" (Lewis & Brooks-Gunn, 1979) (all italics added).

But the referent of "self-concept" is unclear. The referent, if there is one, is certainly less tangible than an arm or a brain; it has neither boundaries nor precise location.

Property as Explanation

In his *Principia,* Newton warned against attributing the slow movement of a liquid to its viscosity. *Viscosity* is a description or property of the movement. We err in using a property of some phenomenon to explain that phenomenon. And yet, in spite of constant reminders from colleagues (e.g., Ebel, 1974), psychologists make this mistake frequently: A chimpanzee is observed to solve a problem in an insightful way. The explanation? The chimpanzee has "insight." A businessman works incessantly and garners many achievements in the corporate world. The explanation? He has a "need for achievement." A girl comes to be able to make accurate predictions about her own behavior. The explanation? She possesses an "accurate self-image." In each case, these so-called explanations are mere descriptions of the behavior observed. One might argue, as does Kagan (1981), that there is a point to such descriptions — that, for example, the "self-concept" can serve as a convenient summary of a great deal of behavior that children normally exhibit by about age 2 — but "convenient summaries," "descriptions," and "properties" don't explain anything.

Causes

Hypothetical constructs such as the self-concept, drives, and traits often obscure the search for more concrete determinants of behavior — for determinants that have physical dimensions, that are manipulable, that allow you to make predictions about or to change behavior. Researchers who appeal to the traditional constructs rarely stray beyond. Some even assert that a more objective analysis is impossible. Gallup (1977b), for example, concludes a paper on the self-concept as follows: "As far as the self-concept is concerned, it would appear that on the morning before God created the great apes [who, according to Gallup, possess self-concepts], maybe he . . . forgot to shave with Occam's razor" (p. 337). But objective accounts are often possible.

The behavior that comes under the rubric of *self* is troublesome because, like language, it is complex, distinctively human, acquired haphazardly over a period of years, and not easily traceable to biological factors or to any obvious instances of conditioning (Epstein, 1986). A wide variety of behavior is said to provide evidence for its existence: pointing to or naming one's picture, body- or mark-directed behavior in front of a mirror, looking at or smiling at one's picture longer than at another person's picture, imitating a videotape of oneself more than a videotape of someone else, and so on (Amsterdam, 1972; Gallup, 1970; Kagan, 1981; Lewis & Brooks-Gunn, 1979).

Presumably, the verbal behavior said to show "self-knowledge," of which Skinner (1945, 1963) has offered accounts, would also apply: describing one's feelings, states of mind, thoughts, aches and pains, actions, and so on.

What all behaviors said to show the existence of a self-concept have in common is that they are controlled in part either by one's own body or one's own behavior. By about age 2, most children respond differently to likenesses of their own faces than to likenesses of other faces. When asked, "Where does it hurt?", they report something about the states of their bodies. When asked, "What are you doing?", they describe their behavior.

Anthropocentrism

Resistance to a factual, scientific analysis of behavior is rooted in part in anthropocentrism. Proponents of human uniqueness have sought to identify psychological or physical qualities, of which the self-concept is but one instance, which set humans apart from the rest of the animal kingdom. But anthropocentrists have suffered numerous setbacks during the past century as, one by one, apparently distinctive human qualities have been observed in other animals. The boundary between humans and non-humans (most notably but not exclusively the great apes) has become increasingly transparent (Beck, 1975; Chiarelli, 1973; Davenport, Rogers, & Russell, 1973; Fouts, 1974; Gardner & Gardner, 1969; King & Wilson, 1975; Mason, 1976; Menzel, 1973; Savage-Rumbaugh, Rumbaugh, & Boysen, 1978; Teleki, 1973; van Lawick-Goodall, 1970, 1971; Wilson & Sarich, 1969; Yeni-Komshian & Benson, 1976; Yunis & Prakash, 1982).

"Bidirectionality" of Consciousness

Always an elusive entity for psychologists, consciousness has been characterized as "bidirectional," in the sense that we both "[have] an experience and [are] aware of having an experience" (Gallup, 1977b). In other words, we can direct our attention outward toward events in the world or inward toward ourselves, or, in still other terms, as we have already noted, behavior comes under the control both of stimuli outside the body *and of the body and behavior of the organism itself.*

To state the matter another way: *We can react not only to the world but to our reaction to the world, since every response is also a stimulus.* To say that an organism is capable of "self-directed consciousness" or "self-awareness" probably means nothing more than that the organism occasionally exhibits behavior that is controlled by its own body or behavior. This may be reductionism, but it also may be true.

Self-awareness has been said to be unique to humans (Ardrey, 1961; Buss, 1973; Kinget, 1975; Lorenz, 1971), and Slobodkin (1977), an evolutionary biologist, has even suggested that it has freed humans from the otherwise deterministic forces of evolution — surely the ultimate in uniqueness among species. The claim that self-directed consciousness is unique has always been limited by the lack of techniques for determining its existence in nonhumans. Klüver (1933) asserted that consciousness in animals was not amenable to study by objective methods, and, more recently, Gardiner (1974) has noted that "there is no way to interview animals to discover the exact point on the evolutionary scale at which [consciousness] emerges. Neither is there any way to determine when 'self' becomes an element within the subjective mass. . ." (p. 207). But if self-awareness in animals is not amenable to study, how can one be confident that it is unique to humans?

A recent line of investigation, notably that of Gallup and colleagues, has suggested that an objective analysis of self-awareness may be possible.

Gallup (1970) suggested a test of self-awareness which, if valid, would repeal the prohibition on comparative scientific study of this phenomenon. This test makes use of *mirror-image stimulation* — stimulation that results from an organism's own reflection in a mirrored surface. The mirror image is, in many ways, unique among the vast array of stimuli used by psychologists.

MIRROR IMAGE STIMULATION

The Mirror as an Unconditional Stimulus

Unconditional responses (UCRs) to mirrors, especially aggressive displays, have been observed in a variety of species, including siamese fighting fish (Thompson & Sturm, 1965), sexually aroused male sticklebacks (Tinbergen, 1951), and the male towhee (Dickey, 1916). Ritter and Benson (1934) reported that wild male towhees, California linnits, Western mockingbirds, robins, cardinals, and blackbirds attack their reflections in mirrors and window panes. Smythe (1962) observed that chaffinches and hedge sparrows occasionally attack their reflections in the hub caps of stationary automobiles, sometimes to the point of exhaustion. Captive California sea lions have been observed to emit underwater clicking-type vocalizations to mirrors, to make rapid runs at mirrors, and to attempt to bite or slap their mirror images (Schusterman, Gentry, & Schmook, 1966). Thompson and Sturm (1965) demonstrated classical conditioning using a mirror as an unconditional stimulus: They brought the aggressive response of siamese fighting fish under the control of a light by pairing the light with mirror exposure.

Among primates, gibbons (Boutan, 1913), rhesus monkeys, and pigtailed and Japanese macaques (Gallup, 1968) respond aggressively to mirrors. MacLean (1964) described penile erection in the squirrel monkey in response to a mirror. Many primates (Yerkes & Yerkes, 1929), as well as cats (Kraus, 1949) and human infants (Dixon, 1957), reach toward or look behind a mirrored surface, as if to make contact with the reflected image. Orangutans (Schmidt, 1878) and chimpanzees (Köhler, 1925) are unusual in that the way they react to their mirror images changes over time: At first they are aggressive, then they appear to be "curious," and eventually they may become emotional if an attempt is made to remove the mirror. Gorillas behave similarly, except that they are aggressive only rarely (Yerkes, 1927).

The Mirror as a Social Stimulus

Organisms do not ordinarily attack themselves. Thus, the aggressive response of an animal to its mirror image suggests that the animal perceives the image as a stranger, and the response may be interpreted as territorial defense (Lorenz, 1966).

It is frequently noted that animals vacillate between approach toward and withdrawal from a mirror. The vacillation would seem to follow from a simple observation by Tinbergen (1968): In general, one animal's approach induces another animal's withdrawal. Moreover, mirrors should enhance such an effect, because you converge with your mirror image twice as fast as you do with a still object.

Adult humans sometimes respond to their mirror images as images of other people. For example, Wolff (1943) noted that many people are startled when they see their own images reflected suddenly in an unexpected mirrored surface; they respond as if they are being confronted by a stranger. Similarly, certain drugs cause some people to report a feeling of strangeness or unfamiliarity with their mirror images (Kraus, 1949). Furthermore, congenitally blind individuals who have had their vision restored report unusual reactions to mirrors. For example, von Senden (1960) told of a man who had to remind himself constantly that a mirror was fastened to a wall in order to compensate for the fact that he "saw" the objects behind the wall.

Retarded humans, too, sometimes respond to their mirror images as if they are seeing another person. Shentoub, Soulairac, and Rustin (1954) exposed 15 retarded children, ages 4 to 19 years, to mirrors and found that many of them tried to escape from the reflection or refused to look at it. One girl, when offered candy before a mirror, offered some to her mirror image. Similar results have been obtained with retarded adults (Harris, 1977).

Schizophrenic humans have also been observed to respond inappropriately to likenesses of themselves. Schizophrenics who were shown photographs of themselves (Faure, 1956) or mirrors (Wittreich, 1959), interpreted these as distorted images of themselves, masks, a twin, or another person. Schizophrenics have also been observed to engage in prolonged mirror gazing (Abély, 1930), and it was even suggested that such behavior might be useful in diagnosis and prognosis (Ostancow, 1934).

Traub and Orbach (1964) developed a full-length mirror that could be adjusted along a continuum, from undistorted to extremely distorted. They presented psychotic humans with the distorted mirror and asked them to adjust it until their reflections appeared undistorted. One subject tried to escape from the distorted image and could not be tested. Many others were unable to look at their distorted reflections. Many subjects repeatedly looked at their bodies, or asked to see themselves in an undistorted mirror before proceeding, indicating they had forgotten what they looked like. Normal subjects given the same task (Orbach, Traub, & Olson, 1966) performed more accurately. As a control, all subjects were asked to adjust the distorted reflection of a door. Accuracy was high for both groups, and there were no significant differences between normals and psychotics.

Mirrors have also been observed to have social facilitation effects. It has been shown that organisms behave differently in the presence of other organisms than they do in isolation (Zajonc, 1965), and mirrors seem to serve sometimes as substitutes for other organisms. For example, isolated pigeons do not normally lay eggs, but they will do so in the presence of mirror-image stimulation (Matthews, 1939). A similar effect has been noted in ring doves (Lott & Brody, 1966). Chickens eat more food in the presence of other chickens than in isolation, and this facilitation effect is also seen with mirrors (Tolman, 1965). Finally, college students who faced a mirror were observed to perform better on tests than students who did not face a mirror (Wicklund & Duval, 1971).

The Mirror as a Reinforcer

Operant conditioning has been achieved using a mirror as a reinforcer. For example, Thompson (1963) conditioned siamese fighting fish to swim through a maze for contingent mirror exposure. Notably, this response extinguished more rapidly than comparable behavior that had been established using food as a reinforcer. Thompson (1964) also established a key–peck response in fighting cocks using mirror exposure as a reinforcer. Reinforcing effects of mirror exposure have also been demonstrated in baby chicks (Gallup, Montevecchi, & Swanson, 1972), paradise fish (Melvin & Anson, 1970), male squirrel monkeys (MacLean, 1964), pigtailed macaques, and rhesus monkeys (Gallup, 1966).

A mirror image may be reinforcing because it is novel (cf. Kish, 1966), or, possibly, simply because it is, in some ways, an ideal consequence. Mirror-image stimulation is unique, because only in front of a mirrored surface are one's movements instantly and perfectly mimicked. Moreover, an animal in front of the mirror has perfect control over the movement of the image, which is to say that the animal's behavior has continuous and virtually instantaneous consequences. Such a scenario would seem to be ideal for the establishment and maintenance of operant behavior.

The correlation between the behavior of the observer and the behavior of the observer's image also means, in effect, that the observer is in a position to control perfectly the behavior of "another organism." The prediction and control of natural phenomena, behavioral and otherwise, is a powerful reinforcer for scientists, gamblers, politicians, managers, teachers, and just about everyone else. Perhaps mirror-image stimulation in reinforcing because it provides the illusion of control over another organism.

Alternatively, Hogan (1967) suggests that the unconditional response (the aggressive display) elicited by mirror-image stimulation is what is reinforcing, not the mirror-image stimulation per se. It seems unproductive to speak of behavior itself as reinforcing, and we suggest that Hogan's statement means simply that mirrors are reinforcing because of the kinds of stimuli they produce, that is, views of aggressive conspecifics, which are, presumably, releasers of aggressive displays.

Moreover, it has been shown that, when given a choice between viewing mirror-image stimulation and viewing a live conspecific — both of which elicit the aggressive UCR — siamese fighting fish (Baenninger, 1966), goldfish (Gallup & Hess, 1971), weaver finches, and parakeets (Gallup & Capper, 1970) prefer mirror-image stimulation.

Some studies suggest that the UCRs elicited by mirror-image stimulation are of greater magnitude than the same UCRs elicited by conspecifics. In effect, then, mirror-image stimulation appears to be what ethologists call a "supernormal stimulus." This effect has been shown for aggressive responses in siamese fighting fish (Baenninger, Bergman, & Baenninger, 1966), adolescent chickens (Gallup et al., 1972), and patas monkeys (unpublished data by Gallup & McClure, cited in Gallup, 1975). It has also been found that distress vocalizations in very young chicks are reduced more by mirror-image stimulation than by a live companion (Gallup et al., 1972).

Although these findings suggest that mirror-image stimulation is a powerful reinforcer, a study by Schulman and Anderson (1972) has introduced a complicating variable. They varied the early social experience of chickens and turkeys and found (a) that group-reared fowl preferred viewing conspecifics, (b) that those raised with a mirror preferred mirror-image stimulation, and (c) that those raised in social isolation showed no preference. The results may be an artifact of a flaw in the procedure, however: A bird was given a choice between viewing its own image or *two* conspecifics.

Controlling for this possible confound, Gallup and McClure (1971) tested feral versus socially isolated, preadolescent rhesus monkeys and found that feral animals preferred a feral conspecific to mirror-image stimulation, whereas isolates preferred mirror-image stimulation over an isolate conspecific. One possible explanation for this finding is suggested by a study by Pratt and Sackett (1967), which showed that rhesus monkeys preferred to view comparably reared conspecifics over monkeys with different rearing histories. Thus, for a feral, socially experienced animal, mirror-image stimulation would present an extremely unfamiliar social situation, in that the image neither initiates an encounter nor reciprocates. The mirror-reflected behavior of an isolate, however, although unfamiliar, would at least be more predictable than a conspecific's behavior. The image would only mimic; it would not initiate behavior with which the subject is unfamiliar.

This explanation, however, contradicts the hypothesis that mirror images are reinforcing because they are novel. Thus, we submit that, at this point in time, there is still much to be learned about (a) what properties of mirror images make them reinforcing and (b) what environmental histories maximize their reinforcing effects.

MIRRORS AND SELF-AWARENESS

Probably the most obvious fact about mirrors—for humans, anyway—is that they are a source of information about one's own body. The responses of nonhuman animals to mirror-image stimulation, as previously noted, appear to be other-directed rather than self-directed. According to Gallup (1977b), in order for "self-stimulation" to become "self-perception" (or "self-aware-ness" or "self-consciousness"), self-recognition must first occur.

Stages of Self-Recognition

Darwin (1877) recorded the responses of a baby to its mirror image, and, in recent decades, more careful and systematic observations have been made. For example, Dixon (1957) noted a series of "stages" through which mirror-controlled behavior seems to pass during the first few years of life: At first, most infants are unresponsive. After a few months, babies react to their images as they would to other children—by vocalizing, reaching, smiling, and so on. By a child's second year, it usually engages in behaviors that suggest "testing" or "discovery." For example, Dixon (1957) observed "repetitive activity while observing the mirror image intently, e.g., alternately observing a hand or foot and its mirror image, opening and closing the mouth with deliberation, or rising up and down slowly while keeping [the] eyes fixed on the mirror image" (p. 253). Amsterdam (1972) describes a similar stage. Finally, toward the end of its second year, the child begins to behave appropriately towards its mirror image.

A Test of Self-Awareness

Gallup (1970), using chimpanzeees, and Amsterdam (1968, 1972), using children, devised an objective test to determine whether an organism had achieved this last stage—the stage at which the daemon Self is said to spring to life, or at least to "mature" (cf. Lewis & Brooks-Gunn, 1979). In Amsterdam's study, a mother smeared rouge on her child's nose—where, supposedly, the rouge would be difficult to see directly—and then encouraged the child to gaze at its mirror image. If the child touched its nose, it was said to have achieved the final stage: The mirror now controlled reaching appropriately. Most children responded in this way by about age 2.

Some Origins of the Appropriate Behavior

Before appropriate control can be established, an organism's social responses to its mirror image (Dixon's second stage) must be extinguished. Gallup (1968) suggested using very narrow mirrors for this purpose, so that only relatively small side-to-side movements by the observer would make the "other animal" disappear and reappear frequently. This seems, however, to be no different than housing two animals adjacent to each other with visual access limited to a small window; social responses of rhesus monkeys do not extinguish under such conditions. Furthermore, contrivances hardly seem necessary, because mirror-image stimulation is such atypical social stimulation: Mimicry is not a typical social response, so, if social responses are going to disappear, they should do so unaided, and, indeed, they often do (Gallup, 1968, 1970).

Mere extinction is not enough, however. An organism's behavior must actually come under the control of the mirror. How might this occur?

When the aggressive behavior has weakened, any arbitrary response—say, arm waving—would be strengthened somewhat by exposure to the organism's mirror image. A self-directed response, such as grooming, could therefore draw two sources of strength: the mirror image of the response, *and the natural consequences of grooming.* If, say, teeth-cleaning occurred by chance before the mirror, a chimpanzee would surely, at some point, gaze at its image and clean its teeth at the same time, in which case *the mirror image would begin to control the topography of the teeth-cleaning, because the image is a guide to more effective movements.* Moving this way or that, according to the image in the mirror, would allow the animal to dislodge bits of food with greater proficiency. The consequences of movements controlled in this way would be detected immediately—the animal would both *see* its hand shift and then *feel* the food in between its fingers (cf. Epstein, 1986).

Does mirror-controlled behavior actually develop in this fashion? Gallup (1968) described the development of self-oriented responses in a chimpanzee after mirror exposure. Initially, responding was aggressive, and then the chimpanzee repeatedly positioned its limbs in unusual positions and tried to inspect its new postures in the mirror. Several contorted facial expressions led to close visual inspection of the reflection. Finally, and most important, while in front of the mirror the animal came to groom parts of its body—for example, its forehead and eyebrows—not visible without the mirror, and it did so while gazing at its mirror image.

"Self-Awareness" in the Chimpanzee

To confirm this observation experimentally, Gallup (1970) isolated four preadolescent chimpanzees in a room with a mirror for 80 hours over a 10-day period. Social behavior declined sharply on the third day, and there was a simultaneous increase in self-directed behavior (including grooming visually inaccessible body parts, picking the teeth or nose while watching the mirror image, making faces at the mirror, and so on). The animals were then anesthetized to unconsciousness with phencyclidine and atropine, and the upper eyebrow ridge and top of the ears were painted red with a dye that has no olfactory or tactile cues when dry.

After they had recovered fully, the chimpanzees were observed for 30 mins in the absence of a mirror, during which time an animal was seen to make a "mark-directed" response only once. A mirror was then reintroduced for 30 mins, whereupon from 4 to 10 "mark-directed" responses per animal were observed. Also, the total mirror-viewing time increased fourfold over the previous mirror sessions, and some of the animals inspected the fingers that had touched the dyed spots. As a control, two chimpanzees that had had no previous mirror exposure were anesthetized, marked, and tested, but they made no mark-directed responses. Critical discussion of this procedure can be found in Epstein (1985a).

Other Primates

Gallup's (1970) finding has apparently been extended to orangutans, another member of the great apes family (Lethmate & Dücker, 1973). However, reports with other primate species have been negative. For example, Tinklepaugh (1928), exposed a female macaque to a mirror for several days and discovered that the animal learned to respond to objects in the environment using the mirror: ". . . if a human being thus viewed makes a threatening movement, she will turn directly from the mirror to the person, as though verifying her indirect picture of the situation" (p. 218). In spite of this proficiency, the monkey showed no sign of responding appropriately to her mirror image. Brown, McDowell, and Robinson (1965) also showed that monkeys could use mirrors to manipulate objects, but they, too, saw no indication that the monkeys responded appropriately to their own images.

Gallup (1970) also tested four adult stump-tailed macaques and two adult rhesus monkeys after 168 hours of mirror exposure. There was little decline in the occurrence of social behavior and no evidence of self-directed behavior during the exposure period. Moreover, no mark-directed responses were observed during testing. Similar results were obtained with four cynomolgus monkeys after 250 hours of exposure. Lethmate and Dücker (1973) tested for but saw no evidence of self-recognition in several primate species: spider monkeys, capuchins, macaques, mandrill and hamadryas baboons, and two species of gibbons. Pribram and Bertrand (cited in Gallup, 1977b) failed to find signs of self-recognition in gibbons and macaques. Benhar, Carlton, and Samuel (1975) gave baboons 250 hours of mirror exposure but, again, found that the baboons responded inappropriately to their mirror images.

Thinking that these failures might have been due to inadequate mirror exposure, Gallup (1977a) exposed a preadolescent crab-eating macaque to a mirror for 2,400 hours, but the subject was still unsuccessful in the test. Furthermore, according to Gallup (1979), Thompson and Radano provided 1 year and Bertrand provided 7 years of mirror exposure to pigtailed macaques, but appropriate responding did not emerge in either case.

Because monkeys are adept at recognizing each other, Gallup, Wallnau, and Suarez (1980) speculated that self-recognition would be facilitated if familiar cagemates were given access to a common mirror. Because each member of the pair would presumably be able to recognize the reflection of its companion, the identity of the remaining individual seen in the mirror would be obvious. In one experiment, a feral adult rhesus monkey and her 6-month-old infant were given over 1,000 hours of mirror exposure. Red dye was applied to the eyebrow and abdomen of both animals. Both the adult female and a control animal without prior mirror exposure touched their marked stomachs, and the infant repeatedly groomed the mark on its mother's eyebrow, but none of the monkeys made self-directed responses to their own marked eyebrows. The experiment was repeated with two 6-month-old rhesus monkeys who were separated from their mothers and maintained together in front of a mirror for 14 weeks. Both infants touched the marks on their cagemate's face upon testing, but neither responded to its own marks.

In contrast, as noted earlier, the behavior of most humans readily comes under the control of a mirror image, though estimates of when the control is normally established vary somewhat. Stone and Church (1968) contend that many children learn to recognize themselves in mirrors by 10 months of age, but earlier sources say that self-recognition is unlikely during the first year (Gesell & Thompson, 1934; Shirley, 1933).

Amsterdam's (1972) study, cited earlier, reported that appropriate control was apparent in 65% of the subjects tested who were between 20 and 24 months old. Unfortunately, the children were marked with a spot of rouge placed on the side of the nose—a visible body part—while fully conscious, and thus the children could detect the marks before they were given the test.

In summary, the results of most of the mirror studies to date suggest a discontinuity in the phylogenetic tree. It seems that the families Hominidae and Pongidae come, with adequate exposure, to respond appropriately to their mirror images; other species do not. It is unusual to find substantial qualitative differences between monkeys and the great apes in learning abilities or other psychological processes (Mason, 1976; cf. Rumbaugh, 1971; Rumbaugh & Gill, 1973).

If there is a discontinuity in the reaction of different species to mirrors, how might we interpret it?

Discontinuity

Because Gallup attributes self-directed behavior in front of a mirror to the daemonic "self-concept," he has concluded that only humans and the great apes (chimpanzees, at least) possess this cognitive entity (e.g., Gallup, 1979).

He mantains that his results "raise serious questions about recent claims (e.g., Griffin, 1976) concerning the evolutionary continuity of mental experience" (Gallup, 1977b, p. 335). His theorizing, furthermore, has become increasingly mentalistic. Writes Gallup:

> . . . most primates lack a cognitive category that is essential for processing mirrored information about themselves. . . (1979, p. 420)

> I do not think their sense of identity or self-concept in any way emerges out of experience with a mirror. A mirror simply represents a means of mapping what the chimpanzee already knows. (1977b, p. 335)

> . . . if you do not know who you are, how could you possibly know who it is you are seeing when you look at yourself in a mirror? (1979, p. 420)

> . . . therein may lie one basic difference between monkeys and the great apes . . . the absence of a sufficiently well-integrated self-concept. (1977b, p. 334)

Gallup has turned to what he calls the "Cooley–Mead" model of self to account for his results. According to Cooley's (1902) "looking glass" theory of self, our self-concept derives from interaction with others. Similarly, Mead (1934) proposed that, in order for the self-concept to emerge, one must see one's self from another point of view.

To evaluate the applicability of the Cooley–Mead model to chimpanzee behavior, Gallup, McClure, Hill, and Bundy (1971) compared the self-recognition responses of feral chimpanzees housed in group cages with those of chimpanzees who were born in the laboratory and reared in isolation. Each animal was exposed to a mirror for 9 days. During the exposure period, feral chimpanzees attended frequently to the mirror at first but paid less attention to it as the days passed. But the isolates attended frequently to the mirror for the entire period. When tested for self-recognition, the feral chimpanzees made 13.5 times as many mark-directed responses as the isolates. Hill, Bundy, Gallup, and McClure (1970) extended these findings with three additional isolation-reared chimpanzees, none of whom showed signs of self-recognition in the test. Two of these animals were then housed together for 3 months. Upon retesting, both animals showed signs of self-recognition, whereas the third chimp, who had remained isolated, did not.

These results were said to support the Cooley–Mead model, and two alternative explanations were summarily — and, in our view, prematurely — dismissed. One possible alternative is that social isolation leads to general deficits in learning ability. Gallup dismissed this possibility on the grounds that apparent learning deficits are complicated by heightened emotionality in novel situations (Harlow, Schlitz, & Harlow, 1968), but those are hardly adequate grounds for dismissal. Indeed, the heightened emotions of the social isolate — that is, the "anxiety" — should interfere with its ability to learn how mirrors work, just as the anxiety of Thorndike's cats made it difficult for them to learn a simple escape response (cf. Gluck & Harlow, 1971). Control by the mirror image would not easily be established if irrelevant emotional behavior were being elicited by the image.

It is also possible that isolates fail to distinguish the atypical behavior of the "other animal" in the mirror because they have not seen the typical behavior of other chimpanzees, and thus they have nothing with which to compare the mirror images. In other words, there were no opportunities for the appropriate discriminations to have been established. Gallup dismissed this possibility because the isolates' interest in the mirror remained high throughout the study, but that seems to be beside the point.

Although conservative explanations for the kinds of data Gallup has gathered do not seem to be in short supply, Gallup persists in attributing successful performances to mental daemons. His speculations have ranged widely. For example, Gallup (1979) has suggested that humans are not unique in their ability to contemplate their own deaths. He has speculated that chimpanzees are aware of, or can be made aware of, their inevitable ends, and Premack (1976), too, has expressed concern over this possibility. Such speculation have given rise to what can only be called *pongidocentrism*.

Continuity

The case for discontinuity is by no means clearcut. Chimpanzees do not always respond appropriately to their mirror images (Gallup et al., 1971; Hill et al., 1970; Russell, 1978), and neither do humans (Harris, 1977; Kraus, 1949; Shentoub et al., 1954; Traub & Orbach, 1964; von Senden, 1960; Wittreich, 1959; Wolff, 1943). And the learning histories of those organisms who can respond appropriately make a difference (Gallup, 1970; Hill et al., 1970).

At best, the self-concept — whatever and wherever it may be — and the behaviors from which it is inferred, are *collateral products* of an organism's genetic endowment and environmental histories. Gallup and his colleagues have helped to discover some of the determinants of the behavior — for example, both chimpanzees and children need extensive exposure to a mirror before control is established. Without the behavior, the daemon would not be invoked. Thus, these determinants are determining both the behavior *and* the "self-concept" (granting, for the sake of argument, that the self-concept is worth talking about). But it makes no sense to attribute the behavior to the daemon — *that is, to attribute one of the products to the other.*

As we noted earlier, daemons are sometimes troublesome because they call attention away from the actual behaviors in question, as well as from the determinants of that behavior. If appropriate behavior with respect to one's mirror image has specific origins in one's learning history, we should be able to find those origins. If particular neural structures are involved, we should be able to find them.

And, finally, once we have identified determinants of the behavior, we should be able to establish such behavior in an organism that does not normally exhibit it.

"Self-Awareness" in the Pigeon

Epstein, Lanza, and Skinner (1981) did so with pigeons. They reported that a normal adult pigeon whose history was supplemented with some simple training could successfully pass the mirror test; that is, it could successfully use a mirror to locate a spot on its body which it could not see directly, *even though it had not been explicitly trained to do so.*

Each of three pigeons was given two types of training over a 10-day period. First, with no mirror present, blue stick-on dots were placed one at a time on parts of the pigeon's body which it could see. Pecking the dots was shaped and maintained on a rich variable ratio schedule of food reinforcement. When the training was complete, each pigeon would readily scan its body, locate a dot, and peck it. The pigeon was thus provided with a repertoire of pecking itself, something a pigeon doesn't ordinarily do.

Second, the pigeon was taught to use a mirror. A mirror was added to the pigeon's chamber and pecks at blue dots placed on the walls and floor were reinforced. Then the dots were flashed only briefly, and pecks at the spot where a dot had been were reinforced. Finally, a dot was flashed only when the pigeon was facing the mirror. It received food when it turned and pecked the position where a blue dot had been flashed. The pigeons were exposed to the mirror for a total of less than 15 hours during the entire training period.

The pigeon was now like some of the chimpanzees and children who have been confronted with the mirror test in recent years. It had a strong tendency to "groom" itself (for blue dots, anyway), which means that, like the chimpanzee or child, it would now try to touch spots that appeared to be on its body. And it had learned — albeit in a more efficient and structured manner than the chimpanzees and children had — how a mirror works.

In some ways the pigeon was now at a disadvantage. For one thing, it had had relatively little mirror exposure. Moreover, it had had little or perhaps even no experience using a mirror to locate an object on its own body. It had learned to use the mirror only to locate spots on the walls and floor of its chamber. It had never seen a spot on its body while the mirror was available. In contrast, chimpanzees and children who are successful in the mirror test have apparently already learned to use mirrors to locate both objects in real space and objects on their own bodies (Gallup, 1968, 1970; Lewis & Brooks-Gunn, 1979).

The following test was conducted: A blue stick-on dot was placed on the pigeon's breast and a white bib placed around its neck so that the pigeon, standing fully upright, could just see the dot in the mirror. Because the bib would drop if the pigeon lowered its head, the pigeon could not see the dot directly. To be certain that the pigeons could not detect the dot either visually or tactually, each pigeon was observed first for 3 mins in the absence of the mirror. Three independent observers scored videotapes for what they judged to be dot-directed responses. None of the birds was observed to peck the dot during this period.

When the mirror was then uncovered, each pigeon approached it and, within a few seconds, began to bob and peck toward the position on the bib that corresponded to the position of the concealed dot. None of the birds pecked the positions on the floor and walls where dots had previously been presented. The three birds were judged by the independent observers to have emitted a total of 29 dot-directed responses within 3 mins of seeing the mirror, though food was not presented. This rate of responding is more than 10 times that reported by Gallup (1970) with chimpanzees.

To control for the possibility that the pigeons were responding simply because the mirror had been uncovered, one bird was tested wearing a bib but with no dot on its breast. The mirror was covered for 5 mins and then uncovered for 5 mins, and no dot-directed responses were observed during either period.

Thus, even though the pigeons had had very limited mirror exposure, and even though they had never been trained to use a mirror to locate spots on their bodies, they successfully used a mirror to do so. Does this mean pigeons have a self-concept?

Implications

The Epstein et al. (1981) study may be interpreted in different ways.

Training.   First, it might be said that because the pigeons had had *training* before the mirror test, the results are not applicable to chimpanzees and children, who, it seems, have had no "training" before the test.

But the word "training" is misleading. The chimpanzees and children who have been successful in the mirror test have had far richer learning histories than our pigeons. Organisms learn constantly, even without teachers! (Some would say especially without teachers!)

Explanation.   However the chimpanzee or child acquired the relevant behaviors — we return to this point later — there is ample evidence that both chimpanzees and children have acquired each of them before they pass the test: They readily touch spots on their bodies, and they have each learned how mirrors work. The pigeon study suggests that successful performances in the mirror test are the outcome of the acquisition of these two repertoires.

If other organisms that are provided with these repertoires prove able to pass the test, the explanation will become more credible. If a chimpanzee or child who lacks one these repertoires proves able to pass the test, the explanation will become less credible (cf. Epstein, 1984a).

Self-Concept.   The results of the Epstein et al. (1981) study will suggest to no one that pigeons have a self-concept. Why not? For one thing, pigeons do not look like people. It is awkward to anthropomorphize with a 12-inch high, armless, feathered creature; it is easier with chimpanzees.

More important, the pigeons acquired only one telltale sign of self-awareness. The self-daemons are typically invoked only after a variety of self-controlled behaviors have been established.

Bad Test.   The Epstein et al. (1981) study could also be said to cast doubt upon the usefulness or informativeness of the mirror test. After all, if an organism that has no self-concept can pass it, what good is the test? The mirror test shows what the mirror test shows — namely, that an organism's behavior is controlled appropriately or inappropriately by a mirror image. That may be worth knowing, but it also may not be a critical sign of self-awareness, as was supposed.

Bad Concept.   Epstein (1986) and Epstein et al. (1981) suggest that the study is significant mainly in calling attention away from self-awareness. Rather, the behavior from which self-awareness is often inferred is brought into focus, along with the learning history that is responsible for the behavior.

Replication

Gallup (1984) cites what he calls a "failure to replicate" the Epstein et al. (1981) study — a convention talk by Gelhard, Wohlman, and Thompson (1982). But these investigators reported having great difficulties in training their two pigeons in preparation for the mirror test. They gave up on one bird after nearly a year. This suggests that they were using inadequate training procedures, not that pigeons cannot pass the mirror test. One of the authors of that study, Roger Thompson (personal communication, December, 1983) stated that he had "no doubt" that Epstein et al. (1981) achieved the result they reported.

Moreover, Cheney (1984) has completed a systematic replication of the Epstein et al. (1981) study, and he has achieved positive results with each of the four pigeons he tested. According to Cheney, "Given the relatively modest level of sophistication and experience of the trainers in this study, the results indicate a rather robust phenomenon" (p. 6).

Contingencies and Species Differences

Under most circumstances, moving toward an object brings it closer and ultimately produces contact with it. However, one must move in a special way to touch an object that is reflected in a mirror. A mirror thus provides a new set of relationships between one's movements and their consequences — a new set of "contingencies."

A pigeon would not normally come under the control of such contingencies, and, therefore, Epstein et al. (1981) supplemented them with the conspicuous and systematically changing contingencies one sometimes calls "training." Epstein (1986) offers further analysis:

> Attending to an object in the mirror and then finding it in real space not only produced the natural consequence — contact with the object — it also produced food, a powerful, effective reinforcer for a hungry pigeon. The food only supplemented the natural contingency; it did not obliterate or override it. The pigeon's behavior had to be under the control of the correspondence between mirrored and real space in order for food to be delivered. . . .

> The period of "testing" or "discovery" that Dixon (1957) described is undoubtedly the period during which a child's behavior comes under the control of the contingencies of reinforcement which govern mirror use. The child slowly learns the correspondence between the locations of parts of its body (and, presumably, of other objects) in real and mirrored space. (p. 104)

The only impressive thing about chimpanzees and children is that they can — *after many hours of activity in front of mirrors* — come under the control of mirror-use contingencies without explicit training. According to the present view, this control is established for the simple reason that chimpanzees and children are extremely sensitive to the consequences of their behavior. Earlier in the chapter we suggested some of the events that might lead to appropriate control. The fact that the mirror image is reinforcing is important, because that means it creates opportunities for further learning. The extinction of UCRs (such as aggressive displays) and of inappropriate reaching (such as reaching toward the image) is also important. Because chimpanzees and children learn quickly, the extinction of these behaviors should occur rapidly — again creating the opportunities for appropriate control to be established.

With inappropriate behaviors eliminated, a chimpanzee gazing at its mirror image should quickly come under discriminative control of that image, because, loosely speaking, *the mirror is a guide to effective action.* We described one possible scenario earlier: While gazing at its image, the animal happens to move its hand toward an irritant on its face or in its teeth which it cannot see directly. The sight of the reflected hand removing the irritant is the occasion upon which the hand successfully removes the irritant, and thus the image should come to control similar movements in the future. It is a "discriminative stimulus," a stimulus that sets the occasion for reinforcement, a stimulus that helps the organism to be effective.

A careful analysis of videotapes of a chimpanzee's interactions with mirrors should show interactions of this sort. We predict that careful study of these interactions will take the mystery out of the acquisition process.

Other Species

Why do so many species — especially other primates — fail the mirror test? Epstein et al. (1981) suggested that monkeys fail because they tend to move so much faster than chimpanzees and children. The contingencies of reinforcement which govern mirror use are more likely to take hold if an organism gazes at its mirror image while it is moving slowly.

But other factors also seem important. If aggressive displays and other UCRs are elicited by the image, appropriate control cannot be established until these have abated. With some species and some individuals, this extinction may not occur. Moreover, inappropriate operant behavior, such as reaching toward the image, must also disappear. With children and chimpanzees, this extinction occurs fairly rapidly, but it may occur slowly or not at all with other species.

Species vary dramatically in the speed with which behavior is acquired or eliminated, and there is significant variation among individuals within a species. In other words, some organisms learn faster than others, and learning ability should make a big difference in the acquisition of mirror-use behavior.

As stated earlier, training that compensates for an organism's deficiencies should also make a difference. With appropriate training, many organisms that would not normally come under the control of their mirror images should do so. Because organisms differ, we should expect that the necessary training should differ for different organisms.

Other Behaviors

Other behaviors said to show the existence of a self-concept demand their own analyses. For example, a child's reply to the question "How do you feel?" has different origins than the child's behavior in front of a mirror. The reply "I feel fine" is the result of years of exposure to speakers and to the contingencies of reinforcement supported by a verbal community; its successful occurrence might also depend on the maturation of language-specific neural structures. It is not reasonable to expect, as some developmentalists seem to hold, that the entire set of behaviors from which the existence of a self-concept is inferred will emerge full-blown if any one member of the set emerges. The behaviors may have little relationship to each other and may have very different origins.

The fact that many self-controlled behaviors appear within a few months of each other during the second year of life (Kagan, 1981) is not surprising, because that is a period of mobility and rapid learning. While the child is acquiring a wide variety of behaviors that are controlled by its own body and behavior, it is also acquiring many other complex behaviors — verbal and other social behaviors, problem solving behaviors, complex motor skills, and so on. The roughly concurrent appearance of many self-controlled behaviors should not in itself be taken as evidence for the validity of the concept of a self-concept.

A WORD ABOUT SIMULATIONS

The Epstein et al. (1981) study is one of a number of so-called "Columban [from the taxonomic name for pigeon] simulations" (Baxley, 1982; Epstein, 1981, 1984a) — simulations of complex human behavior with pigeons.

Rationale

The rationale for these simulations may be briefly stated as follows:

> *If you have reason to believe, based on principles of behavior established in the laboratory and information about a person's past, that certain experiences were responsible for the emergence of some mysterious behavior, you provide support for this conjecture if, after providing an animal that does not normally exhibit such behavior with these experiences, the animal exhibits similar behavior.* (Epstein, 1984a, p. 46)

Outcomes

There have been four outcomes of this research program to date. First, pigeons have been shown to be capable of engaging in a variety of complex behaviors — not just successful mirror-use behavior. For example, with appropriate training histories, pigeons successfully solved the box-and-banana problem, one of Köhler's classic insight problems (Epstein, Kirshnit, Lanza, & Rubin, 1984), as well as a variation on the rake problem (Epstein & Medalie, 1983).

Second, by systematically varying the training histories of different animals, investigators have been able to assess the contributions that different experiences make in the emergence of novel performances (e.g., Epstein et al., 1984).

Third, a set of principles has emerged which allows for the successful prediction of novel performances in the laboratory environment. What Epstein (e.g., 1986) calls "the interconnection of repertoires" has proved to be especially important in understanding how novel performances are generated. The interconnection of three repertoires in pigeon has generated a solution to the box-and-banana problem in just under 1 min (Epstein, 1985b), and, more recently, the interconnection of four repertoires has generated a solution to an even more complex problem in under 4 mins (Epstein, 1985c).

And finally, Epstein (1984b, in press) has offered equations and a computer model, derived from the pigeon studies, which have proved reasonably successful in predicting complex, novel performances in human subjects.

Limitations

Epstein (1984a) has commented at length on the limitations of the simulation research. First, as is true of all simulations, the Columban simulations do not *prove* hypotheses; they don't necessarily shed light on either human or chimpanzee behavior. It would be folly to assert that a history that is responsible for pigeon behavior is necessarily responsible for comparable behavior in chimpanzees or children. Rather, simulations provide "plausibility proofs." They show merely that some conjecture is *plausible*.

Second, not all of the simulations are equally adequate—that is, they do not all meet all of the criteria that good simulations should meet. The "symbolic communication" study (Epstein, Lanza, & Skinner, 1980), for example, was more a demonstration than a simulation. But the "self-awareness" study (Epstein et al., 1981) lives up to most of the criteria that Epstein (1984a) discusses: The behavioral processes it makes use of are applicable to chimpanzees, the pigeon's behavior in front of the mirror has the right topography and function, and chimpanzees who pass the mirror test have acquired the relevant repertoires before they are given the test (see Epstein, 1984a, pp. 46–47, for further discussion of these points).

SOME FINAL REFLECTIONS

The behavior that gives life to the daemonic self has a life of its own. Behavior that is controlled by an organism's own body or behavior seems to be orderly and not fundamentally different from behavior that is controlled in other ways. The origins of such behavior—for example, of appropriate responses to one's mirror image—lie in the genetic and environmental histories of the organisms.

The sharp discontinuity said to exist between the higher primates and other animals has not been conclusively shown, and the concept of a self-concept does not shed light on the differences that have been shown. What differences there are among species and individuals can be accounted for in terms of ontogenic histories, sensitivity to environmental events, and species-specific behaviors elicited by specific stimuli. Further investigations will strengthen such accounts. One may wish to conjure up daemons from the behavior an organism engages in before a mirror, but that won't change the facts, and the facts are worth noting.

A daemon, according to the *Oxford English Dictionary*, is "an attendant, ministering, or indwelling spirit . . . an inward monitor or oracle." Some have been unabashed in their promotion of daemonology in this sense. Freud (1905/1961), for example, spoke of "those half-tamed daemons that inhabit the human breast," and his tripartite mind has been justly characterized as "a dark cellar in which a maiden aunt and a sex-crazed monkey are locked in mortal combat, the affair being referred by a rather nervous bank clerk" (Bannister, 1966, p. 363). An introductory text on information processing (Lindsay & Norman, 1977) has colorful drawings of "feature daemons"— bright-eyed little men who live in one's head, pool their knowledge, and eventually figure out what one is seeing. (Who lives in *their* little heads and makes sense of what *they* are seeing is not specified.) Others have promoted concepts — such as the self-concept — which are less obviously daemonic, in the sense that they lack arms and legs, but which are just as imaginary and troublesome.

As we learn more about how heredity and the environment determine behavior and about how behavior is mediated by the body, we will naturally abandon the myths. Unfortunately, where the daemons rule, the facts may turn up more slowly.

ACKNOWLEDGMENTS

This chapter is an expanded version of an invited address given by the first author at a meeting of the Association for Behavior Analysis (cf. Epstein, 1982). Its preparation was completed while he was in residence at The Neurosciences Institute of the Neurosciences Research Program, New York City. We thank A. Deen for help in the preparation of the manuscript.

REFERENCES

Abély, P. (1930). Le signe du miroir dans les psychoses et plus specialement dans le demence precoce. *Annales Medico-Psychologiques, 88,* 28–36.
Allport, G. W. (1955). *Becoming.* New Haven, CT: Yale University Press.

Amsterdam, B. K. (1968). *Mirror behavior in children under two years of age.* Unpublished doctoral dissertation, University of North Carolina, Chapel Hill, NC.

Amsterdam, B. K. (1972). Mirror self-image reactions before age two. *Developmental Psychobiology, 5,* 297–305.

Ardrey, R. (1961). *African genesis.* New York: Dell.

Baenninger, L., Bergman, M., & Baenninger, R. (1966). Aggressive motivation in *Betta splendens:* Replication and extension. *Psychonomic Science, 16,* 260–261.

Baenninger, R. (1966). Waning of aggressive motivation in *Betta splendens. Psychonomic Science, 5,* 241–242.

Bannister, D. (1966). A new theory of personality. In B. Foss (Ed.), *New horizons in psychology.* Harmondsworth, England: Penguin.

Baxley, N. (Producer). (1982). *Cognition, creativity, and behavior: The Columban simulations* [Film]. Champaign, IL: Research Press.

Beck, B. B. (1975). Primate tool behavior. In R. H. Tuttle (Ed.), *Socio-ecology and psychology of primates.* The Hague, Netherlands: Mouton.

Benhar, E. E., Carlton, P. L., & Samuel, D. (1975). A search for mirror-image reinforcement and self-recognition in the baboon. In S. Kondo, M. Kawai, & A. Ehara (Eds.), *Contemporary primatology: Proceedings of the Fifth International Congress of Primatology.* Basel, Switzerland: Karger.

Boutan, L. (1913). Le pseudo-language. Observations effectuées sur un anthropoide: Le gibbon (*Hylobates Leucogenys* Ogilby). *Actes de la Société Linneenne de Bordeaux, 67,* 5–80.

Brown, W. L., McDowell, A. A., & Robinson, E. M. (1965). Discrimination learning of mirrored cues by rhesus monkeys. *Journal of Genetic Psychology, 106,* 123–128.

Buss, A. (1973). *Psychology—Man in perspective.* New York: Wiley.

Cheney, C. D. (1984). *Mirror use by pigeons: A systematic replication.* Unpublished manuscript, Utah State University.

Chiarelli, A. B. (1973). *Evolution of the primates.* New York: Academic.

Cooley, C. H. (1902). *Human nature and the social order.* New York: Scribner's.

Darwin, C. (1877). A biographical sketch of an infant. *Mind, 2,* 285–294.

Davenport, R. K., Rogers, C. M., & Russell, I. S. (1973). Cross-modal perception in apes. *Neuropsychologia, 11,* 21–28.

Dickey, D. R. (1916). The shadow-boxing of Pipilo. *The Condor, 18,* 93–99.

Dixon, J. C. (1957). Development of self-recognition. *Journal of Genetic Psychology, 91,* 251–256.

Ebel, R. L. (1974). And still the dryads linger. *American Psychologist, 29,* 485–492.

Epstein, R. (1981). On pigeons and people: A preliminary look at the Columban Simulation Project. *The Behavior Analyst, 4,* 43–55.

Epstein, R. (1982). The self-concept and other daemons (abstract). *Behaviour Analysis Letters, 2,* 300–302.

Epstein, R. (1984a). Simulation research in the analysis of behavior. *Behaviorism, 12*(2), 41–59.

Epstein, R. (1984b, September). *A moment-to-moment account of the emergence of a novel performance.* Invited address given at the meeting of the International Society for Comparative Psychology, Acapulco, Mexico.

Epstein, R. (1985a). On the Columban simulations: A reply to Gallup. *Contemporary Psychology, 30,* 417–419.

Epstein, R. (1985b). The spontaneous interconnection of three repertoires. *Psychological Record, 35,* 131–141.

Epstein, R. (1985c, November). *The spontaneous interconnection of four repertoires of behavior in a pigeon.* Paper presented at the 26th annual meeting of the Psychonomic Society, Boston.

Epstein, R. (1986). Bringing cognition and creativity into the behavioral laboratory. In T. J.

Knapp & L. Robertson, (Eds.), *Approaches to cognition: Contrasts and controversies* (pp. 91–109). Hillsdale, NJ: Lawrence Erlbaum Associates.

Epstein, R. (in press). Animal cognition as the praxist views it. *Neuroscience and Biobehavioral Reviews.*

Epstein, R., Kirshnit, C., Lanza, R. P., & Rubin, L. C. (1984). "Insight" in the pigeon: Antecedents and determinants of an intelligent performance. *Nature, 308,* 61–62.

Epstein, R., Lanza, R. P., & Skinner, B. F. (1980). Symbolic communication between two pigeons (*Columba livia domestica*). *Science, 207,* 543–545.

Epstein, R., Lanza, R. P., & Skinner, B. F. (1981). "Self-awareness" in the pigeon. *Science, 212,* 695–696.

Epstein, R., & Medalie, S. (1983). The spontaneous use of a tool by a pigeon. *Behaviour Analysis Letters, 3,* 341–347.

Faure, H. (1956). L'investissement delirant de l'image de soi. *Evolution Psychiatrique, 3,* 545–577.

Fouts, R. S. (1974). Language: Origins, definitions and chimpanzees. *Journal of Human Evolution, 3,* 475–482.

Freud, S. (1961). Fragment of an analysis of a case of hysteria. In J. Strachey (Ed. and Trans.), *The standard edition of the complete psychological works of Sigmund Freud: Vol. 7.* (pp. 1–122). London: Hogarth Press. (Original paper published 1905).

Gallup, G. G., Jr. (1966). Mirror-image reinforcement in monkeys. *Psychonomic Science, 5,* 39–40.

Gallup, G. G., Jr. (1968). Mirror-image stimulation. *Psychological Bulletin, 70,* 782–793.

Gallup, G. G., Jr. (1970). Chimpanzees: Self-recognition. *Science, 167,* 86–87.

Gallup, G. G., Jr. (1975). Towards an operational definition of self-awareness. In R. H. Tuttle (Ed.), *Socio-ecology and psychology of primates.* The Hague, Netherlands: Mouton.

Gallup, G. G., Jr. (1977a). Absence of self-recognition in a monkey (*Macaca fascicularis*) following prolonged exposure to a mirror. *Developmental Psychobiology, 10,* 281–284.

Gallup, G. G., Jr. (1977b). Self-recognition in primates: A comparative approach to the bidirectional properties of consciousness. *American Psychologist, 32,* 329–338.

Gallup, G. G., Jr. (1979). Self-awareness in primates. *American Scientist, 67* 417–421.

Gallup, G. G., Jr. (1984). Will reinforcement subsume cognition? *Contemporary Psychology, 29,* 589–590.

Gallup, G. G., Jr., & Capper, S. A. (1970). Preference for mirror-image stimulation in finches (*Passer domesticus domesticus*) and parakeets (*Melopsittacus undulatus*). *Animal Behaviour, 18,* 621–624.

Gallup, G. G., Jr., & Hess, J. Y. (1971). Preference for mirror-image stimulation in goldfish (*Carassius auratus*). *Psychonomic Science, 23,* 63–64.

Gallup, G. G., Jr., & McClure, M. K. (1971). Preference for mirror-image stimulation in differentially reared rhesus monkeys. *Journal of Comparative and Physiological Psychology, 75,* 403–407.

Gallup, G. G., Jr., McClure, M. K., Hill, S. D., & Bundy, R. A. (1971). Capacity for self-recognition in differentially reared chimpanzees. *Psychological Record, 21,* 69–74.

Gallup, G. G., Jr., Montevecchi, W. A., Swanson, E. T. (1972). Motivational properties of mirror image stimulation in the domestic chicken. *Psychological Record, 22,* 193–199.

Gallup, G. G., Jr., Wallnau, L. B., & Suarez, S. D. (1980). Failure to find self-recognition in mother–infant and infant–infant rhesus monkey pairs. *Folia Primatologica, 33,* 210–219.

Gardiner, W. L. (1974). *Psychology: A story of a search.* Belmont, CA: Wadsworth.

Gardner, R. A., & Gardner, B. T. (1969). Teaching sign language to a chimpanzee. *Science, 165,* 664–672.

Gelhard, B., Wohlman, S., & Thompson, R. K. R. (1982, October). *Self-awareness in pigeons: A second look.* Paper presented at the Northeast Regional Meeting of the Animal Behavior Society, Boston, MA.

Gessell, A., & Thompson, H. (1934). *Infant behavior: Its genesis and growth.* New York: McGraw-Hill.

Gluck, J. P., & Harlow, H. F. (1971). The effects of deprived and enriched rearing conditions on later learning: A review. In L. E. Jarrard (Ed.), *Cognitive processes of nonhuman primates* (pp. 103-119). New York: Academic Press.

Griffin, D. R. (1976). *The question of animal awareness.* New York: Rockefeller University Press.

Harlow, H. F., Schlitz, K. A., & Harlow, M. K. (1968). Effects of social isolation on the learning performance of rhesus monkeys. *Proceedings of the Second International Congress of Primatology.* Basel, Switzerland: Karger.

Harris, L. P. (1977). Self-recognition among institutionalized profoundly retarded males: A replication. *Bulletin of the Psychonomic Society, 9,* 43-44.

Hill, S. D., Bundy, R. A., Gallup, G. G., Jr., & McClure, M. K. (1970). Responsiveness of young nursery-reared chimpanzees to mirrors. *Proceedings of the Louisiana Academy of Science, 33,* 77-82.

Hogan, J. A. (1967). Fighting and reinforcement in the siamese fighting fish (*Betta splendens*). *Journal of Comparative and Physiological Psychology, 64,* 356-359.

James, W. (1890). *Principles of Psychology* (Vol. 1). New York: Henry Holt.

Kagan, J. (1981). *The second year: The emergence of self-awareness.* Cambridge, MA: Harvard University Press.

King, M. C., & Wilson, A. C. (1975). Evolution at two levels in humans and chimpanzees. *Science, 188,* 107-116.

Kinget, G. M. (1975). *On being human.* New York: Harcourt, Brace, Jovanovich.

Kish, G. B. (1966). Studies of sensory reinforcement. In W. K. Honig (Ed.), *Operant behavior: Areas of research and application.* New York: Appleton-Century-Crofts.

Klüver, H. (1933). *Behavior mechanisms in monkeys.* Chicago, IL: University of Chicago.

Köhler, W. (1925). *The mentality of apes.* London: Kegan Paul.

Kraus, G. (1949). Over de psychopathologie en do psychologie van de waarneming van hat eigen spiegelbeeld. *Nederlandsch Tijdschrift voor Psychologie en haar Grensgebieden, 4,* 1-37.

Lethmate, J., & Dücker, G. (1973). Untersuchungen zum selfsterkennen im speigel bei orangutans und einen anderen affenarten. *Zeitschrift fur Tierpsychologie, 33,* 248-269.

Lewis, M., & Brooks-Gunn, J. (1979). *Social cognition and the acquisition of self.* New York: Plenum.

Lindsay, P. H., & Norman, D. A. (1977). *Human information processing.* New York: Academic Press.

Lorenz, K. (1966). *On aggression.* New York: Harcourt, Brace, & World.

Lorenz, K. (1971). *Studies in animal behavior* (Vol. 2). Cambridge, MA: Harvard University Press.

Lott, D. F., & Brody, P. N. (1966). Support of ovulation in the ring dove by auditory and visual stimuli. *Journal of Comparative and Physiological Psychology, 62,* 311-313.

MacLean, P. D. (1964). Mirror display in the squirrel monkey. *Science, 146,* 950-952.

Mason, W. A. (1976). Environmental models and mental modes: Representational processes in the great apes and men. *American Psychologist, 31,* 284-294.

Matthews, L. H. (1939). Visual stimulation and ovulation in pigeons. *Proceedings of the Royal Society of London, 126,* 557-560.

Mead, G. H. (1934). *Mind, self and society: From the standpoint of a social behaviorist.* Chicago, IL: University of Chicago Press.

Melvin, K. B., & Anson, J. E. (1970). Image-induced aggressive display: Reinforcement in the paradise fish. *Psychological Record, 20,* 225-228.

Menzel, E. W., Jr. (1973). Chimpanzee spatial memory organization. *Science, 182,* 943-945.

Ostancow, P. (1934). Le signe du miroir dans la demence precoce. *Annales Medico-Psychologiques, 92,* 787-790.

Pratt, C. L., & Sackett, G. P. (1967). Selection of social partners of peer contact during rearing. *Science, 155,* 1133–1135.

Premack, D. (1976). Language and intelligence in ape and man. *American Scientist, 64,* 674–683.

Ritter, W. E., & Benson, S. B. (1934). "Is the poor bird demented?" Another case of "shadow boxing." *Auk, 51,* 169–179.

Rumbaugh, D. M. (1971). Evidence for qualitative differences in learning processes among primates. *Journal of Comparative and Physiological Psychology, 76,* 250–255.

Rumbaugh, D. M., & Gill, T. V. (1973). The learning skills of great apes. *Journal of Human Evolution, 2,* 171–179.

Russell, I. S. (1978). *Medical Research Council Unit on Neural Mechanisms of Behaviour: Progress report, 1975–1978.* Unpublished document, University of London.

Savage-Rumbaugh, E. S., Rumbaugh, D. M., & Boysen, S. (1978). Symbolic communication between two chimpanzees (*Pan troglodytes*). *Science, 201,* 641–644.

Schmidt, M. (1878). Beobachtungen am Orang-Utan. *Zoologische Garten, 19,* 230–232.

Schulman, A. H., & Anderson, J. N. (1972). *The effects of early rearing conditions upon the preferences for mirror-image stimulation in domestic chicks.* Paper presented at the 1972 meeting of the Southern Psychological Association, Atlanta, GA.

Schusterman, R. J., Gentry, R., & Schmook, J. (1966). Underwater vocalization by sea lions: Social and mirror stimuli. *Science, 154,* 540–542.

Shentoub, S. A., Soulairac, A., & Rustin, E. (1954). Comportment de l'enfant arriere devant le miroir. *Enfance, 7,* 333–340.

Shirley, M. N. (1933). *The first two years: Vol. 2. Intellectual development.* Minneapolis, MN: University of Minnesota Press.

Skinner, B. F. (1945). The operational analysis of psychological terms. *Psychological Review, 52,* 270–277.

Skinner, B. F. (1963). Behaviorism at fifty. *Science, 140,* 951–958.

Slobodkin, L. B. (1977). Evolution is no help. *World Archaeology, 8,* 332–343.

Smythe, R. H. (1962). *Animal habits: The things animals do.* Springfield, IL: Charles C. Thomas.

Snygg, D., & Combs, A. W. (1949). *Individual behavior.* New York: Harper and Row.

Stone, L. J., & Church, J. (1968). *Childhood and adolescence* (2nd ed.). New York: Random House.

Teleki, G. (1973). *The predatory behavior of wild chimpanzees.* Lewisburg, PA: Bucknell University Press.

Thompson, T. (1963). Visual reinforcement in siamese fighting fish. *Science, 141,* 55–57.

Thompson, T. (1964). Visual reinforcement in fighting cocks. *Journal of the Experimental Analysis of Behavior, 7,* 45–49.

Thompson, T., & Sturm, T. (1965). Classical conditioning of aggressive display in siamese fighting fish. *Journal of the Experimental Analysis of Behavior, 8,* 397–403.

Tinbergen, N. (1951). *The study of instinct.* London: Oxford University Press.

Tinbergen, N. (1968). On war and peace in animals and men. *Science, 160,* 1411–1418.

Tinklepaugh, D. L. (1928). An experimental study of representative factors in monkeys. *Journal of Comparative Psychology, 8,* 197–236.

Tolman, C. W. (1965). Feeding behaviour of domestic chicks in the presence of their own mirror images. *Canadian Psychologist, 6,* 227.

Traub, A. C., & Orbach, J. (1964). Psychophysical studies of body images: I. The adjustable body-distorting mirror. *Archives of General Psychiatry, 11,* 53–66.

van Lawick-Goodall, J. (1970). Tool using in primates and other vertebrates. In D.S. Lehrman, R. A. Hinde, & E. Shaw (Eds.), *Advances in the study of behavior.* London: Academic.

van Lawick-Goodall, J. (1971). *In the shadow of man.* Boston: Houghton Mifflin.

von Senden, M. (1960). *Space and sight: The perception of space and shape in the congenitally blind before and after operation.* Glenco, IL: Free Press.

Wicklund, R. A. (1979). The influence of self-awareness on human behavor. *American Scientist, 67,* 187–193.

Wicklund, R. A., & Duval, S. (1971). Opinion change and performance facilitation as a result of objective self-awareness. *Journal of Experimental Social Psychology, 7,* 319–342.

Wilson, A. C., & Sarich, V. M. (1969). A molecular time scale for human evolution. *Proceedings of the National Academy of Science, 63,* 1088–1093.

Wittreich, W. (1959). Visual perception and personality. *Scientific American, 200,* 56–60.

Wolff, W. (1943). *The expression of personality.* New York: Harper.

Yeni-Komshian, G. H., & Benson, D. A. (1976). Anatomical study of cerebral assymetry in the temporal lobe of humans, chimpanzees, and rhesus monkeys. *Science, 192,* 387–389.

Yerkes, R. M. (1927). The mind of a gorilla. *Genetic Psychology Monographs, 2,* 1–193.

Yerkes, R. M., & Yerkes, A. W. (1929). *The great apes: A study of anthropoid life.* New Haven, CT: Yale University Press.

Yunis, J. J., & Prakash, O. (1982). The origin of man: A chromosomal pictorial legacy. *Science, 215,* 1525–1530.

Zajonc, R. B. (1965). Social facilitation. *Science, 149,* 269–274.

3 Origins of Self-Knowledge and Individual Differences in Early Self-Recognition

Michael Lewis
University of Medicine and Dentistry of New Jersey
Rutgers Medical School

The origins of children's knowledge of themselves, their actions, thoughts, and feelings has begun to be considered by developmental theorists. Because of young children's limited language skills and their inability to carry out complex tasks, observational techniques, rather than experimental manipulation, are the mode of exploring the problem. Observation of (a) children's knowledge of their own products (Kagan, 1981), (b) their awareness of internal states (Bretherton & Beeghly, 1982; Lewis & Michalson, 1983), and (c) their response to images of themselves (Bertenthal & Fischer, 1978; Lewis & Brooks-Gunn, 1979b) have all indicated that by 2 years of age children can be said to have knowledge about themselves. Moreover, the emergence of other social skills also point to the children's knowledge about themselves.

Emergence of an active sense of self in the middle of the second year of life constitutes a central milestone and transition in the child's development. Given this view of the importance of self-knowledge, individual differences in this knowledge and the origin of these differences becomes increasingly important to explore. Social, interrelational, temperamental, and cognitive factors have all been suggested and are explored in this chapter.

We, first, explore the phenomenon of self in infancy, pointing to examples of behavior that may require us to hypothesize a developing self-schemata. Next, the definition of self-schema is explored. Following this discussion, a summary of empirical support for an emerging self-schema is presented, focusing on self-recognition. Having shown that self-recognition emerges in the middle of the second year of life, individual differences in self-recognition are discussed with special attention drawn to perceptual–cognitive, familial and experiential factors, parent–child relationships, and temperamental or dispositional differences. Each of these individual factors or their combinations appear to account for some of the individual differences observed.

THE SELF IN INFANCY

Example 1

A 2-year-old child is playing with a toy truck. His friend enters the room and moves over to his side. After a moment, the friend reaches for the truck and tries to take it from him. The 2-year-old pulls it toward himself and says sharply, "Mine."

Example 2

A 2-year-old child is playing with her toys. Her mother enters the room and says, "It is time to go, I need to go to the store." The little girl does not move or stop playing. Her mother calls out again, "Are you coming?" The 2-year-old looks up and says firmly, "No!".

Example 3

Sitting in front of a movie screen a 2-year-old sees a recent holiday scene, in which she, her mother,and father are sledding. The child moves toward the screen and says, pointing to the people, "Mommy," "Daddy," and "Linda." The last, "Linda" is herself. As she says her name she hides her face.

Example 4

Walking with her mother in the supermarket, a 2-year-old wanders down a wrong aisle. She immediately begins to cry and within 30 seconds she is back in her mother's arms. After her crying stops the child says, "Suzy sad."

Or, looking in front of the mirror Suzy smiles, tilts her head and appears embarrassed as she stares at her image.

What do these separate events tell us about the 2-year-old childs' sense of self, and knowledge of others? In the first vignette, the little boy resists the loss of his toy to another by pulling it away. Of interest, in terms of this physical action, is the movement of the toy toward the child's own body accompanied by the word *mine*. In this physical action, one may observe that the movement is toward the self. That is, the movement of the toy away from the other child is not random movement away, but a specific movement toward that same physical location where the physical self resides. That this particular movement also is accompanied by the word *mine* makes this action particularly noteworthy. It could be argued that the movement is defensive and designed just to prevent the other child from getting the toy. In that case, the movement of the toy should have been away from both the other child and self, because this would have been the farthest distance from the threat. That it was not the case suggests the movement represents the physical manifestation of self and the understanding that self (in this case "mine") is to be understood as possessing a particular place in space, the loci occupied by me.

In addition to the movement is the exclamation, "mine." By 2 years of age some children are capable of personal pronouns. Although "me" and "mine" emerge earlier than "I," the use of personal pronoun must have significance for the emerging schema in the mind of the child. Thus, both action and language address the issue of a schema of self already present by 2 years; a schema possessing both location in space and having a verbal/lexical unit — a personal pronoun.

In the next example, a child is engaged in an activity. Although there is insufficient material to judge, we might assume the child was busily engaged in an activity, which might require an elaborate plan or which would evidence symbolic play. Her activity is disrupted by the mother's entrance and plan, which differs from the child's. Although the mother wishes to go to the store, the 2-year-old girl wishes to stay; she does not want to stop playing, nor is she willing to accommodate to her mother's wishes.

Here is the emergence of a conflict of wishes: on the mother's part, a demand to go to the store, on the child's, a desire to play. The conflict and negotiation of these two different wishes give rise to complex social behavior. Sharing behavior, for example, can be said to occur only after it is established that both parties desire the same object, which can be obtained by both only through division. Nevertheless, sharing itself must have at its base the conflict of two wills. The onset of the terrible twos represents a transition from a pleasant, nonconflictive relationship between mother and child, to one of conflict, where the child asserts itself by saying "No." This "No" represents the child's growing will, or for the sake of this chapter, the development of self. The terrible twos, as represented by the assertion of child's self against that of the parent, needs to be viewed as another example of the child's active knowledge of the others wishes as they interact with their own. Relationships, by definition, require the negotiation of two or more selves.

The third example, again, highlights the child's active knowledge of a self-schema. Although it could be argued that the child has simply learned, in some rote fashion, the names to familiar shapes, in this case, mother, father, and self, it appears that by 2 years of age children's ability to discriminate self from other, and others from each other, has achieved a remarkable degree of skill. Children can discriminate themselves in mirrors, stories, and television, and, in static form, such as pictures; and at the same time they can differentiate others, both from themselves, and each other. This ability to differentiate their visual world (and possibly other modes as well — such as auditory, olfactory, and kinesthetic) provides a perceptual–cognitive basis for elaborate schema having to do with objects, events, interactions.

The final example touches on several issues related to the self. To begin with, the child uses her own name as referent. Moreover, and most importantly, she uses an emotional term (one of the few available to children this age [Michalson & Lewis, 1985]). This lexical unit refers to an internal process, a private event located within the individual. As noted earlier, it is not possible to experience an internal action or event until the emergence of a reflecting organism. Such reflection is dependent on the development of self (Lewis & Brooks-Gunn, 1979b; Lewis & Michalson, 1983). Although all organisms may have internal states and state changes (some have called these feelings), they cannot be experienced unless the organism has developed a sense of self. Reflection of emotional states has, as its major characteristic, the facts that (a) the stimulus being referred to is available only to the self (it is a private act), and (b) the organism is capable of reflecting on this state. Bretherton and Beeghly (1982) have commented on the child's growing awareness of internal states, such as feeling and thinking, in children as young as 2 years old.

The child's embarrassed behavior in front of the mirror makes reference to what has been called self-conscious emotions. Emotions like embarrassment, guilt, and shame require consideration of the self because each has the self as a referent vis a vis some ongoing action. Unlike emotions such as fear or surprise, emotional states that need only the self in order to experience them, emotions such as embarrassment, guilt, and shame require the self in order to generate the state itself, because these emotions require that the organism compare the self's own action (thought or feeling) to the self's (and societies') rules. The exhibition of embarrassment requires a self-cognition.

Each of these examples leads us to believe that the concept of self emerges by 2 years of age and that the child's commerce with others and its own action necessitate the consideration of a self-concept. In our study of early development, there are three reasons for consideration of the development of self-knowledge: (a) children's early knowledge about relationships with their social world, (b) children's early emotional development, and (c) children's early control over the object (nonsocial) world. By the end of the first 2 years of life, children enjoy a rich knowledge of their social world and of the assorted people who inhabit it (Lewis, 1982). More importantly, children form significant, complex, and reciprocal relationships with a number of people, usually including their mother, father, siblings, friends, and other caregivers. In fact, these relationships appear in their earliest form within the first year of life. Although more evidence is needed, there is reason to believe that children's early interactions with others contribute to the development of self-knowledge in the infant. These interactions may affect social relationships through their role in the development of these specific self–other schema. It is difficult to imagine social relationships that do not have, as a fundamental feature, the ability of a dyadic member to both distinguish and utilize knowledge about self and other. Relationships, by definition, require the negotiation of two or more selves (Mead, 1934; Sullivan, 1953).

The distinction between private and public acts as it relates to self, has been considered in some detail (Lewis, 1983). In this chapter, one particular class of private acts — feelings and emotions — can be considered in terms of its relationship to self. In considering the difference between emotional states and experiences, the role of the self as object takes on some meaning. My colleagues and I (Lewis & Brooks-Gunn, 1979b; Lewis & Michalson, 1984) have tried to distinguish between signs of emotional states (such as changes in facial, vocal, postural, and physiological activity), and actual emotional experiences, (which include the attending to these behavioral and somatosensory changes and the accompanying thoughts or statements such as "I am fearful" or "I am hungry"). The ability to reflect on a set of events that occurs inside oneself, rather than somewhere else, suggests the importance of considering the development of self.

Finally, the demonstration of the control of behavior, such as in the case of an infant causing a mobile to move, leads us to consider the source of that control. Although early in the child's life the source of the effect may be located in the stimulus itself, or in some combinations of the stimulus with the distinctive stimuli surrounding it, by the time the child is 5 or 6 months old, there is reason to believe that the effect is being caused by the child's intention (Piaget, 1954). Explanations that invoke sensorimotor schemata (in particular, complex circular reactions) appear reasonable. However, these reactions, and the development of a concept of means and ends, also suggest that the self, as agent, is beginning to emerge. Means–ends behavior and the ability to select different means to reach the same goal imply some type of planning on the part of the child. Planning, however primitive, requires goals and subgoals, checking progress against such goals, and the changing of behavior that fails to meet the goals. Goal-setting and executing appropriate motor acts implies the existence of intentions and agency, in whatever way young children might conceptualize them. Whether children know of their agency or intention — that is, whether they have a meta intention — is not clear, and it is not necessary (nor reasonable) to infer it.

Our research focuses on self-development in the first 2 years of life because after this period children's language and their behaviors lead us to believe that a concept of self as subject is already operating. Undoubtedly, children continue to acquire self-knowledge after 2 years of age, but the origins seem to be located in this earlier period.

DEFINITION OF SELF

Although many have written about the self, self-concept, and self-esteem (e.g., Epstein, 1980; Gergen, 1971; Rosenberg, 1965), few have focused on these issues from a developmental perspective, especially in early childhood. Recently, my colleagues and I have initiated a series of studies aimed at finding measures that could be used with preverbal children to provide information about the child's emerging concept of self. The term, development of concept of self, is used to refer to (a) children's construction of agency, (b) a me–other distinction, and (c) knowledge of their own internal states, including emotions and cognitions.

Self-Awareness

The relationship of self-knowledge and self-awareness is particularly important to consider. When organisms are preverbal (infants) or unable to speak (nonhuman primates) it is not possible to explore the issue of awareness, because the organism cannot be easily questioned and because the self, as a phenomenological event, is not easily studied without access to the internal processes of the organism. Because of this, we must make inferences about self-knowledge; although we can study self-knowledge, we cannot explore, at least in infancy, the epistemological issue of knowledge of the knowledge of self. Moreover, self-knowledge can precede the knowledge of self-knowledge. For example, by 8 months infants know — that is, will search for — a hidden object, but cannot tell us if they have awareness of their knowledge of object permanence. We can accept their behavior as demonstrating knowledge, but do not ask about knowledge of knowledge. In the same way, we may speak of a cat's knowledge of spatial properties when it goes around an object rather than trying to go through it. Although we have no idea as to the form this knowledge takes (what is the nature of thought in the young infant or cat), we do infer that their knowledge exists.

In our discussion of self-awareness, we have a similar problem; self-awareness is equivalent to knowledge of the knowledge of self. By referring to adult behavior in this regard, we may be able to discuss this issue more clearly. We agree that adults have knowledge of themselves, citing as evidence their use of self-referents, their ability to recognize themselves, and their use of self-directed behavior. Although adults have self-knowledge, they do not always have self-awareness. Many thoughts and actions do not involve any consideration of self. Moreover, much adult behavior occurs rapidly, with little or no reflective thought. During times of decision-making, when action does not have to be carried out quickly, when we have made an error and need to rethink an action, or when we socially transgress some rule that makes us feel guilty or embarrassed, self-awareness becomes obvious (Lewis & Brooks-Gunn, 1979b).

Low levels of self-awareness do not reflect the absence of self-involvement in ongoing behavior, but suggest that the self has no executive role, leaving for other processes the mechanics of action. The self sets goals, has intentions, and evaluates, but specific behaviors are executed through simpler processes of associations, and learned or overlearned response patterns. Abelson (1976) has linked these lower level processes to scripts that guide behavior. Scripts, as a metaphor, are useful because they assume the organization and maintenance of complex behavior without evoking such executive functions as awareness, thinking, or planning. In brief, self-knowledge and self-awareness may be considered as somewhat separate.

Duality of Self

In our consideration of the meaning of *self*, we have, as have others, emphasized the duality of the self. This distinction is the same as the self as subject and the self as object (Wylie, 1961). My colleagues and I (Lewis & Brooks-Gunn, 1979a; Lewis & Michalson, 1983) have referred to the self as subject the *existential self*, whereas the self as object has been termed the *categorical self*.

Existential Self.   The existential self is the "I," as distinct from other; it is the subjective self. The single, basic premise of the existential self is that this aspect of self is distinct from others; including both people and objects. Like the perceptual metaphor, it is the emergence of a figure–ground relationship, the self being the figure, all else the ground. It is believed that this may be one of the earliest aspects of knowledge. Various theories about this early differentiation have been offered. One such view grows out of the psychoanalytic belief of the infant's need for oral gratification and the tempering of this need through the differentiation of self and mother (Spitz & Wolf, 1946). Another view (Freud 1915/1959) holds to the child's distinction between stimulus events "out there" versus those "in here":

> Let us imagine ourselves in the position of an almost entirely helpless organism, as yet unoriented in the world and with stimuli impinging on it…The organism will soon become capable of making a first discrimination and a first orientation. On the one hand, it will detect certain stimuli which can be avoided by an action of the muscles (flight)—those which it ascribes to an outside world, on the other hand, it will also be aware of stimuli against which action is of no avail…—these stimuli are the tokens of an inner world. (p.62)

The sociological theories of Mead (1934) and Cooley (1912) also treated this problem of the awareness of self as distinct from others, but in these cases the others were persons. Mead (1934), for example, states:

The self has a character which is different from that of the physiological organism proper. The self is something which has a development; it is not initially there at birth but arises in the process of social experience and activity, that is, develops in the given individual as a result of his relations to that process as a whole and to other individuals within that process. (p.135)

More recently, Wallon (1949), Merleau-Ponty (1964), and Heider (1958) have built upon the theories of Mead and Cooley, trying to incorporate them into their concern for social development as well as their concern with the child's changing cognitive development.

The child's notion of existence separate from other develops as the infant differentiates itself from other persons and objects. In regard to persons, the first distinction is probably between child and caregiver. Given the evidence that children are able to differentiate between mother and other people quite early — by the third month — it is not unreasonable to assume that the self-other differentiation is well underway by this time (Banks & Wolfson, 1967; Bronson, 1972).

I have argued that the existential self develops from the consistency, regularity, and contingency of the infant's action and reaction to the world of both objects and people, although the contingency of the social world is viewed as the primary factor (Lewis, 1982). Contingent feedback provides for the general expectancies about the infant's control of his world, and such expectancies should help differentiate the infant's actions from others' actions.

Although the same can be said to be the case for the infant's interactions with its object world, we believe that self–object interactions are less important because (a) object interactions are apt to be less regular, at least very early in life; and (b) one learns less about self through the interaction with in-animate things. Self–object interactions are less regular because they are less contingent early in life. This is due to the lack of the self's agency or permanence that is not established and, therefore, there is little intended connection between the child's action and outcome. Not so in the social realm where social objects, usually caregivers, intend for their actions to be contingent on those of the child. Under these conditions the pairing of infant action–social object response is much more likely to lead to contingency learning for the child.

Categorical Self.   The self as object has been discussed as the empirical self (James, 1961), the social self (Cooley, 1912), and me (Mead, 1934), whereas more recently it has been called self-concept (Wylie, 1961). The development of the categorical self refers to the categories by which the organism defines itself in respect to the external world. Unlike the existential self, which emerges early, the categorical self develops somewhat later and is subject to many lifelong changes. Ontogenetically it should change as a function of the child's other cognitive capacities as well as with changing social relationships. Some categories, like size and strength, change either by being added to or altered entirely. Historically and socially, the categorical self changes. For example, different cultures have different requirements for their members; the little 8-year-old girl playing skip rope in our culture may be a significant caregiver for her 18-month-old brother in another. Given these different values, goals, and expectations of members of a culture, different categories of self should emerge and disappear over time. Of particular importance are those that we hold to be social in nature, learned in every culture, and acquired quite early: familiarity, age, and gender (Lewis & Feiring, 1978, 1979).

The categorical self includes all aspects of the objective self, how one looks and feels, one's beliefs, and what one thinks of oneself. It is the sum total of all those features that go into what we consider ourselves, save the existence of ourselves. Such a conceptualization is not unlike the dual nature of objects the child learns (Piaget, 1963). Thus, the infant first acquires the knowledge that objects have existence, what Piaget calls "object permanence," and after this knowledge the child learns about the specific features of objects such as they have shape or texture, color, or size. In the same way that children can learn about existence prior to learning about the particular features of themselves.

The categorical self continually changes and it is to this aspect of self that many have paid attention. Differences in the categorical self appear as a function of age, cultural, group, and individual differences such as sex. For example, in regard to the category of age, Edwards and Lewis (1978) found that boys were more likely to consider themselves to be older than they were. Girls did not show this pattern. Moreover, girls are less likely to classify themselves as athletic than boys, whereas boys are less likely to classify themselves as physically attractive.

EMPIRICAL SUPPORT FOR AN EMERGING SELF

One way to explore the concept of self is through the study of self-recognition. The only adults who would have difficulty recognizing their faces visually are psychotic patients and those suffering from certain central nervous system dysfunctions (Cornielson & Arsensian, 1960; Frenkel, 1964). However, self-recognition (usually of the face) and the general concept of self are not synonymous, because it is possible to have a concept of self and not be able to visually recognize oneself. Nevertheless, it is hardly possible to recognize oneself and not have a concept of self. Thus, the use of self-recognition provides a simple and straightforward way of exploring the development of self.

In choosing to investigate visual self-recognition as a method for exploring the development of self, three different procedures, each related to naturally occurring situations and using three different types of self-images, have been studied (Lewis & Brooks-Gunn, 1979b). Infants' responses to mirrors, videotapes, and pictorial representations of the self were explored because each of these procedures present the child with different dimensions of self-recognition — contingency and/or feature recognition. Contingency cues allow the infant to learn that the self-image "*acts* like me," whereas feature cues allow the infant to learn that a self-representation "*looks* like me." Both contingent and feature recognition contribute to the differentiation of self and other. A contingent image reproduces one's own actions, whereas others only do so sometimes (as in the case of imitation) and a self-representation always has the features of the self, whereas others only have some similar features in the case of a same-sex and same-age person. Mirror images, videotapes, and pictorial representations of the self may be described in terms of contingency and feature recognition. The findings from the different procedures reveal how infants utilize contingency and feature cues.

The knowledge that a reflection in the mirror is oneself and not another involves contingency as well as feature recognition. Mirrors possess special and unique properties. They are 3-dimensional, relatively distortion-free, and reproduce one's actions simultaneously. The one-to-one correspondence of one's actions, and the reflection of these actions, is naturally present in light-reflecting surfaces. Such contingencies give infants valuable feedback, as they learn that other people do not produce behavior sequences identical to their own and that only a reflected image of self does so. An infant must discover the contingent nature of mirrors, making the inference that a reflection is not another, but is oneself. With this knowledge, the special features unique to oneself may be learned.

Infants' responses to mirrors have been observed in experimental situations. The most commonly used situation was developed by Amsterdam (1968) for infants, and by Gallup (1970) for chimpanzees. In this procedure, the infant's face is marked, either by rouge or tape, and the infant's response to seeing the marked face in a mirror is observed. The operational definition of *self-recognition* is behavior directed toward the mark, because the infant must recognize that the image in the mirror is, in fact, him or herself and that the mark resides not on the image's face, but on his or her own.

Noncontingent self-recognition can be studied through the use of either photographs or the use of videotape feedback. In the former, the infant can be shown a variety of photographs and the infant's responses, including affective, attentional, and verbal, can be measured. In the case of videotape feedback, a variety of procedures have been used, including the delayed feedback of the child's own image. In both types of procedure, verbal response, "That's me," or the subject naming its own name, as well as differences in attention and affect, are used as a means of distinguishing images of self from images of others. Finally, in order to ensure that the infant is responding to its own image, rather than to a class (such as male, blond, etc.), the contrasts for comparison are carefully selected. The results of these studies have already been reported elsewhere (Lewis & Brooks-Gunn, 1979b) so that we present only a summary of our findings.

Period 1: 0 to 3 Months. This period can be characterized chiefly by a biological determinism. There exist both simple and complex reflexes including responses to others that enhance interactions with the caregivers. Reflexive behavior, at first predominant, declines over this period as early schemata and learning begin to predominate (Lewis & Brooks-Gunn, 1979a; Lipsitt, 1980; Papousek & Papousek, 1981). The infant differentiates among social objects and simple circular reactions with objects can be observed. Through both social and object interactions, the beginnings of a self–other differentiation may make its appearance at the end of this period.

Period 2: 3 to 8 Months. During this period, active learning takes precedence over a waning reflex system. Object interactions and social behavior are facilitated by development of more elaborate schemata. Complex action-outcome pairings occur, along with means–ends relationships, in both the social and object domains. Primary and secondary circular reactions are developed as the child learns of its effect on the world; the development of agency and intention can be inferred. The distinction between self and other is consolidated, but cannot be conserved over changes in the nature of the interaction, either in terms of people or objects. Reflected surfaces become of interest due to the contingency between the child's action and the action in the mirror (Dixon, 1957; Rheingold, 1971). Although there is little evidence of self-recognition, children are able to adjust their bodies when placed in a room where visual cues give the appearance that the room is tilted. Such findings would appear to indicate elaborate visual–body schema in spatial knowledge at young ages.

Period 3: 8 to 12 Months. This period can be characterized by two important features: First, at about 8 months infants show general response inhibition when presented with new information or stimuli. Unlike the younger child, the 8-month-old does not respond immediately to the stimulus event; that is, the infant is no longer stimulus bound. This general inhibition, most often observed in one of its manifestations, that of stranger wariness or fear (Schaeffer, 1975), allows the child to think about the stimulus before acting on it. This milestone of central nervous system (CNS) inhibition of action allows for the rapid development of additional schemata.

The second most critical accomplishment of this period is the final establishment of self–other differentiation. This differentiation, which was developing through the earlier period, results in the conservation of the self as distinct from the other across a variety of different situations. This conservation of self represents the first important conservation task and is parallel to the child's growing understanding of object existence. Indeed, object permanence and self-permanence are viewed as part of the same process. At this point in time, the self as unique and permanent in time and space emerges. Although feature recognition does not exist in any appreciable way, self-recognition can be demonstrated in contingent situations (Lewis & Brooks-Gunn, 1979a). The emergence of self as agent facilitates more complex means–ends relationships, and with growing cognitive ability more elaborate plans can be observed.

Period 4: 12 to 18 Months.   The 12- to 18-month period can be characterized as the self-conscious period. During this period, the child's emerging sense of self results in a set of emotional states that can be characterized by self-awareness; that is, children's responses in front of mirrors are ones of coyness or embarrassment if they show self-recognition. Dixon (1957) calls this the "coy stage" and Lewis (Lewis & Brooks-Gunn 1979a; Lewis, Weiss, & Sullivan, 1985) refers to this as the period of "self-conscious emotions." Not only do coyness and embarrassment in front of the mirror become increasingly apparent, fear of the loss of the mother also becomes intense. During this period, self-recognition becomes less dependent on contingency and increasingly more dependent on feature analysis. The self as object becomes more evident in this feature recognition. Pointing behavior emerges, and self-recognition is evidenced through pointing to pictures of the self and through pointing to marks on the nose seen in reflecting surfaces.

Period 5: 18 to 30 Months.   After 18 months, simple language knowledge, the mapping of the lexicon on some features, emerges and allows children to demonstrate knowledge of features of social objects, including themselves. These include gender and age (Edwards & Lewis, 1979; Lewis & Feiring, 1978). Such knowledge supports the belief that the self as object emerges at this time and possesses a number of attributes, including good or bad, efficacy, as well as age and gender. Although more empirical exploration is necessary, this mapping of the critical periods of self-development may be useful as an outline for the emergence of this cognitive capacity.

INDIVIDUAL DIFFERENCES IN MIRROR RECOGNITION

By 15 to 18 months infants start to show self-recognition. However, not all infants show self-recognition. What might be the causes of these individual differences? Four classes of causes are possible: (a) perceptual–cognitive, (b) familial, (c) parent–child relationship, and (d) temperamental. Each of these are considered in turn.

Perceptual–Cognitive

None of the mirror studies reported to date (Lewis & Brooks-Gunn, 1979a) have indicated that an infant can demonstrate mark-directed behavior before the age of 15 months. Even at 15 months only about 25% of the children do so. Thus, it would appear that somewhere between 12 and 15 months mirror recognition emerges. In order to determine whether the emergence of this ability is related to experience or mental age, we observed a group of handicapped infants ranging in chronological age 9–27 months. A majority of the infants had Down Syndrome. The procedure used to assess their self-recognition was the same as that used with normal children. The results indicated that not until the children reached a mental age of 15 months were they able to touch their noses (Brooks-Gunn & Lewis, 1980). Mans, Cicchetti, and Sroufe (1978) found that for Down children a mental age of 18 months or greater was needed in order to show mark-directed behavior.

Other measures of cognition, including object permanence and attentional ability, have been related to self-recognition. The data shown in Table 3.1 are adapted from Lewis and Brooks-Gunn (1979b). Three measures are obtained when observing a child looking at its reflection in the mirror: (a) whether they touch their marked noses (mark-directed), (b) whether they touch their bodies (body-directed) or engage in play behavior, or (c) whether they observe the effects of their own action (imitation).

The cognitive measures presented in Table 3.1 include two measures hypothesized to correlate with the self-recognition measures. The two attentional measures, visual habituation to redundant information and visual re-

TABLE 3.1
Correlations between Self-Recognition and Cognitive Measures

Self-Recognition Measures	Cognitive Measures			
	Habituation	Recovery	Object Permanence	Age
Mirror Measures				
Mark-directed	.17	.46[a]	.45[a]	.64[a]
Body-directed	.11	.08	.15	.18
Imitation	.16	.10	.29[a]	.35[a]
Age	.29[a]	.32[a]	.78[a]	—

[a]p .01
[b]p .05

Note: From (Lewis, M., & Brooks-Gunn, J. (1979b) *Social cognitition and the acquisition of self*. New York: Plenum Press, p. 173).

covery to novelty, have been shown to be measures of cognitive ability (Lewis, 1971; Lewis & Baldini, 1979). Object permanence scores were obtained from a standard object permanence task (see Uzgiris & Hunt, 1978) and is based on Piaget's notion of the child's development of knowledge about object existence.

We have argued that object permanence must be related to self-recognition in that the self, other people, and objects all have permanence, and infants must learn these permanences simultaneously (also see Jackson, Campos, & Fischer, 1978). How can an infant know that an object exists independently of his or her perception of it without concurrent knowledge of self-permanence? If object permanence occurs at the same time or just after self-permanence occurs, we would expect to find a relationship between object and self-permanence.

As expected, mark-directed and imitation behavior were positively related to response recovery, to novelty, and to object permanence scores. Body-directed behavior, which is not held to be related to self-recognition, was unrelated to the cognitive measures.

Age of the child was also found to effect the child's self-recognition measures (mark-directed and imitates measures). Moreover, age was positively related to the cognitive measures. In order to determine whether these reported relationships between self-recognition and cognitive measures were due to age, age was removed from the analysis using a variety of techniques. (These were reported in Lewis & Brooks-Gunn, 1979b.)

When the age dependency of cognition and self-recognition was reduced by looking at the within-age groups correlations or eliminated by the use of regression techniques, a relationship between self-recognition and cognitive performance still emerged, with more advanced cognitive ability being positively related to self-recognition. Bertenthal and Fischer (1978), using a procedure in which five mirror-related tasks were scaled in terms of degree of self-awareness, also examined the relationship between object permanence and self-recognition. They report a significant correlation between the two.

Attentional distribution, in particular response decrement to a redundant signal, and response recovery to novelty, have been shown to be related to later cognitive functioning (Lewis & Baldini, 1979). In terms of self-recognition, the ability to respond to a change after habituating to redundant stimuli seemed especially important because the mark on the nose constitutes an alteration of the situation an infant experiences in a mirror. These data suggest that the visual perceptual–cognitive mode, that is, looking at, attending to, and processing information, exhibit consistencies regardless of the specific task. In the mirror procedure, infants look at, attend to, and respond to self-representations; in the attentional procedure task, they do so to perceptual–cognitive tasks.

These data on the relationship between cognitive ability and self-recognition give rise to the possibility that individual differences in the origins of self-recognition are to be seen in the perceptual–cognitive differences between children.

General Familial Factors

The relationships among self-recognition, familial characteristics, and experiential variables are presented in Table 3.2. The familial variables include the social class level of the family, the mother's educational background, the child's birth order, and the number of other siblings in the family. Several of these familial variables have been found to be related to cognitive development and were included here to see if they also relate to self-recognition. The child's mirror experience was also investigated to observe whether past experience with their images was related to their self-recognition behavior.

With regard to the familial variables, no significant relationships between any of the variables and self-recognition appeared. Sex, maternal education level, birth order, and number of siblings had no relationship to self-recognition. In addition, mirror experience and self-recognition in the mirror were unrelated. Such findings do not support the role of general familial factors such as these. Birth order, number of siblings, mother's education, sex, and socio-economic status (SES) fail to exhibit any relationship with self-recognition, a finding also reported by Amsterdam (1968).

Of interest is the failure to find any relationship between mirror exposure and self-recognition. Self-recognition is related to mirror experience for chimpanzees. Gallup's (1970) chimpanzees did not exhibit self-directed behavior prior to mirror experience, and Kohler (1927, cited in Amsterdam, 1968) reported that people living in nontechnological societies do not recognize themselves in mirrors. However, our data do not support the notion of mirror exposure as a facilitator of mark recognition. Of course, this finding is limited, because the data are based on mothers' reports and because all infants had some previous mirror experience. Perhaps even a limited amount of mirror experience is sufficient for self-recognition. Given the propriocep-

TABLE 3.2
Correlations between Self-Recognition and Social Measures

Self-recognition Measures	Social Measures					
	Sex	SES	Mother's Education	Birth Order	Number of Siblings	Mirror Experience
Mirror Measures						
Mark-directed	− .14	.15	.14	.11	.15	− .18
Body-directed	.01	− .13	− .06	− .06	− .05	− .11
Imitation	− .16	.13	− .01	.04	.05	− .13

Note: From (Lewis, M. & Brooks-Gunn, J. (1979b) *Social cognition and the acquisition of self.* New York: Plenum Press, p. 176).

tive feedback of the facial musculature, a few trials, or even a single trial, may be all that is necesssary to associate facial features to this feedback. That chimpanzees acquire facial recognition with so few hours of learning experience supports the belief that a large degree of experience may not be necessary to identify which features go with one's own face. In any case, amount of mirror experience did not differentiate between those who did and those who did not exhibit self-recognition in the present study.

Social Relationships

The failure to find evidence for the role of familial factors as a mediator of self-recognition in the young has to do more with the gross measurement of these variables than with their potential role. Gallup and McClure (1971), for example, have reported that chimpanzees who have been reared as social isolates do not exhibit mark recognition even after extensive exposure to mirrors. Although no such analog exists in the human literature, it is to the nature of social relationships and their effect on self-recognition that we must turn.

Following Mead (1934) and Merleau-Ponty (1964), we believe that humans come to know themselves through their interactions with others. We have further suggested that the development of self is related to the parent–child relationships (Lewis, 1982) a view shared by Mahler, Pine, and Bergman (1975).

If self-recognition is related, at least in part, to early interactions with others, then two possible models need to be considered. In one, a responsive environment is likely to facilitate a sense of competence and this competence, through affecting the child's means and ends relationships, should further a sense of self (Lewis & Goldberg, 1969). Hence, self-recognition should be enhanced by a responsive environment.

Alternatively, there is some theoretical speculation that some frustration or stress is productive vis-à-vis the development of some skills. Thus, rather than thinking of less-than-ideal child rearing as always leading to slower development, it is possible to consider that some skills are facilitated by less responsive parenting.

For example, Freud (1954) argued that the reality principle and ego development are facilitated by the lack of a totally responsive environment. Ego development is initiated by the inability of the parent to satisfy the needs of the child. Mahler et al. (1975), as well, suggest that individualization can be inhibited by an overly responsive (as well as completely nonresponsive) environment. Thus, self-recognition could be facilitated by less responsivity.

Although hypothesized to be related, until recently there have been no studies looking directly at the connection between the parent–child relationship and self-recognition. Although we emphasize that self-recognition is related to early social behavior, the direction of that relationship is unclear. Although securely attached infants should develop a more healthy concept of themselves than insecurely attached infants (Ahrend, Grove, & Sroufe, 1979; Matas, Ahrend, & Sroufe, 1978), it is not obvious that the onset of self-recognition is facilitated by security of attachment. Indeed, some insecurely attached infants may be too independent too early and, as such, may have earlier self-recognition.

In order to test the relationship between parent–child relationships and self-recognition, children's attachment toward their mothers was assessed in a structured, but modified, Ainsworth strange situation when the infants were 12 months old. Two groups of infants were obtained: those who were securely attached and those who were insecurely attached to their mothers (Ainsworth et al., 1978). Infants were again seen at 18 and 24 months in a standard mirror recognition task (see Lewis & Brooks-Gunn, 1979a). Figure 3.1 presents the data from this study (Lewis, Brooks-Gunn, and Jaskir, in press).

These self-recognition data based on a longitudinal study agree with those already reported on cross-sectional samples (see Lewis & Brooks-Gunn, 1979a for a review) and indicate that mark-directed behavior increases

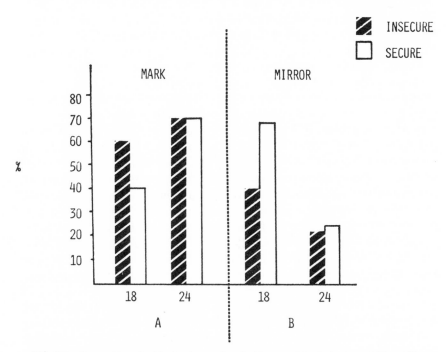

FIG. 3.1   Proportion of subjects who produced self-recognizing behaviors at 18 and 24 months.

whereas mirror-directed behavior decreases with age. Of more concern to the present problem is the fact that individual differences in the infants' relationship with their mothers do seem to influence the age of self-recognition. Insecurely attached infants exhibit the more mature self-recognition pattern earlier.

Similar findings have been reported by Tajima (see Mijake, 1983) working with Japanese infants. He reports that insecurely attached infants showed earlier self-recognition than securely attached infants. In this study, 26 infants were given the mirror self-recognition task at 16 and 20 months of age and their behavior was related to their 12-month attachment classification. Of the total sample, 23.1% touched their noses at 16 months, whereas 43.5% did so at 20 months. When secure and insecure infants were compared, 12.5% of the securely attached and 40% of the insecurely attached were found to touch their noses at 16 months, whereas at 20 months the percentages were 26.4 and 75.0 for the groups respectively.

One might hypothesize that a securely attached child would develop self-awareness earlier than an insecurely attached child. The most parsimonious explanation for the findings obtained to date may be that children who are stressed, who have less effective parents, need to act on their own. This stress may facilitate early self-recognition even though the self-concept being formed may be less positive. That is, from an attachment theory point of view, those infants not able to form a secure base are separated from their mothers, and this separation results in earlier self-awareness. Infants who are more challenged by their environment and less protected from a set of potential behavior perturbations may become more vigilant and may require more rapid development of those skills necessary for this type of coping. Early self-recognition may be one manifestation of this vigilance annd attention.

In order to determine if insecurely attached infants were more attentive and vigilant, Lewis, Brooks-Gunn, and Jaskir (in press) gave the children an attention task that measured information processing and discrimination ability. Insecurely attached infants showed significantly better information processing and discrimination than securely attached infants, although there was no difference between the groups in overall IQ. Increased or advanced vigilance and attention can be seen in maltreated children as well (Belsky, 1978; Lewis & Schaeffer, 1968). Thus, following Mahler et al. (1975) it can be argued that disturbances in the separation–individuation process may occur under conditions that promote both a premature as well as a delayed developmental course. From an attachment point of view, it may be the case that securely attached infants have a better balance between reliance on mother and self (exploration and dependence), whereas insecurely attached infants may have an inbalance, relying less on mother and more on self. Such a view is consistent with the data, showing greater vigilance and attention in the insecurely attached infants.

Temperament and Dispositional Factors

There are some suggestions that certain individual dispositional factors, often referred to as temperament differences, may be related to early self-recognition. For example, at an early age some children have been described as being alert to events around them, socially withdrawn, and fearful. In fact, stranger fear, a phenomenon usually exhibited around 8 months, occurs in these withdrawn children as early as 3 or 4 months. Moreover, these same children are more likely to play by themselves or with objects (toys), than to play with people. In describing them clinically, they appear alert, aware of themselves and others. They are not cuddly and seem in some existential sense to be separated from their parents. They are even reported as looking older. These differences can be seen as early as the first few weeks of life (Brown, 1974). Descriptions of such children and their families suggest that these differences are not a function of poor or inadequate parenting, but rather stem from characteristics of the children themselves (Chess & Thomas, 1982).

Although such individual differences in temperament may make parenting more difficult and, thus, result in insecure attachment (Lerner & Lerner, 1981), temperament may be independently related to early development of self and, thus, to early self-recognition. Such a view is consistent with both Crockenberg (1981), and Goldsmith and Campos (1982), although Belsky, Rovine, and Taylor (1984) have argued that there is little relationship between temperament and attachment.

More directly related to temperament and self-recognition is the study by Tajima (see Mijake, 1983). In the study of Japanese children, he finds a relationship between a temperament variable and self-recognition. Infant inhibition has been described as a temperament variable, that is, an individual subject disposition in which the child shows fear of strangers, is socially withdrawn, and visually alert (see Garcia-Col, Kagan, & Reznick, 1984; Lewis & Brooks-Gunn, 1979a). In the Japanese study, the children who were found to be inhibited also exhibited early self-recognition. Such findings and observations raise the possibility that certain dispositional factors, acting alone or in connection with interpersonal relationships, affects the child's early self-recognition.

It must be kept in mind, however, that early self-recognition may have only a very limited relationship to the content of the self-schemata. As we have made clear in our definition of self, it is important to distinguish between self as subject and self as object. Self-recognition, at least in the mirror, is thought to reflect only the very limited appearance features of the categorical self. Thus, temperamental differences, as described, (or even interpersonal differences) are thought to act as facilitating early self-as-subject development. They have relatively little effect on self as object.

Individual differences in early self-recognition appear to be due to a variety of factors, either in combination or separately. Implicated in almost each of these factors is the child's ability to differentiate its visual world and the ability to describe subtle differences, including differences between self and nonself, and between other nonselves. Where does such an ability come from? Again, in each case children who show early self-recognition appear to show a wariness or vigilance not seen in those without early self-recognition.

Whether this early wariness is a temperamental disposition or a consequence of experience (or both) is still unknown. Clearly, more search is needed in this regard. Likewise, the consequences of early self-recognition are in need of exploration. However, because early self-recognition is believed related to the self as subject, it is difficult to postulate a hypothesis regarding the development of self as object. Nevertheless, if early onset of self as subject is fueled by wariness and attention, it is reasonable to suggest that early self-recognition should be associated with poor self-image (self as object) when the child is older (see Lewis, Feiring, McGuffog, & Jaskir, 1984 for a relationship between insecure attachment and later psychopathology). Exploration of this problem indicates some evidence to suggest that by age 6, the early, as opposed to late self-recognizers, have a less positive image of themselves.

INDIVIDUAL DIFFERENCES IN SELF-KNOWLEDGE

It would seem reasonable to assume that by school age, children have a concept of themselves and that this concept differs between children. Where does this concept come from and what is the cause of these individual differences? The theoretical problem proposed has received some attention, however, little experimental research has been applied to the question. We know, for example, how 6-year-olds conceptualize themselves and how this may change (Livesley & Bromley, 1973). We have theories that relate early parent–child interactions with later psychopathology (Freud, 1954; Mahler et al., 1975), but few theories, and no data, on the parent–child relationship and children's concept of themselves. Moreover, there is relatively little consideration of such factors as other familial relationships (siblings, etc.), or intelligence/cognition, as these factors influence a child's self-concept.

Nevertheless, the examples, as presented earlier, make clear that the child's self-concept (at least in some form) can be said to emerge by the end of the second year. If such examples constitute sufficient reason for inquiry into the development of self-concept by 2 years, then our task is to choose a method of exploring the problem. We have chosen to look at self-recognition, not because it necessarily constitutes the best measure of self-concept, or because it serves as an equivalent of the self-concept in the older organism, but because there are few other techniques that empirically can be used to approach the problem. Such difficulties are not new for those developmental theorists interested in the origins of later complex behavior.

In order to approach any problem with a developmental perspective, it is necessary to assume that behaviors are transformed and their meanings change. Moreover, old abilities and concepts change into new abilities and concepts, often being related to, but showing little structural similarity. Stage theories of development are theories of discontinuities of structure and ability. Such theory suggests that the development of a skill is not merely the accumulative growth of that skill, but a series of transformations. For Piaget (1954), the infant's intellectual ability is not the same, but less, than that of the adult.

In such a fashion, we see self-recognition as a method to explore some aspect of the child's early self-concept. It does not represent the sum total of the infant's self-concept, nor may it be directly related to the self-concept of the 6-year-old. Nevertheless, it does provide a method of experimentally exploring some aspect of the child's self-schemata and for examining individual differences. Our task remains to determine the relationship, if any, between self-recognition and other aspects of the self-schemata as seen in the older child. This task still needs to be performed. Even so, the data both from our laboratory and the work of Tajima as reported, indicate interesting possibilities. First, there is overwhelming support for the developmental unfolding of self-recognition ability. Second, there is growing evidence that individual differences in self-recognition are related to both perceptual/cognitive ability and early parent–child relations. Such findings are encouraging and support our belief that, although self-recognition only constitutes a portion of the self-schemata (and may be related to only limited aspects of later characteristics of that schema), its emergence early in the child's life, and its relationship to factors we have discerned, makes it an important measure of children's development in the first 2 years of life.

REFERENCES

Abelson, R. (1976). Script processing in attitude formation and decision making. In J. S. Carroll & J. Payne (Eds.), *Cognition and behavior.* Hillsdale, NJ: Lawrence Erlbaum Associates.

Ahrend, R., Grove, F. L., & Sroufe, L. A. (1979). Continuity of individual adaptation from infancy to kindergarten: A predictive study of ego-resiliency and curiosity in preschoolers. *Child Development, 50,* 950–959.

Ainsworth, M. D. S., Blehar, M. C., Waters, E., & Wall, S. (1978). *Patterns of attachment: A psychological study of the strange situation.* Hillsdale, NJ: Lawrence Erlbaum Associates.

Amsterdam, B. K. (1968). *Mirror behavior in children under two years of age.* Unpublished doctoral dissertation, University of North Carolina, Chapel Hill, NC.

Banks, J. H., & Wolfson, J. H. (1967, April). *Differential cardiac response of infants to mother and stranger.* Paper presented at the Eastern Psychological Association meetings, Boston, MA.

Belsky, J. (1978). Three theoretical models of child abuse: A critical review. *Child Abuse and Neglect, 2,* 37–49.

Belsky, J., Rovine, M., & Taylor, D. (1984). The origins of individual differences in infant and mother attachment: Maternal and infant contributions. *Child Development, 55,* 718–728.

Bertenthal, B. I., & Fischer, K. W (1978). Development of self-recognition in the infant. *Developmental Psychology, 14,* 44–50.

Bretherton, I., & Beeghly, M. (1982). Talking about internal states: The acquisition of an explicit theory of the mind. *Developmental Psychology, 18*(6), 906–921.

Bronson, G. W. (1972). Infants' reactions to unfamiliar persons and novel objects. *Monographs of the Society for Research in Child Development, 47*(3).

Chess, S., & Thomas, A. (1982). Infant bonding: Mystique and reality. *Journal of Orthopsychiatry, 52,* 213–222.

Cooley, C. H. (1912). *Human nature and the social order.* New York: Scribner's.

Cornielson, F. S., & Arsenian, I. (1960). A study of the responses of psychotic patients to photographic self image experience. *Psychiatric Quarterly, 34,* 1–8.

Dixon, J. C. (1957). Development of self-recognition. *Journal of Genetic Psychology, 91,* 251–256.

Edwards, C. P., & Lewis, M. (1979). Young children's concepts of social relations: Social functions and social objects. In M. Lewis & L. Rosenblum (Eds.), *The child and its family: The genesis of behavior:* (Vol. 2). New York: Plenum.

Epstein, S. (1980). The self-concept: A review and the proposal of an integrated theory of personality. In E. Staub (Ed.), *Personality: Basic issues and current research.* Englewood Cliffs, NJ: Prentice-Hall.

Frenkel, R. E. (1964). Psychotherapeutic reconstruction of the traumatic amnesic period by mirror image projective technique. *Journal of Existentialism, 17,* 77–96.

Freud, S. (1954). *The interpretation of dreams.* New York: Basic.

Freud, S. (1959). *Instincts and their vicissitudes.* New York: Basic.

Gallup, G. G., Jr. (1970). Chimpanzees: Self-recognition. *Science, 167,* 86–87.

Gallup, G. G., Jr., & McClure, M. K. (1971). Preference for mirror-image stimulation in differentially reared rhesus monkeys. *Journal of Comparative and Physiological Psychology, 75,* 403–407.

Garcia-Coll, C. G., Kagan, J., & Reznick, S. J. (1984). Behavorial inhibition in young children. *Child Development, 55,* 1005–1019.

Gergen, K. J. (1971). *The concept of self.* New York: Holt.

Goldsmith, H., & Campos, J. J. (1982). Toward a theory of infant temperament. In R. Emde & R. Harman (Eds.), *Attachment and affiliative systems.* New York: Plenum.

Heider, F. (1958). *The psychology of interpersonal relations.* New York: Wiley.

Jackson, E., Campos, J., & Fischer, K. (1978). The question of decalage between object performance and person performance. *Developmental Psychology, 14,* 1–10.

James, W. (1961). *Psychology: The briefer course.* New York: Harper & Row. (Originally published, 1892).

Kagan, J. (1981). *The second year: The emergence of self awareness.* Cambridge, MA: Harvard University Press.

Lerner, J. B., & Lerner, R. M. (1982). Temperament and adaptation across life: Theoretical and empirical bases. In P. B. Baltes & O. G. Brim, Jr. (Eds.), *Life span development and behavior: Vol. 5.* New York: Academic Press.

Lewis, M. (1971). Individual differences in the measurement of early cognitive growth. In J. Hellmuth (Ed.), *Exceptional infant: Vol. 2.* New York: Brunner/Mazel.

Lewis, M. (1982). The social network systems: Toward a general theory of social development. In T. Field (Ed.), *Review of human development: Vol. 1.* New York: Wiley.

Lewis, M. (1983). Newton, Einstein, Piaget and the concept of self. In L. S. Liben (Ed.), *Piaget and the foundations of knowledge.* Hillsdale, NJ: Lawrence Erlbaum Associates.

Lewis, M., & Baldini, N. (1979). Attentional processes and individual differences. In G. Hale & M. Lewis (Eds.), *Attention and cognitive development*. New York: Plenum.

Lewis, M. & Brooks-Gunn, J. (1979a). *Social cognition and the acquisition of self*. New York: Plenum.

Lewis, M. & Brooks-Gunn, J. (1979b). Toward a theory of social cognition: the development of self. In I. Uzgiris (Eds.), *New directions in child development: Social interaction and comunication during infancy*. San Francisco, CA: Jossey-Bass.

Lewis, M., Brooks-Gunn, J., & Jaskir, J. (in press). Individual differences in early visual self recognition. *Developmental Psychology*.

Lewis, M., & Feiring, C. (1978). The child's social network: Social object, social functions and their relationship. In M. Lewis & L. Rosenblum (Eds.) *The child and its family: The genesis of behavior: Vol. 2*. New York: Plenum.

Lewis, M., Feiring, C., McGuffog, C., & Jaskir, Jr. (1984). Predicting psychopathology in six-year-olds from early social relations. *Child Development, 55*, 123–136.

Lewis, M., & Goldberg, S. (1969). The acquisition and violation of expectancy: An experimental paradigm. *Journal of Experimental Child Psychology, 7*, 70–80.

Lewis, M., & Michalson, L. (1983). *Children's emotions and moods: Developmental theory and measurement*. New York: Plenum.

Lewis, M., & Michalson, L. (1984). The socialization of emotional pathology in infancy. *Infant Mental Health Journal, 5*(3), 121–134.

Lewis, M., & Schaeffer, S. (1968). Peer behavior and mother–infant interaction in maltreated children. In M. Lewis & L. Rosenblum (Eds.), *The uncommon child: The genesis of behavior: Vol. 3*. New York: International Universities.

Lewis, M., Weiss, M., & Sullivan M. (1985). *The self conscious emotions: Theory and proposed research*. Unpublished manuscript.

Lipsitt, L. P. (Ed.), (1980). *Developmental psychobiology: The significance of infancy*. Hillsdale, NJ: Lawrence Erlbaum Associates.

Livesley, W. J., & Bromley, D. B. (1973). *Person perception in childhood and adolescence*. New York: Wiley.

Mahler, M. S., Pine, F., & Bergman, A. (1975). *The psychological birth of the infant*. New York: Basic.

Mans, L., Cicchetti, D., & Sroufe, L. A. (1978). Mirror reactions of Down's Syndrome infants and toddlers: Cognitive underpinnings of self-recognition. *Child Development, 49*, 1247–1250.

Matas, L., Ahrend, R. A., & Sroufe, L. A. (1978). Continuity of adaptation in the second year: The relationship between quality of attachment and later competence. *Child Development, 49*, 547–556.

Mead, G. H. (1934). *Mind, self, and society: From the standpoint of a social behaviorist*. Chicago: University of Chicago Press.

Merleau-Ponty, M. (1964). *Primacy of perception*. (J. Eddie, Ed., & W. Cobb, Trans.). Evanston, IL: Northwest Universities Press.

Michalson, L., & Lewis, M. (1985). What do children know about emotions and when do they know it? In M. Lewis & C. Saarni (Eds.), *Socialization of emotion*. New York: Plenum.

Mijake, K. (1983). Infant's temperamental disposition, mother's mode of interaction, quality of attachment, and infant's receptivity to socialization. *Research and Clinical Center for Child Development, Annual Report*. Saporro, Japan: Hokkaido University.

Papousek, H., & Papousek, M. (1981). The common in the uncommon child: Comments on the child's integrative capacities and on initiative parenting. In M. Lewis & L. Rosenblum (Eds.), *The uncommon child: The genesis of behavior: Vol. 3*. New York: Plenum.

Piaget, J. (1954). *The construction of reality in the child*. (M. Cook, Trans.) New York: Basic. (Originally published, 1937.)

Piaget, J. (1963). *The origins of intelligence in children*. (M. Cook, Trans.) New York: Norton.

(Originally published 1936.)

Rheingold, H. L. (1971). *Some visual determinants of smiling infants*. Unpublished manuscript.

Rosenberg, M. J. (1965). *Society and the adolescent self-image*. Princeton, NJ: Princeton University Press.

Schaeffer, H. R. (1975). Cognitive Components of the infants response to strangeness. In M. Lewis & L. A. Rosenblum (Eds.), *Origins of fear*. New York: Wiley.

Spitz, R. A., & Wolf, K. M. (1946). The smiling response: A contribution to the ontogenesis of social relations. *Genetic Psychology Monographs, 34,* 57–125.

Sullivan, H. S. (2953). *The interpersonal theory of psychiatry*. New York: Norton.

Uzgiris, I. C., & Hunt, J. (1975). *Toward ordinal scales of psychological development in infancy*. Urbana, IL: University of Illinois Press.

Uzgiris, I. C., & Hunt, J. (1978). *Assessment in infancy: Ordinal scales of development*. Chicago: University of Illinois Press.

Wallon, H. (1949). *Les origines du caractere chez l'enfant; les precludes du sentiment de personalite*. [The origins of character in the infant's home: the precursors of emotion in personality.] (2nd Ed.) Paris: Presses Universitaires de France.

Wylie, R. C. (1961). *The self concept*. Lincoln: University of Nebraska Press.

4 The Psychoanalytic Ego in Lacan: Its Origins and Self-Serving Functions

John P. Muller
Austen Riggs Center

For an American audience, what is, perhaps, most troubling in Lacan's work is his persistent and insulting attack on what he calls the American hymn to "the autonomous ego" (Lacan, 1977, p. 306). Historically, and culturally, we place a high value on individualism, and you can hardly pick up a psychoanalytic or psychological text that does not put in a central place so-called healthy ego functioning, where the ego is the measure of reality, the analyst's ego is the norm and model for the patient's ego, and strengthening the ego is taken to be a desirable end of treatment — the current focus on self and narcissism, I think, being a variation of the same theme (see Blanck & Blanck, 1979). In Lacan's view, all of this radically distorts the Freudian revolution, a revolution that Freud, himself, (1917, p. 139) compares to two major previous dislocations: First, when Copernicus dislodged the earth from the center of the universe, and then, when Darwin dislodged the human species from its privileged position in the order of beings, a dislocation whose consequences are still being felt in our schools. Freud, in turn, reveals that the ego is not master in its own house, and Lacan takes this third revolution very seriously, going so far as to view the ego as "the mental malady of man" (1975, p. 22).

It must be stressed that Lacan is speaking from the psychoanalytic field of experience, which he takes to be the very same field of Freud's discoveries. For Lacan (as for Freud) the ego that is present in the psychoanalytic field is surely the conscious ego of the speakers, but because psychoanalysis is the talking cure, and not a cure by physical contact, pharmaceutical agents, or hypnotic or pedagogic suggestion, the emphasis in any serious science of psychoanalysis must be on the central characteristics of the talking. In examining these characteristics, Lacan stresses that the ego is not to be equated with the presence speaking, and that the laws governing speech are basic patterns elucidated by structural linguistics; these are largely unconscious and account for unconscious phenomena such as dreams and symptoms.

Lacan's point rests on the fact that speech always says more than the speaker intends, given the many levels of discourse in any analysis, ranging from the intrusive Freudian slips, to the body speech of symptoms, to the punning and ordinary homophonies of speech, to the ongoing fantasies and intermittent dreaming we all engage in. The Nobel laureate Czeslaw Milosz (1978) writes: "The purpose of poetry is to remind us how difficult it is to remain just one person, for our house is open; there are no keys in the doors and invisible guests come in and out at will." The ego tries precisely to pretend that I am just one personality, possessing an identity, assuming a status, and master of the house (see Greenwald, 1982, for a useful challenge to this position). The ego does this by maintaining a defensive rigidity and by functioning, Lacan says, as "the armor of an alienating identity," (1977, p. 4) demanding to be recognized, ever-ready to mirror the other in order to win approval, and resisting the implications of unconscious desire. Rather than providing veridical access to reality, the ego has shaped reality to preserve its position of mastery. The distortions reach such outlandish proportions that we must invoke the category of social psychosis to understand such things as the massacre of American natives by New England colonists in the name of waging God's war against the devil, the holocaust executed in the service of good order, the massive stockpiling of weapons that annihilate in order to maintain peace, and so forth.

This paper attempts to extend the psychoanalytic perspective, specifically that of Jacques Lacan, to embrace recent experimental research on the self, depression, and aggression as an elaboration of an earlier paper (Muller, 1982). Within Lacan's framework we can approach the ego as a set of cognitive constraints whose distorting effects are especially prominent in the domain of oneself, one aspect of which is "the self" as a set of schemata. For Lacan, the ego originates, is rooted in, takes its structure from, the mirroring mode of relating. Moreover, there is ample experimental evidence that the functions of the ego are essentially self-serving, with depression, in part, resulting from the ego's inability to sustain illusions. Aggression, in turn, can be considered as a defensive response of the ego. It is hoped that a more disseminated understanding of the Lacanian ego will serve several purposes: (a) to revitalize thinking about psychoanalytic concepts, (b) to provide a fertile theoretical ground for experimental research, and (c) to broaden the understanding of behavior.

JACQUES LACAN'S READING OF FREUD:
AN OVERVIEW

Biography

Jacques Lacan was born in Paris in 1901 and died in 1981. He received a classical education before going into medical studies, which he completed in 1932 with a doctoral dissertation on paranoia. At this time he was also involved with surrealism, with Hegel's philosophy as expounded in the lectures of Alexandre Kojève (Miller, 1981), and with psychoanalytic training, with Rudolf Loewenstein as his analyst, from 1932 to 1938.

In 1936, Lacan delivered an unpublished paper on the origins of the ego in the "mirror phase" of child development at the 14th International Psychoanalytic Congress in Marienbad; his later published paper, *The Mirror Stage as Formative of the Function of the I as Revealed in Psychoanalytic Experience* was delivered at the 16th International Congress of Psychoanalysis in Zurich in 1949. This paper, together with *Aggressivity in Psychoanalysis,* delivered in 1948, were published in a collection of Lacan's (1966) papers titled *Ecrits.* Our attention will return to these two papers in detail once we have examined some central features of Lacan's framework.

The Freudian Discovery

Lacan (1977) claims his work is a "return to Freud" (p. 114) and no one has been more diligent in rereading the corpus of Freud's work, in German, with a close attention, even devotion, to Freud's style. Freud's early work, such as *Project for a Scientific Psychology* (1895), *Interpretation of Dreams* (1900), *The Psychopathology of Everyday Life* (1901), *Jokes and Their Relation to the Unconscious* (1905), and the case histories and letters to Fliess are especially important to Lacan because they reveal Freud's discovery of unconscious processes with a freshness, a directness, as yet unobscured by Freud's later reinterpretations under the influence of his jostling band of followers (Roustang, 1982). This discovery, according to Lacan, was that the unconscious consists of inscriptions whose registration and interconnections are governed by the laws of language. Such laws, as expressed by Saussure (1966) and Jakobson (1956), were, of course, not yet formulated when Freud made his discovery, and, therefore, Freud attempted to make his discovery scientifically acceptable by locating it in the domain of a "hard" science like biology or physics. But when his actual descriptions of the workings of the unconscious (as evidenced in dreams, slips of the tongue, case histories, or symptomatology) are viewed through the lens of structural linguistics, there is no doubt, Lacan stresses (and the reader can experience this, too), that Freud's discovery dealt with linguistic properties (see also Forrester, 1980, for the linguistic aspects of the early Freud). This is why Lacan (1977) quite plainly states, "The unconscious is neither primordial nor instinctual; what it knows about the elementary is no more than the elements of the signifier" (p. 170).

The Lacanian Unconscious Structured Like a Language

But what is this notion of the signifier, and how can we understand its function in the Freudian unconscious? Saussure (1966), the fount of structural linguistics, distinguished speech from language, where speech is taken as an individual psychomotor act occurring in time (and therefore diachronic), and language is conceived as an organized system of signs (a synchronic whole), making speech possible. The linguistic sign for Saussure is composed of a relationship between a signifier and a signified, the signifier being the sound–image, and the signified a concept. Saussure (1966) stresses two things about the sign: First, the relationship between sound–image and concept is arbitrary, unmotivated, without intrinsic connection, and simply the result of convention; and second, that no signifier or signified has meaning in itself, but receives its linguistic value by way of reciprocal differentiation from all the other signs in a given system. Phonemic features, therefore, have no so-called natural affinity to meaning and no positive substance, but achieve salience only in opposition to all other phonemes in a given language. This perspective of Saussure lays down a basic tenet of structuralism, namely, the fundamental priority of the patterned system to any of its components.

Lacan (1977) adapts this Saussurian framework and formulates the linguistic sign as signifier-over-signified, $\frac{S}{s}$, with a bar separating signifier from signified. This bar has all the force of a barrier and includes the notion of a dynamic repression of the signified. Thus, he can speak of the symptom as a signifier whose signified is repressed from consciousness. But he complicates this further, for the signified, so repressed, turns out to be another signifier embedded in an associative chain of signifiers. An illustration of this is given by Freud (1909) in his analysis of the Rat Man:

> In this way rats came to have the meaning of "*money.*" The patient gave an indication of this connection by reacting to the word "*Ratten*" ["rats"] with the association "*Raten*" ["installments"]. In his obsessional deliria he had coined himself a regular rat currency. When, for instance, in reply to a question, I told him the amount of my fee for an hour's treatment, he said to himself (as I learned six months later): "So many florins, so many rats." Little by little he translated into this language the whole complex of money interests which centered round his

father's legacy to him; that is to say, all his ideas connected with that subject were by the way of the verbal bridge "*Raten — Ratten,*" carried over into his obsessional life and brought under the dominion of his unconscious. Moreover, the captain's request to him to pay back the charges due upon the packet served to strengthen the money significance of rats, by way of another verbal bridge "*Spielratte,*" which led back to his father's gambling debt. (pp. 213–214)

Additional material was associated with "*heiraten,*" or "to marry."

The repressed signified, then, turns out to be an endless chain of associated signifiers. There are at least two reasons for this: First, signifiers always refer to other signifiers, retrospectively giving meaning, for example, to the preceding words in a sentence and anticipating meaning until the sentence is punctuated. Signifiers do not refer directly to things, for there is no one-to-one correspondence between words and things. Second, in Lacan's notion of metaphor, the Saussurian signifier–signified formula is altered: in metaphor a substitute signifier replaces another signifier in an associative chain, but the replaced signifier does not vanish. It goes "below the bar" to another level of discourse where it continues to function in an unconscious associative chain marked by certain "nodal points" or "switch-words" (as in Freud & Breuer, 1895, p. 290). Thus, Lacan writes the formula for metaphor, substitute signifier over original signifier, as $\frac{S'}{S}$, where the place of the signified is, henceforth, occupied by a signifier. It is the structure of metaphor that makes symptoms possible, that gives symptoms their meaning, and accounts for the power of "the talking cure." For the symptom is a metaphor and is rendered unnecessary once the repressed signifier, replaced by the substitute signifier — the symptom — can be articulated (see Muller, 1979).

It is Lacan's main thesis that Freud understood this, and that the essential Freudian discovery, lost in the process of transmission, is that the unconscious is structured linguistically — it operates according to laws of language; its "stuff" is the stuff of language. The laws of language constitute an all-pervasive, largely unconscious, patterning of the human sociocultural world, and this structure is what we take Lacan to mean, following Levi-Strauss, by "the symbolic order," a framework, in which Lacan (1977) can say, "Man speaks, but it is because the symbol has made him man" (p. 65). The symbolic order is also the Other, other to consciousness and to the individual, for "this locus also extends as far into the subject as the laws of speech, that is to say, well beyond the discourse that takes its orders from the ego, as we have known ever since Freud discovered its unconscious field and the laws that structure it" (p. 141). The ego, in essence, functions to mask the subject's desire, disclosed in unconscious discourse, and to promote its own position as narcissistic object of desire. Laplanche (1970) goes so far as to call the ego an object that passes itself off as a desiring subject.

The Ego in Freud

Lacan (1953) claims there is a basic ambiguity in Freud's view of the ego. On the one hand, the ego functions as a narcissistic love object; on the other hand, the ego is the center of consciousness, resisting the id and fostering reality relations. Lacan sees the first conception as more basic in Freud coming to the forefront as, "His Majesty the Ego" (Freud, 1908, p. 150; 1914, p. 91). The second conception, part of the new topology after 1920, has become associated with the adaptation theory of American ego psychology. Rapaport (1967) finds four phases in the history of psychoanalytic ego psychology. In Phase 1, Freud lays stress on the role of defenses against remembering and re-encountering certain experiences of reality. In Phase 2, begun when Freud made his assertion (now in question, as we read in Malcolm [1983]) that reports of infantile seduction were actually fantasies, the stress was placed on repression as the result of ego instincts. This is consistent with Lacan's view of the ego as distorting, defensive, and self-protective (although Rapaport, of course, does not say this). This congruence extends into Phase 3, beginning after the 1914 paper on narcissism. Rapaport (1967) writes that in this period "Freud repeatedly indicated that he expected the theory of the ego to arise from the study of narcissistic neuroses [i.e., psychosis]" (p. 74). In *The Ego and the Id,* the ego is presumed to differentiate out of the id, arises from identifications with abandoned objects, includes the structures responsible for resistance, and "is first and foremost a bodily ego" (Freud, 1923, p. 26). Ego functions are still organized around the perception–consciousness system, and in that context the ego has an adaptive function insofar as it is self-protective in the face of external dangers, such as the threat of death, the loss of the protecting mother, or the fear of castration (1923, pp. 57–59). This self-protective function, however, is not commensurate with a notion of ego autonomy, and Rapaport (1967) can only speak of "Freud's implied conception of autonomous synthetic functions of the ego" (p. 750).

In Phase 4, coming after Freud and centering on the work of Hartmann and Erikson, Lacan locates what he calls the American glorification of the autonomous ego. In this phase, Rapaport lends his support to the admittedly post-Freudian reconceptualization of the ego and the id wherein both differentiate from a common matrix that includes the ego's independent roots. Such roots, called the "ego apparatuses of primary autonomy," consist of functions such as motility, perception, and memory. These apparatuses enable instinctual drives to coordinate with their objects, and this link-up, in turn, provides the means for coordinating with external reality, viewed in this reconceptualization as "an average expectable environment." Such coordination is seen as a "state of adaptedness which is prior to conflict and not a product of conflict solution" (p. 751) – and by taking this circuitous route we can finally speak of an ego autonomously developing relationships with reality.

If we find warranted Rapaport's judgment that such a view of the ego is post-Freudian, then Lacan's (1977) heralding of a "return to Freud" (p. 114) is an appeal to take seriously Freud's view of the ego as radically narcissistic. The evidence for such a view of the ego in Freud is summarized by Duruz (1981) in his diligent rereading of the Freud texts.

THE EGO IN LACAN: ORIGINS IN THE MIRROR PHASE

Lacan may have been aware of the pioneering conceptualizations of the early American social psychologists: Baldwin (1902, 1906; see also Cairns [1980]), Cooley (1962), and Mead (1934) whose attempts to situate the origins of the self in a social dialectic remain fertile even today. At any rate, Lacan does refer to Baldwin (whose work was translated into French) in his 1949 essay on the ego. (Freud, too, refers to Baldwin [1905, p. 174n.]; see also Letter 74 to Fliess [1887-1902, p. 228].) But it is the French psychologist Wallon (1949) who is credited with providing observational data regarding the experience of the infant before the mirror. Wallon reports examples of infants responding to their reflections between their eighth and ninth months, and for Lacan this observation provides a major paradigm. Lacan's thesis is that the ego originates through the process wherein the infant visually recognizes its reflection in a mirror and responds to it with evident delight. Lacan stresses three central features of this archetypal moment:

1. The experience of visual self-recognition is positively charged for the infant (it is not trivial).
2. The essential structure of this experience is one of identification, wherein the assumption of an image has tranformative impact on the subject.
3. This identification, to be called "ego," will go on to have primarily self-serving, defensive, and alienating functions.

Visual Self-Recognition in the Infant

Gallup (1977) reports that chimpanzees and orangutans are the only non-humans that show mirror self-recognition in his laboratory procedure (see also Gallup's chapter in this volume). Lacan (1977) called attention, in 1949, to this "fact of comparative psychology" (p. 1), and asserted that whereas in the case of the chimpanzee the act "exhausts" itself "once the image has been mastered and found empty," by contrast the infant engages in play, gesturing before the mirror, in a "jubilant assumption of his specular image" (p. 2). Although "jubilation" may not be observable in the chimpanzee, Gallup (1977) reports that the animal does go on to make pragmatic use of the mirror for grooming, and Köhler (1976) earlier described how his chimpanzees sought out their reflections in pools of water, polished tin, and so forth.

Borrowing Gallup's experimental technique, Lewis and Brooks-Gunn (1979; see also Lewis, this volume) provide an empirical base of controlled observations that essentially support Lacan's description of the infant before the mirror. Among the 9-month-old infants, 81% showed smiling behavior before the mirror, 80% cooed or babbled, 88% touched the mirror, and 38% engaged in rhythmic imitative behavior before the mirror. Although, perhaps, this constellation of behavior is not quite the jubilant response described by Lacan, Lewis and Brooks-Gunn (1979) conclude "the infants were quite interested in the mirror" (p. 37). More to the point, however, is the finding that such measures of interest decreased with age, especially after 1 year of age, for the younger children showed significantly more longer looks at the mirror, more touching of the mirror, and tended to show more smiling behavior. The decline in such measures of interest with age suggests that the initial moment of recognition, what Lacan (1977) calls the "Aha-Erlebnis," had already taken place, for the most part, by the age of 1 year. None of the younger children, moreover, acted coy or silly before the mirror, as some of the older children did; Lewis and Brooks-Gunn (1979) note that acting "silly or coy has been seen as a measure of self-admiration" (p. 44) and we can interpret that such narcissistic engagement can only occur after the mirror identification is firmly established (as in the older children).

Thus, we have ample experimental evidence for Lacan's description of the mirror-phase infant, which Lacan tells us includes the period from 8 to 18 months. This period also coincides with the consolidation of object permanence (Baer & Wright, 1974; Lewis & Brooks-Gunn, 1979) and also with the capacity for long-term memory as evidenced in delayed visual recognition of previously presented complex forms (Cohen, 1979; Rose, 1981). The recognition of and identification with a visual Gestalt as oneself would require both object permanence and long-term memory.

This visual Gestalt, the mirror-reflection of the human body, that the infant takes to be oneself, is, for Lacan, not to be confused with the self or the subject. To call this mirroring identification the ego emphasizes its structure as the foundational identity for all subsequent identifications, and, in this sense, precisely what Freud (1923) stated when he defined the character of the ego as "a precipitate of abandoned object cathexes" (p. 29). Nor is the psychoanalytic ego, for Lacan, to be equated with what Freud calls the perception-consciousness system as structured by "the reality principle"; rather, Laccan (1977) stresses, "(o)ur experience shows us that we should start, instead, from the *function of méconnaissance* [mis-understanding] that characterizes the ego in all its structures" (p. 6). As a structuring of reflected attributes the ego is related to a schema, along the lines of contemporary work on self-schemata; for example, the self as "a complex, person-specific, central, and attitudinal schema" (Greenwald & Pratkanis, 1984). Yet, we may be able to make more precise distinctions if we keep in mind the fundamental difference, found in Freud, between the level of unconscious processes, unconscious knowing, unconscious speaking, unconscious desire, and the level of consciousness. For Lacan, the true subject is the subject of the unconscious, not to be confused with the ego, which functions in consciousness as a structure of identification. Thus, we may distinguish:

1. Subject as unconscious knowing and desiring.
2. Ego as structure of identification.
3. Self as set of attributes posited in light of the ego.
4. What we will go on to call the "domain of oneself": that field of experience that includes the eight senses of ego described by Allport (1964) as well as the body, one's possessions, and one's desired objects.

In this framework the self is always in quotation marks as a set of propositions, a kind of propaganda script promoted by the ego in order to sustain a sense of identity and continuity (see Jones & Pittman, 1982, for an extended formulation). The ego, moreover, is an object for the subject, in part, because it is an other for the subject, for its origin as reflection grounds it in exteriority. To see oneself in the mirror is to see another looking back.

Sometimes this "other" of the reflection, with whom the child is identified, is confused by the child with the image of another child: The other child is experienced as a counterpart whose visual image exerts a "veritable captivation" on the child's behavior. The child sees its own self in the other. Following the work of Bühler (1927) and Köhler (1926), Lacan (1977) calls this phenomenon "transitivism." He writes that it occurs between 6 months and 2½ years of age:

> During the whole of this period we will record the emotional reactions and the articulated evidences of a normal transitivism. The child who strikes another says that he has been struck; the child who sees another fall, cries. (p. 19)

This effect of the nascent ego as reflected image, namely, to become confused with the image of the counterpart, may explain some curious findings made by Lewis and Brooks-Gunn (1979) in a second series of studies using videoscreen presentations.

Infants, ranging in age from 9 to 24 months, were seated one meter from a television screen with the mother sitting to the side, but behind the child. Three types of video presentations were made in counter-balanced order: (1) a recording of the infant made at home 1 week earlier, (2) a recording of another child of the same age and sex at home, and (3) a live display of the infant's actual behavior in the laboratory. A variety of infant responses to the viewings were analyzed. When contingent play was examined (the cluster of responses consisting primarily of facial movements and playing peekaboo by moving one's head, hand, or body out of the camera's view, and, therefore, off the screen and back again), children of all ages exhibited this response more to the live video presentation than to either the 1-week-old recording of themselves, or the recording of another child. In this experiment, 28% of the 9–12-month-old group, 75% of the 15–18-month-old group, and 97% of the 21–24-month-old group showed contingent play behavior, taken as a measure of self-recognition in the videoscreen. Behavior imitative of the nonlive tapes was infrequent: None of the 9-month-olds showed it, but there was a trend for the older groups to show it more in response to their own image than in response to another child's image on the screen. All age groups smiled more in the live video condition, whereas the proportion of time spent looking, as well as exhibiting facial expressions of concentration, was greatest in response to the videotape of another child and least in response to the live condition.

A second video study that added 2½ and 3-year-olds used the same kind of presentation, but also examined the effects of a taped or live approach of a stranger from the rear of the child or that of a counterpart (thus, the child, in live format, could see on the screen that a stranger was approaching from his or her rear and then could turn around to look). In this key experimental condition, it was found that all age groups turned around to look at the stranger on about one-half of the live trials, with no overall mean effect due to age, indicating that all age groups (from 9 months to 3 years) included children who demonstrated self-recognition. It was also observed, however, that the children over 18 months of age also turned their heads in about the same proportion on the taped stranger-approach trials as well. Lewis and Brooks-Gunn (1979) state: . . . "only the youngest infants responded solely to the contingency cues" mirroring live behavior (p. 95), although in the older groups, "turning behavior was also affected by the development of specific feature recognition" tied to the taped child's identity (whether self or other), (p. 97). But we are not certain about what constitutes the structure of such recognition in the nonlive tape conditions (tape of self as well as tape of another child) so that turning behavior ensues. Lewis and Brooks-Gunn (1979) report evidence from another study indicating that "infants often spend a great deal of time watching but not interacting with peers in small group situations," suggesting that the visual features of counterparts are of keen interest to infants (p. 111). Lacan's notion of "transitivism" may help us here if we assume there has been an identification with one's image. Given that structure of identification (from 8 to 18 months), Lacan (1977) writes that we can then observe a "deflection of the specular *I* into the social I" (p. 5); that is, there is a tendency toward an identification with images of counterparts. Lacan describes such subsequent identification as suffused with jealousy and competitiveness. Thus, we interpret, when the older infants (over 18 months), viewing the noncontingent tapes of themselves or another infant, saw the stranger approaching on the screen and then turned around to look, they were demonstrating transitivist behavior. The specific feature recognition at work here can, thus, be viewed as a form of identification with and captivation by the image of the other-as-counterpart.

Lewis and Brooks-Gunn (1979) are also hard-pressed to shed light on the generally positive responses made by the infants to their own images (cooing, smiling, laughing, etc.). Bossert (1983), in a videoscreen study of self-recognition among 2-year-olds, also reports that children were more likely to smile more when viewing contingent images of self compared to noncontingent (delayed) tapes of self; children also looked longer at a live contingent image of self compared to a delayed noncontingent image of self. Children also made faces more frequently in the live rather than delay condition. (Thus, we can interpret, deliberately promoting and enjoying mirroring effects.) In their interpretation of such positive interest, Lewis and Brooks-Gunn (1979) postulate an "attraction" that:

> . . . may be a reflex of our species (and perhaps other species) to respond to their young. As unlearned behavior, young infants find their reflections interesting from the first, since their own image is an image of an infant. Thus the first organizing feature of self-knowledge may be an unlearned response to behave positively and be attracted to images of young organisms. (pp. 222–223)

This explanation lacks the conceptual richness Lacan offers when he relates the perception of the human form as a Gestalt to the specific prematurity of the human infant at birth (1977, p. 4; see also Freud, 1926, p. 154). Gould (1976) argues that such prematurity is essential in the human species if the infant's head (only one-quarter of its eventual size) is not to exceed the limits of the maternal pelvic cavity. He cites evidence that leads him to conclude: "Human babies are born as embryos, and embryos they remain for about the first nine months of life" (p. 2)—that is, at about the very time that Lacan placed the mirror phase, the moment of readiness to recognize and identify with the Gestalt of the human form.

Lacan stresses that the infant is "jubilant" in this moment of recognition and identification because in this moment there is an experience (structured in the visual image) of the mastery, stature, and coherence that is in sharp contrast with the consequences of prematurity. For Lacan, these consequences are more than just the prolonged dependency stressed by Freud and others. The infant's prematurity comports a neuro-muscular discoordination and felt bodily fragmentation and, along with this, a visual precocity. Thus, Lacan wrote in 1948:

It is in function of this delay in development that the precocious maturation of visual perception takes its value of functional anticipation. There results from it, on the one hand, the remarkable salience of the visual structure in the recognition — so early, we have seen — of the human form. On the other hand, the opportunities to identify with this form, if I can put it so, receive from it a decisive pay-off which goes to constitute in man this imaginary knot, absolutely essential, that obscurely and across inextricable doctrinal contradictions psychoanalysis has, however admirably, designated under the name of *narcissism*. (1966, p. 186, author's own translation)

We do not know, to be sure, if and how the infant is actually conscious of its biological status, but this is not Lacan's point in any case. He, like Freud, lays great emphasis on the retroactive impact of subsequent experiences. Thus, adolescent sexual excitement retroactively influences how childhood experiences are experienced and viewed from the vantage point of adolescent knowledge (see Laplanche & Pontalis, 1973, pp. 111–114 for further elaboration of this notion of "deferred action"). Likewise, to threaten the place of the ego causes anxiety insofar as it allows a resurgence of the experience of bodily fragmentation. The visual Gestalt of the human form, coherent, erect, and masterful, promises a stability, unity, and wholeness that are in contrast to the experience of bodily fragmentation, what Lacan (1953) calls the "corps morcelé," the "body in bits and pieces" (p. 13). The identification with this visual Gestalt (that cognitive act whereby the infant affirms that its reflected image is oneself: this does not necessarily involve an actual mirror, but more pragmatically in the form of the body of the parent) allows the body image to serve as a defensive mask, concealing the actual state of fragmentation, functioning as a kind of camouflage and lure, a kind of covering over of the true state of affairs. Thus, when the integrity of the body image is attacked or threatened (as, for example, in competition or in the process of psychoanalysis when ego defenses begin to be dismantled) then the subject experiences the anxiety associated with bodily fragmentation (there is also an impulse to aggression, and we shall return to this). The infant's jubilation before the mirror, therefore, is meaningful precisely with reference to the conditions of human natal prematurity.

Recognition, Identification, and the Transformative Effects of the Image

Lacan wrote in 1946: "We think we can designate in the *imago* the proper object of psychology, precisely in the same way that Galileo's notion of the inert material point was the foundation for Physics" (1966, p. 188, author's own translation). The Latin word *imago* is defined as "an imitation, copy of a thing, an image, likeness" (Lewis & Short, 1955, p. 888). The reflection in the mirror is an *imago*, then, insofar as it is a visual image and representation of oneself. In emphasizing the transformative effect of such visual images, Lacan introduces examples from ethological research (1953; 1966, pp. 188–191, summarized by Ver Eecke [1983], pp. 115–116). Matthews (1938–1939) provides data indicating that what is necessary for ovulation to occur in female pigeons is the sight of another pigeon: Ovulation can occur in the case of two female pigeons confined together, in female pigeons separated from either male or female pigeons by a plate of glass, or even in a pigeon confined alone with a mirror present, but does not occur in the presence of other pigeons when the pigeon has no sight of others or of its own reflection. (The pigeon treating its reflection as equivalent to another pigeon is relevant to issues debated by Gallup and by Epstein and Koerner in their chapters in this volume.) Matthews (1938–1939) concludes, "the stimulus which causes ovulation in the pigeon is a visual one" (cited in Ver Eecke, 1983, p. 115). Lacan also draws on the work of Chauvin (1941) regarding the grasshopper *Schistocerca,* for whom two lines of development are possible, solitary or gregarious, with differences in behavior, size, color, shape, and food intake. The transition from solitary to gregarious type is determined by contact with members of its own species during an early stage of development; such contact may be visual or (unlike the pigeons) tactile. But Lacan (1953) stresses that "the mere sight of a member of the closely similar *Locusta* species (itself nongregarious) is sufficient, whereas even association with a *Gryllus* (cricket) is of no avail" (p. 14) to produce a gregarious outcome. Visual recognition of a counterpart, therefore, can have decisive impact on development.

From a psychoanalytic perspective, what is at stake here is the way self-recognition in a mirroring mode impacts on the subject. For Lacan, the impact is decisive both for the subject and for a correct appraisal of the role of the ego. When the subject identifies with its mirror reflection (either in the mirror or in a relationship in which the other reflects oneself) it becomes caught up in what Lacan calls "the imaginary order," the order of visual images where lure, disguise, and captivation are the salient features. Essential to the imaginary order is the potential for point-to-point correspondences in spatial extensions, as when a lens projects an image on a screen (1978, p. 86). It is this visual, spatial framework for luring, disguising, posturing, and preening that is the ego's main arena for activity. Contrary to the neo-Freudians (especially the Americans in the tradition of Hartmann, Rapaport, Kris, and Erikson) who proclaim that the ego and its correlative, the reality principle, provide objective access to what is, the ego in Lacan is essentially narcissistic and biased. The ego is primarily concerned with defending its position and appearance, is prone to luring and being lured, is ready to distort and deny facts to preserve illusions, and works toward creating mirroring objects — not just in others but also in statues, monuments, automobiles, and so on. This is accompanied by an exaggerated sense of its own importance, as we shall see, as well as a pervasive use of projection, so much so that Lacan states that the subject's ordinary cognitions are a form of "paranoiac knowledge," which Lacan (1977) defines as "the most general structure of human knowledge: that which constitutes the ego and its objects with attributes of permanence, identity, and substantiality, in short, with the form of entities or 'things' that are very different from the Gestalten that experience enables us to isolate in the shifting field. . ." (p. 17). As a result of the identification with the Gestalt of the human form as coherent, whole, erect, masterful (and, thus, an identification of oneself as possessing these attributes), these same attributions are made about reality so that things are taken to be separate identities, unities, perduring substances, and isolated out of the context of experiential flux. Thus, the world as reflected in the mirror (with right and left reversed, with surface distortions and virtual images) becomes the model for understanding "reality."

It would be instructive to apply the Lacanian framework to the large body of research on imitation (Yando, Seitz, & Zigler, 1978). Kagan (1981) presents data indicating that infants begin to imitate an adult's behavior around 9–10 months of age, but, thereafter, peer imitation increases with age, especially after 2 years (coinciding with the phase of transitivism). This period also includes the appearance of mastery smiles occurring while pursuing or having attained a goal in solitary play (after 1 year, according to Kagan, 1981) and the emergence of evaluative standards (at 18–24 months) as indicated by attention to broken toys, missing upholstery buttons, and so on, as well as distress following an adult model's performance, taken to be an indication of apprehension "because of a self-imposed obligation to perform actions" that the child is not sure he or she can implement (Kagan, 1981, p. 54). Imitation, as a central variable for self-serving concerns, appears in the findings of Thelen and Kirkland (1976) who summarize research indicating that "being imitated leads to increased attraction toward the imitator, increased allocation of rewards, and reciprocal imitation." (p. 692) They found that among school children, subjects tend to like and imitate, in turn, not the younger, but those older children (presumably of higher status because of their age and observable mastery) who imitated them. The same subjects also rated their own performances as above average when they were imitated by an older child than when a younger child imitated them. Indeed, being imitated by a younger child appeared to be aversive.

The effects of mirroring and being mirrored even serve to influence punitiveness. Berkowitz and Dunand (1981) found that subjects in a hot room punished a peer most severely when the peer was not bothered by the heat (as they were), and were least punitive when the peer seemed to share in the suffering: "In sum, we come to like those who (we believe) have the same emotional feelings we do when they are exposed to the same unpleasant condition" (Berkowitz, 1983b, p. 114).

SELF-SERVING FUNCTIONS OF THE EGO

Without mentioning the work of Lacan, Greenwald (1980) presented a review of findings from the areas of memory, persuasion, and attribution research that support Lacan's view of the ego as distorting, defensive, and self-serving. Cognitive biases such as egocentricity (self as the focus of knowledge), conservatism (resistance to cognitive change), and a self-serving feature Greenwald calls "beneffectance," (perception of responsibility for desired, but not undesired, outcomes) all "play a role in some fundamental aspect of personality" and, moreover, "are pervasive in and characteristic of normal personalities" (p. 603). Subsequent research (e.g., Ross, McFarland, & Fletcher, 1981) has supported Greenwald's thesis. These biases are much more in evidence when a specific domain is at issue, namely, the domain of oneself, or when there is greater ego-involvement as indicated by actual or manipulated arousal levels (Gollwitzer, Earle, & Stephan, 1982).

The self-serving function of beneffectance, "the tendency to take credit for success while denying responsibility for failure" (Greenwald, 1980, p. 605) is illustrated in a study by Johnston (1967). Subjects were told that each had a partner with whom they had to perform a task of skill, and feedback was given to each "team" (there was, in fact, no partner). Afterward, in cases of above average performance, subjects took credit for the success, while the assumed partner was blamed in cases of below average performance. Even with average performance feedback designations, a subject tended to believe that his or her above-average performance had been lowered by the below-average performance of the assumed partner. Ross and Sicoly (1979) also reported that subjects accepted more responsibility for the group's product than was attributed to them by the other participants. In an equally self-serving manner, subjects tend to deny responsibility for negative consequences of their actions. Harvey, Harris, and Barnes (1975) had subjects believe they were administering shocks to someone in a learning task (as in Milgram, 1963). Subjects believing they gave severe shocks claimed less responsibility for the learner's distress than those giving mild shocks, even less responsibility than subject observers attributed to them.

This pattern of "asymmetrical attributions" after success and failure is now judged to be a "firmly established finding" (Gollwitzer, Earle, & Stephan, 1982, p. 702). The motivational versus cognitive aspects of this phenomenon, however, have been debated. Miller and Ross (1975) proposed that an information theory model rather than self-esteem enhancement would account for the findings in the following way: (1) people expect success more than failure, (2) people take responsibility for expected outcomes (and, therefore, take credit for success), and (3) people tend to perceive a relation between effort and intended outcome (and, therefore, take credit for success). However, Sicoly and Ross (1977) found ample evidence for the motivational hypothesis. They asked 70 female college students to read pairs of suicide notes and to discriminate the genuine from the fake. Being told this was a social-sensitivity task, they were systematically given either successful or failing scores, were asked to rate their degree of responsibility for success or failure, and were asked to rate the accuracy of a confederate's feedback that took the form of systematically overevaluating or underevaluating the subjects' observed self-ratings of responsibility. Once again, the results indicated that subjects were more willing to take responsibility for success than for failure. Subjects also rated the confederate's evaluations of their responsibility as more accurate when they received excessive credit for success or exoneration for failure. In addition, these same subjects (in the success-more responsibility and failure-less responsibility conditions) went on to rate the confederate as more perceptive, more likable, more confident in their judgments, and as having more information on which to base them. Stephan, Bernstein, Stephan, and Davis (1979) in a laboratory study of male undergraduates, manipulated high versus low expectation for success on a task and also the basis of these expectations (ability or task difficulty). Task outcomes were then varied to confirm or disconfirm these given expectancies. In a second field-test study (a course exam), the same subjects were asked to predict their own exam scores and to state the basis for their expectations. The actual exam performance, in fact, either confirmed or disconfirmed these expectations. The results of both studies supported the self-serving bias, namely, that subjects claim they are responsible for success, while failure is blamed on task difficulty, independent of the basis for their expectations or whether the expectation is confirmed. In another field study, Lau and Russell (1980) coded newspaper articles covering sports events. It was found that players, coaches, and sportswriters tend to attribute internal reasons more for winning than for losing, that those with greater ego-involvement (players and coaches) do this more than others, and that, once again, these results were not a function of expectancies.

In a review of more than 75 attribution studies, Zuckerman (1979) concluded that "the motivational explanation is more effective than any of its informational alternatives" (p. 276). Zuckerman (1979) found that in studies where the task is to influence the other (as in teacher–student or therapist–client paradigms), subjects tend to give credit to the other; "in general there is very little evidence of self-serving attributions" (p. 248). In attribution studies regarding the outcome of subjects' own performance, however, self-enhancing and self-protective effects appeared in 27 of the 38 studies falling into this class (showing that subjects take more credit for success and less for failure). In studies comparing attributions about one's own behavior with attributions about the behavior of others, no self-serving bias was found when both self and other performed independent tasks; but studies in which self competed with other provided clear support for the self-serving bias (that success results from skill or effort, while failure is due to luck). In a review of more than 30 studies, Bradley (1978) also finds support for the self-serving bias. Green and Gross (1979), likewise, confirm this pattern of findings. Subjects were asked to attribute reasons why positive or negative evaluations were given by another person, and targets were varied: In one condition, the subjects, themselves, were the target of these evaluations, while in the other condition a third person was evaluated. When subjects were the target persons, they attributed the positive evaluations to themselves and the negative evaluations to situational circumstances; when a third person was evaluated, positive and negative evaluations had no effect on the attributions.

The ego's distorting functions can be seen in other cognitive processes that are, quite literally, self-serving. Sackeim (1983) stresses the adaptive value of self-deception. Taylor (1983) analyzed the beliefs and treatment course of women with breast cancer. It was found that patients who do best make exaggerated (and illusory) attributions that they or their physicians can control the illness and they also make self-enhancing social comparisons (no matter how severe their illness, they claim to be better off than some others). As Taylor indicates, loss of such illusions appears associated with depression. When depressed subjects are compared with nondepressed subjects, a self-serving pattern of attributions characterizes the nondepressed: they exaggerate others' positive views of them (Lewisohn, Mischel, Chaplin, & Barton, 1980); they are more likely to attribute control over uncontrollable events (Alloy, Abramson, & Viscusi, 1981); they tend to minimize the amount of negative feedback others give them (Nelson & Craighead, 1977); they over-reward their own performances (Rozensky, Rehm, Pry, & Roth, 1977); and they make internal attributions for their successes, while their failures are blamed on external factors (Abramson & Alloy, 1981). These and other findings are highly consistent with a Lacanian view of the ego that places, in the forefront, its self-serving, distorting, and defensive cognitive features.

EGO AS SOURCE OF AGGRESSION

Toward the end of his life Freud wrote:

> The desire for a powerful, uninhibited ego seems to us intelligible; but, as we are taught by the times we live in, it is in the profoundest sense hostile to civilization. (1938, p. 185)

Ten years later, Lacan delivered a paper at the Eleventh Congress of French-language Psychoanalysts in Brussels, titled *Aggressivity in Psychoanalysis* (1977, pp. 8–29; see also Muller & Richardson, 1982, pp. 42–66). In this paper, Lacan roots the impulse to aggression squarely in the narcissistic structure of the ego. By adapting the Hegelian master–slave dialectic regarding the origin of self-consciousness (Muller & Richardson, 1982, pp. 64–66), Lacan is able to consider aggression in the intersubjective framework of the desire for recognition.

Lacan's View of Aggression

In his 1948 paper, Lacan presents psychoanalysis as a technique that amounts to "inducing in the subject a controlled paranoia" (p. 15). The analyst's deliberately reduced ego-involvement frustrates the analysand's attempts to engage in seductive and mirroring operations, and, thereby, encourages the analysand to become angry and project "complexes" (constellations of impulse and behavior) onto the analyst, thus making available for analysis customary modes of relating and responding. There is nothing original, of course, in this view of the psychoanalytic process, and Lacan repeatedly asserts that he is, indeed, following Freud.

Lacan (1977) then turns to the major thesis of the essay: "Aggressivity is the correlative tendency of a mode of identification that we call narcissistic, and which determines the formal structure of man's ego and of the register of entities characteristic of his world" (p. 16). Lacan states that a specific image accompanies aggressive intentions: "These are the images of castration, mutilation, dismemberment, dislocation, evisceration, devouring, bursting open of the body, in short, the *imagos* that I have grouped together under the apparently structural term of *imagos of the fragmented body*" (1977, p. 11). He then makes a series of observations in support of his claim. He sees "a specific-relation here between man and his own body that is manifested in a series of social practices (p. 11)" — rites involving tattooing, incision, circumcision, and even fashion. He points to the play of children aged between two and five in which "the pulling off of the head and the ripping open of the belly are themes that occur spontaneously to their imagination" (p. 11). The paintings of Hieronymous Bosch provide "an atlas for all the aggressive images that torment mankind" (p. 11). Dream fragments reveal the same themes. We see the same focus on bodily fragmentation in the "cruel refinement" of man's weapons at the earlier, "craft stage" of his industry (1977, p. 12). In this way, we are led to see the image of the fragmented body as the core psychological content of the impulse to aggress.

In the phenomenon of transitivism, wherein children identify with one another's visual image, Lacan finds the groundwork for what he calls the "aggressive relativity" that marks the ego from its very origin (1977, p. 19). As a result of such identification with the other, the subject desires what others desire in the arena of competition and admiration. In addition, under the critical pressure of an essentially unattainable ideal ego, we observe "the depressive disruptions of the experienced reverses of inferiority" (1977, p. 20). When one's "bad internal objects" are reevoked in situations of inferiority in the adult, there can follow a "disconcerting" and "fragmenting effect on the *imago* of the original identification" (1977, p. 21). The unifying effect of the original identification serves to bind the infantile image of the fragmented body; when this identification is challenged by the competing image of another, or when the subject's demand for recognition is refused, or when the bodily coherence, so maintained, is attacked physically, the response is aggression. Thus, the aggressive imagery of bodily fragmentation is the inverse of the Gestalt of the unifying ego and, thereby, aggression is held in correlative tension with narcissism.

Lacan (1977) ends his essay by relating his view of aggression to the social, global arena of war: "The pre-eminence of aggressivity in our civilization would be sufficiently demonstrated already by the fact that it is usually confused in 'normal' morality with the virtue of strength" (p. 25). A view of human activity that sanctions aggression in the name of moral strength and competition is disruptive of social bonds; the "promotion of the ego today," furthermore, leads to isolation (p. 27). Therefore, the "instinct of self-preservation" must be reexamined given the link between aggressive mastery, and, for example, heart disease (Carver & Glass, 1978). We see how the fear of death can become psychologically subordinate in man "to the narcissistic fear of damage to one's own body" (Lacan, 1977, p. 28), and, specifically, to the narcissistic desire to maintain the coherence of the body image, grounded in the original mirror identification that dispelled fragmentation.

From this perspective, we can hypothesize the following:

1. The impulse to aggress will follow any challenge to the narcissistic position of the ego, in increasing severity of retaliation for: (a) disagreement with one's opinion, (b) refusal of praise or recognition, (c) insults and direct assaults on self-esteem, (d) direct physical injury as a challenge to felt bodily coherence, mastery, and unity;

2. To the extent that strength, control, and coherence have been valued as masculine in a given culture, men will show more overt aggression than women and androgymous women more than feminine women;

3. All of the above will vary with situational and social factors that mediate and structure an individual's aggressive responses. Just as the ego maintains self-serving functions in the sphere of cognitive attributions (as discussed earlier), so, also, it can be seen that the ego will mediate aggressive responses to any challenge of its position.

This viewpoint attempts to encompass both a body-based as well as a cognitive approach to aggression. It is body-based insofar as physical pain "can be a fairly potent stimulus to aggression in a wide variety of species" (Berkowitz, 1983a, p. 1136), precisely because pain threatens the experience of bodily integrity. The cognitive aspects, in human beings, are crucial insofar as "anger is a response to some perceived misdeed . . . more than anything else, anger is an attribution of blame" (Averill, 1983, p. 1150). We become angry most often at those we know and love (Averill, 1983), not simply because of frequency of contact, but because it is precisely from them that we desire to be recognized and to be mirrored, and when we are denied such recognition, we become angry. And this applies equally to men and women (Frodi, Macaulay, & Thome, 1977). But such cognitive factors are not necessarily conscious, for a Lacanian framework, stressing the unconscious network of signifiers that structure responses, also concurs with an emphasis on the conditioning of associations that cue aggressive responses, in accordance with what is now termed "associative network theory" (Bower, 1981). When a cue is perceived, it is, without conscious awareness, (Marcel, 1983a, 1983b; Shevrin, 1980; Shevrin & Dickman, 1980; Silverman, 1976) contextualized in both its surrounding network of place, time, and people, as well as in the unconscious associative network wherein it functions as a signifier for the subject.

A CONSTRAINTS MODEL OF THE EGO

The Lacanian view of the ego can, I think, be conceptualized in terms of constraints placed on knowledge of a domain. In particular, we can view the ego as a set of constraints that govern the way we come to know the domain of oneself—come to know it, that is, in a distorted manner. The ego also influences how we view others and the world.

The notion of constraints governing domains is pursued with regard to cognitive development by Keil (1981). Greenwald (1982) also considers personality development as including a "self-system" that functions as a "protected domain" and is "associated with a set of cognitive biases" (p. 159). Keil, following Peirce (1931–1935), Chomsky (1968), and others, reasons that in any domain of knowledge there is a near infinite range of hypothetically learnable structures. Keil (1981) writes: "Peirce was preoccupied with the following question: Given the multitude of hypotheses that can be based on a particular set of observations, how is it that science makes any progress?" (p. 198). Peirce's answer was that we are predisposed to generate some hypotheses rather than others. Chomsky argues for such a predisposition in the case of the child learning to speak. Keil (1981), thus, reasons: "Knowledge acquisition can not proceed successfully unless the inductive devices that apply to various cognitive domains are constrained in their outputs" (p. 199). Following Chomsky, Keil (1981) defines constraints:

> . . . as formal restrictions that limit the class of logically possible knowledge structures that can normally be used in a given cognitive domain. Constraints

reduce such a class toward a limited class of naturally learnable concepts. This does not mean absolute learnability — that is, that non-natural concepts cannot be taught with extensive training — but merely that such concepts are much less natural. A dog can, with extensive training, be taught to walk on its hind legs, but such behavior is still non-natural. (p. 198)

Keil (1981), thus, argues for the existence of detailed constraints because "much of cognitive development cannot be understood without reference to them" (p. 197). He goes on to say that "knowledge [in a given domain] undergoes change but nonetheless honors a uniform set of constraints throughout development" (p. 202). This implies, therefore, that the preschooler's knowledge is not essentially different from the adult's:

Recent research in cognitive development may be interpreted as providing implicit support for a constraints-oriented approach. Increasingly, studies are finding that the cognitive systems of children and adults are governed by many of the same restrictions and are, consequently, much more similar than is immediately apparent. It is becoming evident that cognitive development cannot be fully characterized unless these restrictions are understood. (p. 198)

For examples of such work on knowledge domains and constraints, Keil points to the work of Chomsky, Wexler and Culicover (1980), and Fodor (1975) on language, Osherson (1977) on natural deduction systems, Keil (1979) on basic categories of existence, and Gelman and Gallistel (1978) on numbers. Gelman (1979), for example, suggests five basic principles for successful counting:

(1) The one-one principle — each item in an array must be tagged with one and only one unique tag. (2) The stable-order principle — the tags assigned must be drawn from a stably ordered list. (3) The cardinal principle — the last tag used for a particular count serves to designate the cardinal number represented by the array. (4) The abstraction principle — any set of items may be collected together for a count. (5) The order-irrelevance principle — the order in which a given object is tagged as one, two, three, and so on, is irrelevant as long as it is tagged but once and as long as the stable-order and cardinal principles are honored. Number words are arbitrary tags. The evidence clearly supports the conclusion that preschoolers honor these principles. (p. 901)

And she asserts that preschoolers can do this by the age of 2½ years.

Now, for Keil (1981), these principles, as such, are not constraints, for Gelman's principles "are probably not stated in sufficiently general or formal terms and are probably consequences of more powerful, abstract constraints that are yet to be discovered. Nonetheless, they illustrate how natural knowledge of counting might be restricted" (pp. 211–212). Keil proposes that similar sets of constraints can be found that are specific to such domains as moral reasoning, aesthetics, naturalistic knowledge of mechanics, certain spatial and orienting skills, classification skills, causal thinking, etc. He does not address himself to the possibility of a domain of oneself, but such a domain appears to be at least as important as the others. But because this domain is prone to so much distortion and illusion, whether it can be properly called a domain of knowledge is another matter to be left open at the present time.

Keil (1981) then asks whether there are "general principles that enable one to tell what aspects of knowledge are and are not likely to be tightly constrained" (p. 223). While awaiting further empirical support, he offers five "suggestive guidelines" that are useful for exploring the notion of a domain of oneself whose constraints constitute the ego. Keil's first guideline is that "the more complex and abstract the knowledge, the more constraints are needed at the cognitive level" (p. 23). He argues that the "richer the knowledge to be acquired, the more tightly constrained it will have to be at the highest possible levels of description, if acquisition is to proceed successfully" (pp. 223–224).

The domain of oneself is surely among the more complex and abstract domains of knowledge (is this not what the history of philosophy, a good part of theology, and numerous other disciplines, including psychoanalysis, reveal?); but we must leave open for now the issue of whether and in what ways such knowledge is "scientific." What kind of "tight constraints" are specific to this domain? We do not yet know, but clues are suggested (in Keil's sense, perhaps, of suggested guidelines) by Greenwald's biases of egocentricity in the fabrication of memory, conservatism as resistance to change, and beneffectance, biases (along with others) that are consistently operative in how we construe this domain — or, rather, misconstrue this domain. To insist that the ego, as the set of such constraints specific to the domain of oneself, intrinsically involves a misconstrual, is just what Lacan (1977) means when he writes of "a misconstruing that is essential to knowing myself [*un méconnaître essentiel au me connaître*]" (p. 306).

Keil's (1981) second guideline is that "strongly constrained knowledge is knowledge that is acquired relatively effortlessly and rapidly, and usually without formal tutelage. Moreover, it is knowledge that is universally acquired" (p. 224). This describes, quite adequately, certain features of how we come to know the domain of oneself, features that include vision, the construction of space, properties of the image, and the mirror phase in which self-recognition originates through the child's spontaneous identification with the reflected image of the body as Gestalt. The mirror phase and the knowledge that comes from it (the reflection is recognized as "I") operate effortlessly and, presumably, universally.

Keil's third guideline for discerning when a domain is tightly constrained is that "tightly constrained knowledge appears to be less open to conscious introspection. This principle is a likely corollary of the prior principle that such knowledge is acquired without specific instruction. . . . In a related vein, this principle suggests that the acquisition of constrained knowledge is less susceptible to manipulation by means of learning strategies and other sorts of conscious manipulations" (p. 224). In the case of the domain of oneself, this principle is central because it opens the way to an eventual elaboration of the unconscious/conscious distinction as well as to a more rigorous delineation of how the set of constraints (ego), by necessity, skews this domain and results in an intrinsic misconstrual of it. This domain of oneself, moreover, is seen to have limited accessibility to conscious thought, as argued by Freud, (1900a) and, more recently in Bowers and Meichenbaum (1984). In addition, there is widespread skepticism about the degree to which once-acquired knowledge (or misconstrual) of this domain is open to conscious manipulation (Argyris, 1976).

Keil's (1981) fourth guideline states that "highly constrained knowledge may also carry a much stronger sense of anomaly than less restricted knowledge. Anomalies in different domains might include ungrammaticality, certain perceptual illusions, anomalous number systems, and bizarre moral laws" (p. 224). Every therapist witnesses to anomalies in the domain of oneself: peculiar obsessional thoughts and compulsions, strange notions about oneself felt as unique phenomena, hysterical bodily symptoms, many of the neurotic phenomena that we are ordinarily told are unwanted, incomprehensible, crazy.

Keil's (1981) fifth guideline takes the form of "an intuition that restrictive constraints are better characterized as constraints on structure than as constraints on process" (p. 224). This seems reasonable with regard to the domain of oneself, where the constraints of the ego set limits not on content or on processes as such, but rather on how they are structured through the mirroring mode, looking and being seen, competitiveness, egocentricity, conservatism, defensiveness, beneffectance, etc. By conceptualizing the ego in this way (as constraints that structure the domain of knowledge of oneself), we need not view the ego as an organization of knowledge (Greenwald, 1980), but rather as the organization whereby knowledge about the domain of oneself is structured. The ego, therefore, is not the substantive content, but rather the skewing lens, the source of *méconnaissance* about the domain of oneself. It is precisely this distorting function of the ego that Lacan claims has been overlooked by the ego psychologists in their zeal to defend its autonomy, synthetic functions, and verdicality.

CONCLUSION

The experience of self-recognition before the mirror, then, is no casual, passing moment. It constitutes an identification with an image and, thereby, has a transformative effect. By identifying with its reflected image, the infant affirms "That is I" and, thereby, makes a profound shift from its actual experience to an idealization. The idealized form of this "I" promises a cohesion that is in contrast to felt bodily fragmentation, a mastery that is lacking to its insufficiency and helplessness, and an imposing stature that is not apparent in its lowliness.

This first captivation by an external image forms the basis and provides the model for all subsequent identifications and, therefore, for what is commonly spoken of as "ego identity." But contrary to the prevalent perspective that prizes such ego identity and makes the ego the agency of adaptation to reality, Lacan calls attention to the ego's fundamentally defensive and distorting role. The ego, spawned in the mirror phase, is defensive insofar as it structurally serves to camouflage the anxiety of bodily fragmentation. Once installed, it is prone to competitive threats by the images of others, and it maintains its own position with rigidity (Argyris, 1976). The subject, in mistakenly identifying its image as itself, locates itself externally, measures itself against an external idealization, and, thereby, distorts its own reality. A fundamental misconstrual is, thereby, structurally ingrained in self-consciousness, so that, henceforth, the ego will mark for the subject "his discordance with his own reality" (Lacan, 1977, p. 2.) Thus, Lacan repeatedly speaks of "the *méconnaissances* that constitute the ego," "the *function of méconnaissance* that characterizes the ego in all its structures" (p. 6), especially in its speech, "in those reactions of opposition, negation, ostentation, and lying that our experience has shown us to be the characteristic modes of the agency of the ego in dialogue" (1977, p. 15). When the distorting illusion of ego mastery is lost, depression ensues; when it is threatened, aggressivity follows.

REFERENCES

Abramson, L. Y., & Alloy, L. B. (1981). Depression, nondepression, and cognitive illusions: Reply to Schwartz. *Journal of Experimental Psychology: General, 110,* 436–447.

Alloy, L. B., Abramson, L. Y., & Viscusi, D. (1981). Induced mood and the illusion of control. *Journal of Personality and Social Psychology, 41,* 1129–1140.

Allport, G. (1964). The ego in contemporary psychology. *Personality and Social Encounter, Selected Essays.* Boston, MA: Beacon Press.

Argyris, C. (1976). Theories of action that inhibit individual learning. *American Psychologist, 31,* 638–654.

Averill, J. R. (1983). Studies on anger and aggression: Implications for theories of emotion. *American Psychologist, 38,* 1145–1160.

Baer, D. M., & Wright, J. C. (1974). Developmental psychology. In M. Rosenzweig & L. Porter (Eds.), *Annual Review of Psychology,* Palo Alto, CA: Annual Reviews. (pp. 1–82).

Baldwin, J. M. (1902). *Fragments in philosophy and science.* New York: Scribner.

Baldwin, J. M. (1906). *Thoughts and things: A study of the development and meaning of thought or genetic logic:* (Vol. 1). New York: Macmillan.

Berkowitz, L. (1983a). Aversively stimulated aggression: Some parallels and differences in research with animals and humans. *American Psychologist, 38,* 1135-1144.

Berkowitz, L. (1983b). The experience of anger as a parallel process in the display of impulsive, "angry" aggression. In R. Geen & E. Donnerstein (Eds.), *Aggression: Theoretical and empirical reviews: Vol. I. Theoretical and methodological issues* (pp. 103-133) New York: Academic Press.

Berkowitz, L., & Dunand, M. (1981). [Misery wants to share the misery]. Unpublished raw data.

Blanck, G., & Blanck, R. (1979). *Ego psychology II: Psychoanalytic developmental psychology.* New York: Columbia University Press.

Bossert, L. D. (1983, August). *Self recognition in 2-year-olds: Roles of contingency and feature cues.* Presented at the 91st Annual Convention of the American Psychological Association, Anaheim, CA.

Bower, G. H. (1981). Mood and memory. *American Psychologist, 36,* 129-148.

Bowers, K., & Meichenbaum, D., (Eds.). (1984). *The unconscious reconsidered.* New York: Wiley.

Bradley, G. W. (1978). Self-serving biases in the attribution process: A re-examination of the fact or fiction question. *Journal of Personality and Social Psychology, 36,* 56-71.

Buhler, C. (1927). *Soziologische und psychologische Studien uber das erste Lebensjahr.* Jena: Fischer.

Cairns, R. B. (1980). Developmental theory before Piaget: The remarkable contributions of James Mark Baldwin. *Contemporary Psychology, 25,* 438-440.

Carver, C. S., & Glass, D. C. (1978). Coronary-prone behavior pattern an interpersonal aggression. *Journal of Personality and Social Psychology, 36,* 361-366.

Chauvin, R. (1941). Contribution à l'étude physiologique du criquet pèlerin et du déterminism des phénomènes grégaires. *Annuales de la Société entomologique de France, 110,* 133-272.

Chomsky, N. (1968). *Language and mind.* New York: Harcourt Brace Jovanovich.

Cohen, L. B. (1979). Our developing knowledge of infant perception and cognition. *American Psychologist, 34,* 894-899.

Cooley, C. H. (1962). *Social organization.* New York: Schocken Books. (Original work published 1909).

Duruz, N. (1981). The psychoanalytic concept of narcissism. *Psychoanalysis and Contemporary Thought, 4,* 3-67.

Fodor, J. A. (1975). *The language of thought.* New York: Thomas Y. Crowell.

Forrester, J. (1980). *Language and the origins of psychoanalysis.* New York: Columbia University Press.

Freud, S. (1887-1902). *The origins of psychoanalysis: Letters to Wilhelm Fliess, drafts and notes.* In M. Bonaparte, A. Freud, & E. Kris (Eds.), Trans. E. Mosbacher and J. Strachey. New York: Basic Books, 1954.

Freud, S., & Breuer, J. (1895). Studies on hysteria. *Standard Edition, 2.* London: Hogarth Press, 1955.

Freud, S. (1900a). The interpretation of dreams. *Standard Edition, 4 & 5.* London: Hogarth Press, 1953.

Freud, S. (1900b). Die Traumdeutung. *Gesammelte Werke, 2 & 3.* London: Imago, 1942.

Freud, S. (1901). The psychopathology of everyday life. *Standard Edition, 6.* London: Hogarth Press, 1960.

Freud, S. (1905). Three essays on the theory of sexuality. *Standard Edition, 7.* London: Hogarth Press, 1953.

Freud, S. (1908). Creative writers and day-dreaming. *Standard Edition, 9.* London: Hogarth Press, 1959.

Freud, S. (1909). Notes upon a case of obsessional neurosis. *Standard Edition, 10.* London: Hogarth Press, 1955.

Freud, S. (1914). On narcissism: An introduction. *Standard Edition, 14.* London: Hogarth Press, 1957.

Freud, S. (1917). A difficulty in the path of psycho-analysis. *Standard Edition, 17.* London: Hogarth Press, 1955.

Freud, S. (1923). The ego and the id. *Standard Edition, 19.* London: Hogarth Press, 1961.

Freud, S. (1926). Inhibitions, symptoms and anxiety. *Standard Edition, 20.* London: Hogarth Press, 1959.

Freud, S. (1938). An outline of psycho-analysis. *Standard Edition, 23.* London: Hogarth Press, 1964.

Frodi, A., Macaulay, J., & Thome, P. R. (1977). Are women always less aggressive than men? A review of the experimental literature. *Psychological Bulletin, 84,* 634–660.

Gallup, G. G. (1977). Self-recognition in primates: A comparative approach to the bidirectional properties of consciousness. *American Psychologist, 32,* 329–338.

Gelman, R. (1979). Preschool thought. *American Psychologist, 34,* 900–905.

Gelman, R., & Gallistel, C. R. (1978). *The child's understanding of number.* Cambridge, MA: Harvard University Press.

Gollwitzer, P. M., Earle, W. B., & Stephan, W. G. (1982). Affect as a determinant of egotism: Residual excitation and performance attributions. *Journal of Personality and Social Psychology, 43,* 702–709.

Gould, S. J. (1976). Human babies as embryos. *Natural History, 84,* 22–26.

Green, S. K., & Gross, A. E. (1979). Self-serving biases in implicit evaluations. *Personality and Social Psychology Bulletin, 5,* 214–217.

Greenwald, A. G. (1980). The totalitarian ego: Fabrication and revision of personal history. *American Psychologist, 35,* 603–618.

Greenwald, A. G. (1982). Is anyone in charge? Personalysis versus the principle of personal unity. In Jerry Suls (Ed.), *Psychological perspectives on the self: Vol. 1* (pp. 151–181). Hillsdale, NJ: Lawrence Erlbaum Associates.

Greenwald, A. G., & Pratkanis, A. R. (1984). The self. In R. S. Wyer & T. K. Srull (Eds.), *Handbook of social cognition.* Hillsdale, NJ: Lawrence Erlbaum Associates.

Harvey, J. H., Harris, B., & Barnes, R. D. (1975). Actor–observer differences in the perceptions of responsibility and freedom. *Journal of Personality and Social Psychology, 32,* 22–28.

Jakobson, R. (1956). Two aspects of language and two types of aphasic disturbances. In R. Jakobson & M. Halle (Eds.), *Fundamentals of language* (pp. 53–87). The Hague: Mouton.

Johnston, W. A. (1967). Individual performance and self-evaluation in a simulated team. *Organizational Behavior and Human Performance, 2,* 309–328.

Jones, E. E., & Pittman, T. S. (1982). Toward a general theory of strategic self-presentation. In Jerry Suls (Ed.), *Psychological perspectives on the self: Vol. 1* (pp. 231–262). Hillsdale, NJ: Lawrence Erlbaum Associates.

Kagan, J. (1981). *The second year: The emergence of self-awareness.* Camridge, MA: Harvard University Press.

Keil, F. C. (1979). *Semantic and conceptual development: An ontological perspective.* Cambridge, MA: Harvard University Press.

Keil, F. C. (1981). Constraints on knowledge and cognitive development. *Psychological Review, 88,* 197–227.

Kohler, E. (1926). *Die Personlichkeit des dreijahrigen Kindes.* Leipzig, Germany.

Kohler, W. (1976). *The mentality of apes.* (E. Winter, Trans.). New York: Liveright.

Lacan, J. (1953). Some reflections on the ego. *International Journal of Psycho-analysis, 34,* 11–17.

Lacan, J. (1966). *Ecrits.* Paris: Editions du Seuil.

Lacan, J. (1975). *Le Seminaire de Jacques Lacan.* Book 1: *Les Ecrits Techniques de Freud,* 1953–1954. Ed. J. A. Miller. Paris: Editions du Seuil.

Lacan, J. (1977). *Ecrits: A Selection*. (A. Sheridan, Trans.) New York: Norton.

Lacan, J. (1978). *The four fundamental concepts of psycho-analysis*. (A. Sheridan Trans.) Ed. J. Miller. New York: Norton.

Laplanche, J. (1976). *Life and death in psychoanalysis*. (J. Mehlman, Trans.) Baltimore, MD: Johns Hopkins University Press.

Laplanche, J., & Pontalis, J.-B. (1973). *The language of psychoanalysis*. New York: Norton.

Lau, R. R., & Russell, D. (1980). Attributions in the sports pages. *Journal of Personality and Social Psychology, 39,* 29–38.

Lewisohn, P. M., Mischel, W., Chaplin, W., & Barton, R. (1980). Social competence and depression: The role of illusory self-perceptions, *Journal of Abnormal Psychology, 89,* 203–212.

Lewis, C. T., & Short, C. (1955). *A Latin dictionary*. Oxford, England: Clarendon.

Lewis, M., & Brooks-Gunn, J. (1979). *Social cognition and the acquisition of self*. New York: Plenum.

Malcolm, J. (1983). *In the Freud archives*. New York: Knopf.

Marcel, A. J. (1983a). Conscious and unconscious perception: Experiments on visual masking and word recognition. *Cognitive Psychology, 15,* 197–237.

Marcel, A. J. (1983b). Conscious and unconscious perception: An approach to the relations between phenomenal experience and perceptual processes. *Cognitive Psychology, 15,* 238–300.

Matthews, L. H. (1938–1939). Visual stimulation and ovulation in pigeons. *Proceedings of the Royal Society of London* (pp. 557–560). London.

Mead, G. H. (1934). *Mind, self, and society: From the standpoint of a social behaviorist*. Chicago: University of Chicago Press.

Milgram, S. (1963). Behavioral study of obedience. *Journal of Abnormal and Social Psychology, 67,* 371–378.

Miller, D. T., & Ross, M. (1975). Self-serving biases in the attribution of causality: Fact or fiction? *Psychology Bulletin, 82,* 213–225.

Miller, J. A. (1981). "Jacques Lacan: 1901–1981," *Ornicar?* N. 24, 9 Septembre 1981, pp. 5–14.

Milosz, C. (1978). *Bells in winter*. (C. Milosz & L. Vallee, Trans.). New York: Ecco Press.

Muller, J. P. (1979). The analogy of gap in Lacan's *Ecrits: A Selection*. *Psychohistory Review, 8* (3), 38–45.

Muller, J. P. (1982). Cognitive psychology and the ego: Lacanian theory and empirical research. *Psychoanalysis and Contemporary Thought, 5,* 257–291.

Muller, J. P., & Richardson, W. J. (1982). *Lacan and language: A reader's guide to Ecrits*. New York: International Universities Press.

Nelson, R. E., & Craighead, W. E. (1977). Selective recall of positive and negative feedback, self-control behaviors, and depression. *Journal of Abnormal Psychology, 86,* 379–388.

Osherson, D. N. (1977). Natural connectives: A Chomsky approach. *Journal of Mathematical Psychology, 16,* 1–29.

Peirce, C. S. (1931–1935). *Collected papers of Charles Sanders Peirce*. In C. Hartshorne and P. Weiss (Eds.), Cambridge, MA: Harvard University Press.

Rapaport, D. (1967). A historical survey of psychoanalytic ego psychology. In M. Gill (Ed.), *The collected papers of David Rapaport* (pp. 745–757). New York: Basic Books.

Rose, S. A. (1981). Developmental changes in infants' retention of visual stimuli. *Child Development, 52,* 227–233.

Ross, M., & Sicoly, F. (1979). Egocentric biases in availability and attribution. *Journal of Personality and Social Psychology, 37,* 322–336.

Ross, M., McFarland, C., & Fletcher, G. (1981). The effect of attitude on the recall of personal histories. *Journal of Personality and Social Psychology, 40,* 627–634.

Roustang, F. (1982). *Dire mastery: Discipleship from Freud to Lacan*. (N. Lukacher, Trans.). Baltimore, MD: The Johns Hopkins University Press.

Rozensky, R. H., Rehm, L. P., Pry, G., & Roth, D. (1977). Depression and self-reinforcement behavior in hospitalized patients. *Journal of Behavior Therapy and Experimental Psychiatry,* *8,* 31–34.

Sackeim, H. A. (1983). Self-deception, self-esteem, and depression: The adaptive value of lying to oneself. In J. Masling (Ed.), *Empirical studies of psychoanalytic theories: Vol. 1* (pp. 101–157). Hillsdale, NJ: The Analytic Press.

Saussure, F. de (1966). *Course in general linguistics.* (W. Baskin, Trans.). New York: McGraw-Hill. (Original work published 1916)

Shevrin, H. (1980). Glimpses of the unconscious. *Psychology Today, 13,* 128.

Shevrin, H., & Dickman, S. (1980). The psychological unconscious: A necessary assumption for all psychological theory? *American Psychologist, 35,* 421–434.

Sicoly, F., & Ross, M. (1977). Facilitation of ego-biased attributions by means of self-serving observer feedback. *Journal of Personality and Social Psychology, 35,* 734–741.

Silverman, L. H. (1976). Psychoanalytic theory: "The reports of my death are greatly exaggerated." *American Psychologist, 31,* 621–637.

Stephan, W. G., Bernstein, W. M., Stephan, C., & Davis, M. H. (1979). Attributions for achievement: Egotism vs. expectancy confirmation. *Social Psychology Quarterly, 42,* 5–17.

Taylor, S. E. (1983). Adjustment to threatening events: A theory of cognitive adaptation. *American Psychologist, 38,* 1161–1173.

Thelen, M. H., & Kirkland, K. D. (1976). On status and being imitated: Effects on reciprocal imitation and attraction. *Journal of Personality and Social Psychology. 33,* 691–697.

Ver Eecke, W. (1983). Hegel as Lacan's source for necessity in psychoanalytic theory. In J. H. Smith & W. Kerrigan (Eds.), *Interpreting Lacan: Vol. 6 psychiatry and the humanities* (pp. 113–138). New Haven: Yale University Press.

Wallon, H. (1949). *Les Origines du caractere chez l'enfant: Les preludes du sentiment de personnalite* (2nd ed.). Paris: Presses Universitaires de France.

Wexler, K., & Culicover, P. W. (1980). *Formal principles of language acquisition.* Cambridge, MA: MIT Press.

Yando, R., Seitz, V., & Zigler, E. (1978). *Imitation: A developmental perspective.* Hillsdale, NJ: Lawrence Erlbaum Associates.

Zuckerman, M. (1979). Attribution of success and a failure revisited, or: The motivational bias is alive and well in attribution theory. *Journal of Personality, 47,* 245–287.

II

SELF-ESTEEM AND SELF-CONCEPT FROM CHILDHOOD TO ADOLESCENCE

5 Self-Concept From Middle Childhood Through Adolescence

Morris Rosenberg
University of Maryland

Although the self-concept is of enormous importance to all human beings be-yond the early years, it appears to be of particular interest in adolescence. Rice (1978) ventures the opinion that, among students of adolescence, proba-bly more has been written about the self-concept than any other single topic. This is not to say that the self-concept is more important during adolescence, but that it is particularly problematic at this life stage; adolescence appears to be a time of self-concept difficulty. Whether or not it is appropriate to char-acterize adolescence as a period of crisis (for differing views, see Blos, 1962; Douvan & Adelson, 1966; Erikson, 1959; Offer, 1969; Offer, Ostrov, & Howard, 1981), there is ample evidence to indicate that it is a difficult life stage (e.g., Jersild, Brook, & Brook, 1978). It is noteworthy that, in their study of "four stages of life," Lowenthal, Thurner, and Chiriboga (1975) found that 40% of their respondents identified adolescence as the "worst time of life;" this proportion is higher than that of any other life stage, including old age.

Given the enormous interest in the topic, one would assume that a body of certified knowledge dealing with adolescent self-concepts would, by now, be available. This is far from the case. According to Savin-Williams and Demo (1983a), "despite 1,500 articles on adolescent self-esteem published since 1967, we know relatively little of its correlates, determinants or predictors" (p. 131). Furthermore, we know even less about how the self-concept changes between middle childhood and adolescence. Many of our conclusions, then, must be considered tentative.

In this chapter, two broad features of the self-concept are considered. The first is the *content* of the self-concept. What do people see when they look at themselves (e.g., do they view themselves as fat or thin, smart or dull, interesting or boring). The second broad feature of the self-concept might be described as its *dimensions* or facets. For example, are people's general attitudes toward the self favorable or unfavorable (self-esteem), stable or volatile (stability), salient or peripheral (self-consciousness), and so on. Although certain common developmental processes affect both the content and the dimensions of the self-concept, these two features are so fundamentally different that it is best to treat them separately.

CONTENT OF THE SELF-CONCEPT

In this chapter we have elected to view the self-concept as a body of self-knowledge (Lewis & Brooks-Gunn, 1981) or, in Murphy's (1947) terms, "the individual as known to the individual" (p. 996). The virtue of this approach is that it organizes our thinking about self-concept development in two ways:

First, this approach highlights the degree to which the self-concept, as a cognitive structure (Sarbin, 1962), is governed, controlled, and constrained by the processes of cognitive development. Thoughts about the self are viewed as similar to thoughts about other aspects of the individual's world. It thus follows that the individual's capacity for thought governs his or her capacity for self-thought. For example, if people have memory, then they can have memory about the self. If they are capable of classification, then they are capable of classifying the self as a specific instance of a general category. If they have discovered formal logical operations, then they can reason logically about the self. Whatever cognitive abilities the individual possesses can be applied to the self as an object of his or her own reflection.

But this means that cognitive development represents a limiting condition on the construction of the self-concept. If individuals have not yet acquired certain cognitive capacities, then they cannot conceptualize the self in these terms. Self-concept development, then, is inextricably interwoven with cognitive development, and must take account of ontogenetic processes.

Second, because the object toward which the attitudes are held is a person, self-perception may be viewed as a specific instance of person perception (Tagiuri, 1968), and may follow a similar developmental course. It is no accident, we believe, that some of the most important developmental studies of the self-concept (Livesley & Bromley, 1973; Secord & Peevers, 1974) are essentially person-perception studies, with self-concept included as a "buffer item" (Livesley & Bromley, 1973), or, what appears to be an afterthought (Secord & Peevers, 1974). Although there are differences in how people conceptualize themselves and others (e.g., Livesley & Bromley, 1973; Mullener & Laird, 1971; Rosenberg, 1965; Secord & Peevers, 1974), it is surprising how parallel the ontogenetic processes are. It is for this reason that

Damon and Hart (1982) conclude that "self-concept development may show a sequence of development that parallels the sequence found in the development of person perception" (p. 290).

Knowledge of the content of self-concept development stems chiefly from what McGuire and Padawer-Singer (1976) describe as nonreactive research. The characteristic procedure involves presenting a general, relatively unstructured question to respondents and permitting them to formulate their answers in their own terms.

What changes in the content of the self-concept occur between middle childhood and adolescence? Although the evidence supporting some of these generalizations is limited, we discuss five developmental tendencies associated with advancing age:

1. With advancing age, there is a decreased tendency to conceptualize the self exclusively as a social exterior and an increased tendency to conceptualize the self as a psychological interior.

2. With advancing age, there is a decreased tendency to conceptualize the self in terms of interpersonal linkages (the connection of the self to specific others) and an increased tendency to conceptualize it in terms of interpersonal sentiments and relationships (one's feelings toward others and others' feelings toward self).

3. With advancing age, there is a decreased tendency to conceptualize the self in concrete, specific, material terms and an increased tendency to conceptualize it in abstract, conceptual terms.

4. With advancing age, there is a decreased tendency to conceptualize the self as a simple, global, undifferentiated object and an increased tendency to conceptualize it as a complex, differentiated object.

5. With advancing age, there is a decreased tendency to rest the self-concept on an arbitrary, capricious and external foundation and an increased tendency to rest it on a logical, evidential, and autonomous foundation.

Each of these developments is considered in turn.

From Social Exterior to Psychological Interior

When we speak of a social exterior, we refer to those aspects of the self that are overt and visible, such as one's physical, demographic, or behavioral characteristics. A psychological interior, in contrast, refers to a private world of thoughts, feelings, or wishes that are not directly accessible to outside view.

The shift from a social exterior to a psychological interior is consistently demonstrated in developmental studies (Bernstein, 1980; Broughton, 1978;

Damon & Hart, 1982; Livesley & Bromley, 1973; Montemayor & Eisen, 1977; Rosenberg, 1979; Secord & Peevers, 1974; Selman, 1980). For example, in a study of 1,988 Baltimore school pupils selected randomly from grades 3-12 (Rosenberg & Simmons, 1972), one question asked was: "Who knows best what you really feel and think deep down inside? . . . What does this person know about you that others do not?" One of the most common responses to this question among the younger children was some kind of behavior, action, or activity. "She (my mother) knows I cross (Bradley) Road when I shouldn't but she doesn't tell my father because he gets so mad. I tell her but not my father." Another little boy replied: "That I watch adult shows more than kid shows." Keller, Ford, and Meacham (1978) report that, among preschoolers, activity is the most frequently mentioned self-concept component.

Second, younger children are more likely to focus on abilities or achievements. What the person who knows the self best is "how smart I am," "good in arithmetic and bad in reading," "she knows I can skate," "I can read well."

Third, younger children are more likely to describe themselves in terms of physical characteristics, such as appearance ("what I look like," "what I wear," "tall"), or health status ("they know I've got stitches in my head, and no one knows it except my family"), and material and demographic facts ("my real age," "that I have a new pair of shoes").

Thus, when young children are asked what the person who knows them best knows that others do not, they tend, more than the older, to answer in terms of overt, visible, external, and public categories. The child's reply will either be in terms of behavior (especially good or bad behavior); talents, abilities, or accomplishments; and certain objective facts (e.g., physical or social identity elements).

A similar pattern of findings (Rosenberg, 1979) emerged when these respondents were asked about their points of pride (best things about you), shame (things not so good), distinctiveness (how you differ from others), commonality (ways you are the same as others), and desired adult self (like to be as a grown up).

Other self-concept studies show similar results. According to Montemayor and Eisen (1977), the younger the child, the greater the likelihood that he or she will identify the self in terms of the following three categories: (a) territoriality–citizenship (I am an American; I live on Oak Street); (b) physical self-body image (I have blonde hair; I'm skinny); and (c) possessions, resources (I own a bike; I have a dog).

Livesley and Bromley (1973) found that the younger children were more likely to describe themselves in terms of (a) physical appearance (tall, pretty, blue eyes, fair hair); (b) general information and identity (name, age, sex, nationality, religion, school; e.g., "lives at," "Catholic," "10 years old,"); (c) possessions (has a pet rabbit; has a new bicycle).

These data rather strikingly support Piaget's (1976) contention that in childhood thought tends to be tied to "concrete operations," that is, to the tangible features of reality, and that this mode of thought is as applicable to the self as to the rest of the world. The self, in the child's eyes, is matter in motion (Rosenberg & Rosenberg, 1981). The self of the child takes up space, engages in action, and consists chiefly of concrete material elements.

Although adolescents' self-concepts also include overt and visible elements (adolescents, for example, are greatly concerned with physical appearance or characteristics), they differ from children's in incorporating a larger proportion of interior elements. In response to the Baltimore question asking respondents about what they are like "deep down inside," the majority of older children cite (a) general inner thoughts and feelings; (b) specific interpersonal feelings, or (c) private wishes, desires, or aspirations.

Similarly, Livesley and Bromley (1973) found that, first, older children were much more likely to describe themselves in terms of internal thoughts, that is, beliefs, attitudes, and values (standards, values, and ideals that the individual conforms to). Second, older subjects were more likely to respond in terms of general personality qualities (friendly, selfish, kind, moody, changeable). Although some of these traits are expressed in overt behavior, they also entail the examination of internal feelings. Third, adolescents were more likely to describe themselves in terms of what Livesley and Bromley call "orientation" (expectations, wishes, fears, self-reproaches). These cognitive elements tend to be largely internal and invisible. Montemayor and Eisen's (1977) study yielded similar results.

In sum, the data are consistent in indicating that, when asked to describe how the self appears, the older child is decidedly more likely than the younger to answer in terms of a psychological interior — a world of general emotions, attitudes, beliefs, wishes, feelings, motives — while the younger child is more likely to respond in terms of a social exterior — a world of action or activities (Keller, Ford, & Meacham, 1978; Secord & Peevers, 1974), objective facts, material possessions, and overt achievements. The younger child's gaze is turned outward, toward the overt and visible. Although the older children are not indifferent to such overt components as appearance, they are, nevertheless, much more likely than younger children to turn their gaze inward, toward the private and invisible. With increasing age, the child becomes less of a Skinnerian or demographer, more of a Freudian or clinician.

It is noteworthy that this development parallels the development in person perception. Shantz (1975), speaking of person perception, observes, "There is a developmental trend toward conceiving of people less in terms of their surface appearance, possessions, and motor behavior and more in terms of an underlying reality (values, beliefs, intentions)" (p. 314).

This focus on an internal world reflects the adolescent's greater capacity and inclination to introspect, that is, to look inward and inspect their thoughts and feelings. With advancing age, there is an increased tendency for thought to become conscious of itself. Individuals monitor their own thoughts, attempting to discover what they believe or value. By adolescence, individuals become aware of themselves as persons who have thoughts and feelings about their thoughts and feelings and who view themselves as capable of affecting these internal elements. Given these developments, it is readily understandable that the self-concept, which is the product of these psychological processes, would come to consist increasingly of internal psychological components.

Interpersonal Linkages and Interpersonal Sentiments

In attempting to understand the role that other people play in the individual's self-concept, it is useful to distinguish between interpersonal linkages, on the one hand, and interpersonal sentiments and relations, on the other. Interpersonal linkages refer to specific others to whom the individual is connected. These other people are often included in an individual's description of his or her self-concept. For example, a respondent, asked to say something about him or herself, may reply that he or she has a friend named Helen or a brother named Danny or a mother with blond hair. The other person is part of the individual's visible and objective world and is prominent in the individual's awareness — indeed, often more prominent than the self.

The term *sentiment* is used in Heider's (1958) sense of referring to a positive or negative evaluation of, or feeling toward, someone. In the present context, however, the term *sentiment* is meant in a two-way sense — as the individual's feelings toward others (I am friendly; I like people; my mother doesn't know how I feel about her), and the individual's view of others' feelings toward him or her (I am well-liked; I am popular). In addition, people's self-concepts may include the nature of their interpersonal relationships (I am easy to get along with; I seem to get into fights with people). People may also characterize themselves in terms of certain qualities that have desirable or undesirable interpersonal effects (e.g., kind, hot-tempered).

Although the evidence is limited, the Livesley and Bromley (1973) data suggest that younger children are more apt to characterize themselves in terms of interpersonal linkages. In the early years, there is a greater tendency for children to describe themselves in terms of "friendships and playmates" (e.g., the individual's friends, acquaintances, playmates), or "family and kinship" (e.g., the person's family and other relatives, such as the number and identity of siblings or other family members). Essentially, the child identifies those people who enter his or her field of vision or are important features of his or her objective reality. Following their sociological bias already observed, younger children tend to conceptualize their interpersonal worlds as a series of connections between themselves and others.

Adolescents, in contrast, are more apt to characterize themselves in terms of interpersonal feelings. Three findings from the Baltimore study appear to support this conclusion. Asked what kind of personality they would like to have or what kind of person they would like to be as an adult, 73% of the oldest, but only 36% of the youngest cited some interpersonal trait. Similarly, 28% of the oldest, but only 9% of the youngest cited an interpersonal trait as their chief point of pride ("best thing about you"). And when asked about their chief deficiency or drawback, 18% of the oldest cited some interpersonal trait or some interpersonal difficulty, whereas only 6% of the youngest answered in these terms.

Adolescents are particularly likely to focus on interpersonal attraction, that is, liking or being liked by others. Asked what kinds of persons they desire to be as adults, adolescents gave such answers as "a person that's well liked by most people," "easy to talk to," "a nice person with a good reputation," "charming, outgoing, friendly, honest," "nice, sweet personality," "easy to get along with," "very friendly and active–sociable."

The adolescent's stronger tendency to view the self in terms of interpersonal sentiments is, of course, a consequence of improved role-taking. Insofar as the child's thought is egocentric, he or she is less capable of seeing the world from other people's viewpoints or perspectives. The little boy may be aware that Tommy is his brother, but not that he is Tommy's brother. When children, as a consequence of interaction, increasingly attempt to understand others' viewpoints, however, they come to recognize that an important feature of other peoples' thought is themselves. They discover that other people hold attitudes toward them, that they exercise an impact on other people's minds. As a consequence of role-taking, they become aware of themselves as having interpersonal effects, and conceptualize themselves accordingly.

It is important to stress that we are not describing differences in the actual sentiments of children or adolescents, but in their tendency to conceptualize themselves in terms of sentiments they possess or elicit from others. Younger children, as Livesley and Bromley (1973) show, are very likely to feel "preferences and aversions." It is not that the young child is less likely to feel love or feel loved, but that he or she is less likely to think of the self in these terms.

Children's description of the self in terms of interpersonal linkages is consistent with their perception of the self as a social exterior. Just as one has a bike or plays with one's toys, so one has a brother and plays with one's friends. Other people are concrete, tangible features of the child's world and, hence, self-concept. There is little probing either of one's own or the other person's internal interpersonal feelings.

Adolescents, on the other hand, are more likely to focus on the nature of the interaction and, especially, the interpersonal feelings involved. This is consistent with the adolescent's greater sensitivity to a psychological interior, both of other people and the self. In late childhood and adolescence, there is a greatly intensified interest in "role-taking" or "people-reading" (Flavell, 1974; Flavell, Fry, Wright, & Jarvis, 1968). Adolescents strive to enter the minds of others, to discover what others are thinking and feeling. One of the important items of information they attempt to obtain is others' feelings toward them. At the same time they give increased attention to discovering their own feelings toward other people. In the course of development, the self-concept comes to include the individual's feelings toward others and others' feelings toward the self.

Finally, the more mature interaction of adolescence is characterized by what Selman (1980) has called "mutual perspective taking." With the advent of mutual perspective taking, the self comes to be described in terms of the nature of its interaction with others — as easy to get along with, as someone with the ability to make friends, as someone who maintains harmonious relations with people, as someone who has difficulties with people. Seeing matters from others' viewpoints and recognizing that they are seeing matters from ours effects an important change in the self-concept.

From Percept to Concept

In speaking of the "development of a terminology of trait names and similar abstractions," Murphy (1947) notes that in time "the vocabulary of the self becomes, so to speak, less and less visual and in general less and less sensory. . . . the child forms general ideas of himself. In short, the self becomes less a pure perceptual object, and more and more a conceptual trait system" (pp. 505–506).

That advancing age brings with it a shift from a concrete to a more abstract mode of thought, is amply documented (Bourne & O'Banion, 1971; Elkind, Medvene, & Rockway, 1970; Harvey, Hunt, & Schroder, 1961; Lunzer, 1965; Penk, 1971). We noted earlier that younger children, insofar as they are anchored in the stage of concrete operations rather than formal operations (Inhelder & Piaget, 1958), tend to describe the self in objective material terms. Older children, in contrast, are more apt to characterize themselves in terms of stable personality traits (Bernstein, 1980). Consider the responses to the following question in the Baltimore study: "What kind of personality would you like to have, or what kind of person would you like to be, when you are an adult?" Whereas 58% of the youngest children cited some trait, this was true of 93% of the oldest. These traits were varied in nature. Some referred to desired emotional characteristics (cheerful, happy), to matters of emotional control (doesn't lose temper, avoids fights), to qualities of character (mature, brave, dependable, honest), to interpersonal characteristics (friendly, outgoing, sociable, well-liked), and others. Montemayor and Eisen (1977), Livesley and Bromley (1973), Secord and Peevers (1974), Bannister and Agnew (1977), and Bernstein (1980), all document the adolescent's greater tendency to conceptualize the self in abstract terms. In part, these changes are rooted in the shift from a social exterior to a psychological interior (since the private aspects of the self lack concrete, external referents), in part to maturation and learning.

The capacity for conceptualization again represents a limiting condition on self-conceptualization. A child who lacks the capacity for abstract thought lacks the capacity for conceptualizing the self in abstract terms. The consequence is that children's and adolescents' self-concepts differ radically because of these differing capacities for thought.

From Global to Differentiated Self-Concepts

In their discussion of self-concept development over the age span, Montemayor and Eisen (1977) adopt as their springboard Werner's (1957) ontogenetic principle that stipulates "whenever development occurs, it proceeds from a state of relative globality and lack of differentiation to a state of increasing differentiation, articulation, and hierarchic integration" (p. 126). (See also Mullener & Laird, 1971; Scarlett, Press, & Crockett, 1971; Secord & Peevers, 1974).

What are some of the expressions of this developmental tendency? First, according to Livesley and Bromley (1973), when young children express their feelings toward people, their answers tend to be vague, global, and nonspecific. People are described as kind, nice, good, bad, weird, horrible. With increasing age, the descriptions become more precise and differentiated. Instead of good or nice, the adolescent describes a person as cheerful or generous or sociable or considerate, and so forth. Instead of bad or not nice, the adolescent describes the person as bad tempered, boastful, jealous, selfish, and so forth.

Second, person perception research (Livesley & Bromley, 1973) shows a developmental shift from a univalent to a bivalent or multivalent mode of conceptualization. To the young child, something is either all good or all bad; to the adolescent, people can be good in certain respects and bad in others, or good under certain circumstances and bad under others. Harter's (1983) example of the self-assessment of intelligence is illustrative. To the young child, "One is dumb because one does poorly at math, science, and social studies." With development, "trait labels become differentiated, such that the child comes to appreciate that while one is dumb with regard to math, science, and history, one can simultaneously be smart at art, music, and creative writing" (p. 307).

Third, adolescents are able to recognize that self-concept elements are hierarchically organized, with higher order concepts subsuming lower order ones. According to Harter (1983), "Attributes in the self-theory would also show some hierarchical organization, for example, 'I'm smart' (higher order trait) because I'm good at reading, spelling, and math" (p. 294). Similarly, the child may describe the self as a fast runner, whereas the adolescent sees the self as a good athlete; or the child sees the self as having pretty eyelashes, whereas the adolescent sees the self as physically attractive. In the final stage described by Harter, still higher order abstractions may develop that subsume the lower order constructs.

Adolescents are thus better able to recognize complexity and to connect the general and the specific. They can identify the specific traits that form the basis of the general assessment; they can provide different assessments of different features of the self; they can recognize that different elements are hierarchically organized, with broader elements subsuming more specific ones. The adolescent self-concept is, thus, more differentiated than that of the child (Secord & Peevers, 1974).

From Arbitrary and External to Evidential and Autonomous Foundations

Not only may the content of the self-concept change between middle childhood and adolescence, but so, too, may the foundations on which the self-concept rests. By foundations, we refer both to the use of evidence (the mode of reasoning used to draw conclusions about the self), and the source of evidence (the person whose judgment about the self is respected).

It may be argued, of course, that if children and adolescents reach the same conclusions about themselves, then the way they reached these conclusions is an entirely separate issue. We suggest, however, that identical conclusions resting on different foundations may be viewed as qualitatively different. For example, assume that two people, given a mathematics problem, produce the correct answer. In the first case, the answer was derived by consulting the textbook, whereas in the second case it was solved by one's own reasoning. The understanding that the second person has achieved is qualitatively different from that of the first. The same may hold for self-concepts.

There are at least two important differences in the foundations on which children's and adolescents' self-concepts rest. The first is the change from a syncretic, arbitrary, and capricious self-concept to a logical and evidential one. The second is the shift from an externally based to an autonomously based self-concept.

The evidence supporting the argument that the child's self-concept tends to be arbitrary whereas the adolescent's rests more on logic and evidence is admittedly flimsy. Livesley and Bromley's data (1973), however, are consistent with this position. They show that older children, in describing persons, are more likely to buttress their conclusions with "collateral facts and ideas" (p. 126). These are described as "specific statements in support of a previous assertion, illustrations of personal qualities, explanations of behavior"

(p. 235). This is not to suggest that adolescents generally offer such supportive information, but simply to say that they are more likely than children to do so.

Although some recent critiques (e.g., Gelman, 1978) have called into question some of Piaget's generalizations, his ideas nevertheless remain highly suggestive. The young child, according to Piaget (1951), is never in doubt. When Piaget asks the young Genevan where Lake Geneva comes from, the child may immediately reply that men dug a big hole and poured water into it. No evidence is offered to support this conclusion, logical inconsistencies remain unexamined, and no defense of the judgment is attempted or provided. Thus, the young child has an immediate answer to everything, however devoid of logic or inconsistent with evidence. Truth is instantaneous and given; it has neither an inductive nor deductive foundation.

In contrast to the child, the adolescent is characterized by a tendency to formulate hypotheses and to attempt to test and verify provisional conclusions. For example, a little girl, overhearing someone say that she has nice eyelashes, may conclude that she is pretty. An adolescent girl, in contrast, may make the investigation of her attractiveness a major research project. She may spend an enormous amount of time in front of the mirror, give the closest and most careful attention to her appearance, be keenly sensitive to how she is perceived by others (e.g., aware of admiring sidelong glances), compare her specific features or general appearance with an admired cultural model or with specific peers, and so on. The fundamental principles of self-assessment — reflected appraisals, social comparison, self-attribution, and psychological centrality (Rosenberg, 1979) — are all brought into play in an effort to reach a conclusion about physical attractiveness. A substantial body of evidence may be weighed, balanced, and evaluated in reaching a judgment. Thus, even if children and adolescents were to come to the same conclusion about a particular feature of the self, these conclusions might rest on fundamentally different foundations and would be, we believe, qualitatively different.

A second difference in the foundation of children's and adolescents' self-concepts is to be found in the locus of self-knowledge. In the child's view, the truth about the self tends to be vested in external authority; for the adolescent, autonomous judgment predominates. In the Baltimore study, for example, respondents were asked: "If I asked you and your mother how smart you were, and you said one thing and she said another, who would be right — you or your mother?" Similar questions were asked about how "good" and how "good-looking" the child was, and whether the father's judgment was also more valid than the respondent's. In the 8–11 year age group, between two thirds and three fourths of the children attributed superior wisdom about themselves to the adults; among those 15 years or older, between one half and two thirds attributed more accurate knowledge to themselves.

Similar findings appear when we focus on knowledge of the psychological interior — one's thoughts, feelings, wishes, and so forth. Respondents were asked: "Who do you feel really understands you best? I mean, who knows best what you really feel and think deep down inside?" The options provided were "your mother, your father, yourself, your best friend." Whereas 52% of the 8–11-year-olds identified a parent as the person who knew best what they were like deep down inside, this was true of only 24% of those 15 or older. The adolescents were much more likely to affirm that they, themselves, knew best.

To the adolescent, then, there exists a world of internal thoughts, wishes, and feelings to which they have privileged access and about which, in general, they are the ultimate authorities. To an important extent their views of themselves stem from their examination of these inner worlds and the conclusions that they draw from this inspection. To the child, in contrast, the truth about the self is to a much greater extent the property of an external omniscient authority. Conclusions about the self resting on these different foundations are, in our judgment, qualititatively different.

Summary: Self-Concept Content

In summary, as children move in and through adolescence, there are interesting and significant changes in how they conceptualize the self. First, there is a gradual and consistent shift from defining the self in terms of objective visible features (e.g., where one lives, what one looks like, what one owns) to internal psychological characteristics (what one thinks and believes, what one feels, what one's personality qualities are, etc.). This does not mean that older adolescents do not conceptualize the self in external terms (indeed, the oldest, according to Livesley and Bromley, 1973, or Montemayor and Eisen, 1977, are greatly concerned with their appearance), but that they are also aware of an inner world of thought, feeling, and desire, and characterize themselves accordingly. Second, the adolescent is more likely than the child to conceptualize the self in terms of interpersonal sentiments or the quality of interpersonal relations, that is, they are aware of themselves as having feelings toward others, and of others' feelings toward them. Third, adolescents are much more likely to think of themselves in abstract rather than concrete terms. Whereas the children's self-concepts consist largely of specific information about the self, the adolescents are more apt to think of themselves dispositionally — in terms of response tendencies. Fourth, with advancing age the self comes to be seen as a complex, differentiated entity, rather than a vague global entity. Finally, adolescent self-concepts come to be based more on autonomous judgments resting on logic and the sifting and evaluation of evidence.

These are not the only changes in self-concept content that occur between childhood to adolescence. According to Damon and Hart (1982), there is also an increased awareness of the self as a continuous object (with a past, present, and future) (see also Peevers, 1984); as a distinct object (similar to, and different from others, that is, a comparative self); as a volitional object (observing one's wants and acting on them); and as a reflective object (having thoughts about the self as a thinker).

The most general conclusion to be drawn from this discussion is that the chief reason why children and adolescents think about the self differently is that they think differently. Two influences are especially important. The first is cognitive development, expressed in the shift from concrete to abstract modes of thought, and from global undifferentiated to differentiated and hierarchically ordered modes of thought (Horrocks, 1976). The second is the process of role-taking that permits the individual to see the world, including the self, from the other's point of view (Flavell et al., 1968; Mead, 1934; Selman, 1980; Stryker, 1980; Turner, 1968). It is through role-taking and social interaction that the individual discovers an inner psychological world, conceptualizes the self in terms of interpersonal relationships, rests conclusions about the self on logical and evidential foundations, and anchors knowledge about the self within the self.

DIMENSIONS OF THE SELF-CONCEPT

An adequate description of self-concept development must include consideration of certain general or overarching self-concept dimensions. For example, are people's self-feelings generally favorable or unfavorable? Are their self-concepts firm and stable or shifting and volatile? Is the self a tender and delicate object or a tough and robust one? Is the self in the forefront or background of awareness? These dimensions, too, may change between childhood and adolescence, and may have profound effects on young people's psychological well-being.

Space limitations compel us to confine our discussion to two dimensions of the self-concept: self-esteem and self-concept stability. How do youngsters change in these respects as they move from childhood into adolescence? What is the bearing of these dimensions on such emotional dispositions as depression, anxiety, life satisfaction, and so forth? Do males and females differ in terms of these dimensions?

Self-Esteem

Far and away the preeminent topic of self-concept research has been self-esteem. No one knows how many articles on the self-concept have been published, but in 1982 Ostrow estimated the number to be about 7,000. About 90% of these publications, according to McGuire and Padawer-Singer (1976), have focused on self-esteem.

The reason for this extraordinary interest in global self-esteem lies not in its success in predicting behavior — indeed, its record in this respect is rather unimpressive and, to many hopeful investigators, disappointing — but in its significance for psychological well-being. The evidence is by now overwhelming that low self-esteem is associated with psychological distress (Rosenberg, 1985). In surveys of normal populations it is consistently associated with depression (Bachman, 1970; Kaplan & Pokorny, 1969; Luck & Heiss, 1972; Rosenberg, 1965). Low self-esteem people are also more apt to manifest psychophysiological indicators of anxiety (Bachman, 1970; Kaplan & Pokorny, 1969; Luck & Heiss, 1972; Rosenberg, 1965), as well as psychological anxiety (Bachman, 1970). (For other references, see Wylie, 1979, and Burns, 1979). Low self-esteem is also significantly associated with "negative affective states," irritability, impulse to aggression, and anomia (Rosenberg, 1985), as well as low life satisfaction (Campbell, 1981). It is also relevant to observe that various psychodiagnostic instruments measuring depression, such as the Beck (1967) Depression Inventory, the Center for Epidemiologic Studies-Depression Inventory (Radloff, 1977), and the Depression syndrome of DSM-III (American Psychiatric Association, 1980) include low self-esteem as a symptom.

Self-esteem, in our view, does not involve feelings of superiority (believing that one is better than others), or of perfection (believing that one is free of faults or limitations). Self-esteem, we suggest, primarily involves feelings of self-acceptance, self-liking, and self-respect, both conditional and unconditional. Feelings of competence or efficacy contribute importantly to self-esteem, but are not identical with it or exclusively responsible for it.

The literature dealing with self-esteem change between middle childhood and adolescence yields inconsistent findings. Wylie's (1979) thorough review of the literature led her to conclude that the available research had failed to demonstrate a consistent association between age and self-esteem. But, in reexamining the studies considered by Wylie (1979), McCarthy and Hoge (1982) pointed out that:

> Of the seven studies that showed increases in self-esteem with age, six were longitudinal in design. Of the studies showing no relationship between self-esteem and age or showing declining self-esteem with age, 21 out of 22 were cross-sectional in design. Since longitudinal studies, when well carried out, are less subject to distortion from sampling errors, we believe that they are more credible than cross-sectional studies as evidence regarding the relationship between self-esteem and age. (p. 373)

McCarthy and Hoge's (1982) longitudinal study revealed significant improvement in self-esteem between grades 7–12. Their careful methodological analysis of the findings supports their claim that the changes "cannot be explained by invalid or unreliable scales, attrition effects, testing effects, or error introduced by careless subjects" (p. 378). O'Malley and Bachman's (1983) review of a number of studies utilizing excellent national samples of adolescents and young adults have concluded that "reasonably solid evidence exists that there are age-related differences in self-esteem between the ages of about 13 and 23" (p. 258). One of the studies discussed by O'Malley and Bachman (1983) is the "Monitoring the Future" project that studied four student cohorts between 1976 and 1979. Two of these studies used a 4-item self-esteem measure and two used an 8-item measure. The self-esteem level increased each year. There was an average increase of about one-tenth to one-twelfth of a standard deviation each year in the first 4 years after high school (O'Malley & Bachman, 1983). Bachman, O'Malley, and Johnston (1978), Engel (1959), Kaplan (1975), and Simmons, Rosenberg, and Rosenberg (1973) also provide evidence of self-esteem improvement during the adolescent years.

Between the ages of 13 and 23, then, there appears to be a consistent improvement in global self-esteem. Furthermore, the cumulative impact is substantial, exceeding a full standard deviation over an 8-year span (O'Malley & Bachman, 1983).

But what about those younger than 13? Few comparative data are available. In a study of school pupils ranging from grade 3–12 (Simmons, Rosenberg, & Rosenberg, 1973), self-esteem reached its low point at age 12. The data, however, are sparse and inconsistent (see Demo & Savin-Williams, 1983; Simmons & Blyth, 1984), and it is not possible to reach any firm conclusions at this point. To offer a tentative best guess, we think it is probable that self-esteem tends to decline at age 11, reaches a low point at about ages 12–13, and gradually improves by age 14, an improvement that continues at least into early adulthood.

Whether self-esteem is lower at age 12 or 13 may depend in part on whether one experiences the transition from elementary to junior high school or whether one remains in the same school. For those youngsters moving into junior high school in the seventh grade, this change in school context is associated with depressed self-esteem among boys and girls in the Baltimore study (Simmons, Rosenberg, & Rosenberg, 1973), and among girls in the Milwaukee study (Simmons, Blyth, Van Cleave, & Bush, 1979). In addition, studies using the Perceived Competence Scale, which measures cognitive, social, and physical competence as well as general self-worth (Harter, 1981, 1982; Harter & Connell, 1982), also found that scores on the Perceived Competence Scale decline in the seventh grade. On the other hand, in studies of middle level schools (grades K–8), the shift from sixth to seventh grades (which does not involve a change of school) is associated with improved self-esteem (Demo & Savin-Williams, 1983; Simmons et al., 1979). Whether self-esteem rises or falls between the sixth and seventh grade thus depends in part on whether there has been a change in school context.

Although the vast majority of studies focus on global self-esteem, it is also relevant to consider whether judgments of specific characteristics also change with increasing age. The Baltimore study (Simmons, Rosenberg, & Rosenberg, 1973) asked pupils to rate themselves on eight characteristics and to indicate how much they cared about each of these qualities. The qualities under consideration were the following: smart, good-looking, truthful or honest, good at sports, well-behaved, work hard at school, helpful, good at making jokes. Restricting the analysis to those qualities judged to be important by the respondents, the data showed that in every case the self-ratings of 12–14-year-olds were lower than 8–11-year-olds, and in six cases significantly so. The differences between the 12–14 and the 15 or older adolescents, however, were generally weak and insignificant. Thus, with regard to certain specific qualities that matter to them, adolescents are consistently less likely than children to evaluate themselves favorably.

McCarthy and Hoge (1982) have suggested several possible reasons for the improvement in global self-esteem as adolescence progresses. They point out, first, that if people have a universal desire for high self-esteem, then high self-esteem people will work to maintain it, whereas low self-esteem people will work to improve it. Engel (1959) and Kaplan (1980) show that in adolescence, high self-esteem youngsters tend to remain high whereas low self-esteem youngsters tend to become higher. Hence, the mean level improves over time. Second, they suggest that adolescents may enhance their competence and interpersonal skills, producing improved reflected appraisals, social comparisons, and self-attributions (Rosenberg, 1979). Third, enhanced freedom and autonomy in adolescence may enable youngsters to select peers and contexts that are likely to enhance self-esteem.

Gender. What about male and female self-esteem? Although rather abundant literature has emerged in recent decades detailing the various ways in which society damages the self-esteem of females, the data, at least in school populations, show only modest support for these arguments. The careful review of this subject by Maccoby and Jacklin (1974) and the more exhaustive review by Wylie (1979) find little consistent difference in the global self-esteem of boys and girls, although boys show somewhat greater self-confidence. A recent report by O'Malley and Bachman (1979) indicates that in adolescence the difference in self-esteem level between boys and girls is about one-tenth of a standard deviation in the boys' favor. Similarly, studies conducted among school populations in Baltimore (Rosenberg & Simmons, 1972) and Milwaukee (Bush, Simmons, Hutchinson, & Blyth, 1977–78; Simmons & Blyth, 1984) find boys' self-esteem to be significantly higher than girls'. In our judgment the self-esteem advantage of adolescent males is probably small.

There is one particular self-concept element, however, which appears to be decidedly more negative among girls. This is the quality of physical attractiveness. According to the Baltimore data, girls (especially white girls) are decidedly less likely than boys to be satisfied with their physical appearance. Although this difference is found in middle childhood, it is much greater in adolescence. Consider the proportion of white respondents who said that they were "very satisfied" with their looks and who thought they were good-looking. Among 8–11-year-olds, the male–female differences are 4% and 9%, respectively. For 12–14-year-olds, however, the differences rise to 20% and 18%, and for those 15 or older, the differences are 19% and 21%. (A similar pattern appears among black respondents, but the differences are smaller.) (Simmons & Rosenberg, 1975). The Milwaukee (Simmons & Blyth, 1984) study also found that girls were less satisfied than boys with their physical attractiveness. Jersild, Brook, and Brook (1978), too, report that: "At all grade levels from the sixth through the twelfth, the number of girls who complained about their physical characteristics was larger than the number who spoke favorably about such characteristics" (p. 83), a pattern decidedly different from that of boys. Finally, Offer, Ostrow, and Howard (1981) report that, "Particularly notable are the decidedly negative feelings the girls expressed toward their bodies, with over 40 percent of the normal girls saying they frequently feel ugly and unattractive" (p. 95). In this important respect, adolescent girls appear to be at a distinct self-esteem disadvantage.

In addition to changes in the level of self-esteem with advancing age, it is important to consider changes in the influences that bear on self-esteem as children mature. Even if global self-esteem were to remain the same over the age span, the forces that shape and form it might change radically. Little is currently known about this intriguing subject. We suggest that four types of influences worth special consideration are the sociodemographic, behavioral, interpersonal, and contextual. On the sociodemographic level, for example, Demo and Savin-Williams (1983), and Rosenberg and Pearlin (1978) have demonstrated that social-class background more powerfully affects the self-esteem of adolescents than of children, and Rosenberg and Pearlin (1978) indicate that the effect of social class on adult self-esteem is still stronger. On the behavioral level, Bachman, O'Malley, and Johnston (1978) show that as one moves through high school and into the world of work, school marks recede in importance as an influence on self-esteem whereas occupational success plays a greater role. In the interpersonal realm, the data in Rosenberg (1979) suggest that it is highly likely that, among children, perceived parental attitudes toward the self are of almost exclusive significance for self-esteem formation whereas, among adolescents, peer judgments gain increasing importance. Finally, with regard to contextual influences, Gecas (1972) has shown that, among adolescents, feelings of self-esteem and of authenticity are highest when one is among friends and lowest when one is in the classroom. Much remains to be learned about the forces shaping self-esteem as youngsters move from middle childhood through adolescence.

Barometric and Baseline Self-Concept Stability

Although there are exceptions (Bachman, O'Malley, & Johnston, 1978; Carlson, 1965; Engel, 1959; Franzoi & Reddish, 1980; Mortimer & Lorence, 1981; O'Malley & Bachman, 1983), the causes, correlates or consequences of self-concept stability have received little attention in the literature. And yet, from a motivational perspective, the need for a stable self-concept is readily apparent.

The self-concept, as Lecky (1945) once expressed it, is the basic axiom of the individual's life theory. It is the most constant feature of the individual's experience and the most important basis for human action. Without some picture of what one is like — one's traits, statuses, or other qualities — the individual is virtually immobilized. As Mead (1934) pointed out, the individual is obviously an important factor in the empirical situation of which it is a part; and without an idea of what one is like, rational action is impossible.

The need for a stable self-concept is evidenced by the elaborate system of "self-verification" devices described by Swann (1983). Swann and his colleagues have shown that people may exercise the most remarkable ingenuity and expend the most enormous effort to resist change in the self-concept. (For other evidence, see Rosenberg, 1979). Although there appears to be some disagreement about whether self-esteem or self-maintenance is the more powerful motive (Dipboye, 1977; Kaplan, 1975; Korman, 1970; Jones, 1973), it seems reasonable to conclude that both are powerful needs.

At first glance, the meaning of stability would appear to be self-evident. And yet, Mortimer, Finch, and Kumka (1982) have aptly documented their conclusion that "stability has no uniform definition" (p. 265). (They distinguish four types of stability: structural, normative, level, and ipsative.) One consequence is that different writers have conceptualized stability in different ways, and have reached diametrically opposite conclusions.

To some writers, especially symbolic interactionists, the self is so variable, mutable, and situation-dependent that it is scarcely meaningful to think of a transsituational self-concept at all. Gergen (1972) claims that the happy, healthy personality has multiple selves that vary in accordance with social norms or situational requirements. In this view, "the individual is so responsive to the pressures of immediate situations that the idea of a coherent self is entirely illusory" (Mortimer & Lorence, 1981, p. 9).

But it is not simply self-presentation but self-feelings that are said to be governed by situational or contextual factors. Gecas (1972) has demonstrated that feelings about the self vary with the context. For example, when respondents are asked how they feel about themselves when they are in the classroom, the family, among friends, in heterosexual relations, and with adults, the adolescents tend to describe their feelings about themselves as being very different in these varying contexts. The importance of contextual factors for self-attitudes has frequently been demonstrated (e.g., Pitts, 1978; Rogers, Smith, & Coleman, 1978; Rosenberg, 1975, 1977), and recent research (McGuire & McGuire, 1981) has shown its bearing on the salience of self-concept components.

Additional evidence of the mutability of the self-concept appears in research demonstrating its ready responsiveness to experimental manipulation. Morse and Gergen (1970) showed that when they placed their subjects in the company of an apparently highly efficient and competent person ("Mr. Clean"), the person's feelings of self-assurance declined. On the other hand, when an incompetent and inept person ("Mr. Dirty") was present, their self-assurance rose.

Epstein (1981) has shown that self-feeling may be highly variable. People may have a positive feeling about themselves when they receive an A on a test, make a favorable impression on someone they have met, successfully repair a mechanical appliance, and so on. The opposite self-feeling may accompany the experience of failure.

Thus, one might be disposed to concur with Gergen's (1981) conclusion that the idea of a firm self-concept is an illusion, that it is totally governed by situational influences. At the same time, if we examine changes in general self-attitudes over an extended period of time, these self-concept dimensions appear to be impressively stable. In their Monitoring the Future study, O'Malley and Bachman (1983) report "that stability in the 1st year after high school is just under .700 . . . . Annual stabilities are estimated to be higher (.883 and .917) in the next 2-year interval . . .; and over the 3-year interval, the estimated annual stabilities are .815 and .826" (p. 263). Engel (1959) found self-concept stability over a 2-year period, corrected for unreliability, was .78.

Self-concept stability among adults appears to be even greater. In their study of a sample of successful men, Mortimer and Lorence (1981) find "a striking stability of five dimensions of the self-concept over a 14-year period spanning late adolescence to early adulthood" (p. 32).

It has thus been persuasively argued that the self-concept is highly variable and that it is highly stable. The question is: Which is correct? The answer, obviously, is both. As has so often happened in this field, James (1950) provided the answer before other people thought of the question. In his classic chapter on the self, he observed that "we ourselves know how the barometer of our self-esteem and confidence rises and falls from one day to another through causes that seem to be visceral and organic rather than rational, and which certainly answer to no corresponding variations in the esteem in which we are held by friends" (p. 307). At the same time, he observed that "there is a certain average tone of self-feeling which each of us carries about with him, and which is independent of the objective reasons we may have for satisfaction or discontent" (p. 306). Murphy (1947) agreed, holding that, "The individual has an attitude toward his own person that is comparable to his attitude toward music: it is general and also specific, varying in generality from one person to another but also varying from day to day, hour to hour, in the same person" (p. 487).

Empirical support for these views appears in a study by Savin-Williams and Demo (1983a), who show that, "Self-feelings are apparently global and context dependent. The largest number of our adolescents had a baseline of self-evaluation from which fluctuations rose or fell mildly, most likely dependent on features of the context" (p. 131). (See also Mortimer, Finch, & Kumka, 1982; Savin-Williams and Demo, 1983b).

Following James (1950), we suggest that it is useful to differentiate two types of self-concepts: the *barometric self-concept* and the *baseline self-concept*. The barometric self-concept refers to whether the individual experiences a rapid shift and fluctuation of self-attitudes from moment-to-moment. At a given instant, a person's self-respect may be high, but in the following moment an unkind word, a gentle frown, or a slight setback may cause it to plunge sharply. Such fluctuations are inevitably characterized by uncertainty, doubts about the self, or, to use Erikson's (1959) term, *identity diffusion*. Baseline stability, in contrast, refers to the self-concept change that may take place slowly and over an extended period of time. It is possible for the barometric self-concept to fluctuate greatly, even if the baseline self-concept shows little change. (See Jackson & Paunonen, 1980; Mortimer, Finch, & Kumka, 1982.) A parallel would be that of a baseball player who consistently has about a .300 average, season after season, and yet who has a reputation as a streak hitter, alternating frequently between streaks and slumps. In our judgment, it is the shifting volatile type of instability, rather than the long-term gradual change, that is apt to be particularly distressing. When self-attitudes and self-feelings fluctuate wildly, the individual is apt to be baffled, uncertain, and anxious.

Measures of the barometric self-concept appear in four studies: New York State (Rosenberg, 1965), Baltimore (Rosenberg & Simmons, 1972), Youth in Transition (Bachman, Kahn, Mednick, Davidson, & Johnston, 1967), and Milwaukee (Simmons & Blyth, 1984). These measures ask subjects whether their opinions about themselves change greatly or tend to remain the same; whether their ideas about themselves change quickly; whether on one day they have one opinion of themselves and on another day a very different opinion; and so on. (For specific items, see Rosenberg, 1979).

All four studies reveal that a volatile and uncertain self-concept is experienced as psychologically distressing. In each study adolescents with fluctuating self-concepts are found to score higher on measures of depression, and one of the studies (Youth in Transition) finds stability to be directly related to measures of "happiness" and inversely related to "negative affective states." Furthermore, adolescents with volatile self-concepts are strikingly more likely to be anxious, whether this anxiety is reflected in general measures of anxiety, in somatic symptoms, or in a specific anxiety-tension measure. Finally, these adolescents receive higher scores on measures of impulse to aggression, overt aggression, irritability, resentment, and anomia. All relationships are significant beyond the .001 level (Rosenberg, 1985). Although these relationships are partly explained by the fact that youngsters with volatile self-concepts are more likely to have lower self-esteem, self-concept volatility continues to be significantly associated with psychological discomfort even when self-esteem is statistically controlled.

Does self-concept volatility rise or fall in adolescence? According to the Baltimore data, the self-concept becomes much more volatile in early adolescence. During childhood (age 8–11), the self-concept is moderately sure and stable, but at the age of 12–13, there is a sharp increase in volatility. After age 14, the barometric self-concept shows some improvement, though it does not reach the childhood level of stability. Because we believe that self-concept volatility and uncertainty is one of the most important features of adolescent turmoil, it is appropriate to consider this development in detail.

The first reason for increased self-concept volatility is that, in late childhood and adolescence, young people experience a greatly increased concern with the impression they are making on others, on what other people — especially peers — think of them. Virtually every writer on the subject of adolescence has remarked on how desperately the adolescent wants peers to like and accept him or her. This heavy dependence on, and concern with, what other people think of the self tends to produce uncertainty and fluctuation for several reasons.

The first is the inevitable ambiguity of others' attitudes toward the self. Serious efforts at role-taking make people aware that no human being can have direct access to another's mind. We discover that, just as we are seeking to produce a certain effect on the other's mind, so they are trying to produce one on ours. In doing so, it becomes evident that, in speaking to us, people are fashioning their messages, editing and constructing their thoughts, revealing and concealing their ideas about us in various ways (Flavell, 1974; Selman, 1980). We learn that the world of interpersonal interaction is a world of euphemism, indirection, impression management (Goffman, 1956), disclaimers (Hewitt & Stokes, 1975), selective self-disclosure (Jourard, 1964). And precisely because adolescents depend so heavily on what others think of them, the ambiguity of others' attitudes accentuate adolescents' uncertainty about what they are like.

Second, self-concept variability is fostered by other people's differing views of us (e.g., the respect of the peer group counterposed to the critical stance of the parents). These differing viewpoints are not simply idiosyncratic variations; they are, on the contrary, rooted in the social structure. It is inherent in the nature of role-relationships that different members of a person's role-set (Merton, 1957) should view the individual from different perspectives. Different others pay attention to different aspects of the self, and thus "see" different persons when they look at us. Insofar as the individual depends heavily on reflected appraisals — and adolescents are particularly apt to do so — the contradictory information provided must inevitably generate uncertainty about the self.

Third, the heightened concern with reflected appraisals in adolescence produces enhanced efforts at self-presentation or impression management (Goffman, 1955, 1956; Jones & Pittman, 1982; Schlenker, 1980). Adolescents become heavily engaged in attempting to influence other people's thoughts about the self. In the process, they pay attention to how they look, how they sound, what impression they are making, and so on. In any given situation, they "take a line" (Goffman, 1955), advance a claim to be a certain type of person, and seek to make their performance dramaturgically convincing. Varying roles may be tentatively adopted — the world-weary sophisticate, the sweet young thing, the model son and daughter, the rebellious youth — and perhaps quickly abandoned. As young people observe themselves experimenting with these different roles, they may readily come to experience their selves as highly mutable.

Fourth, self-concept shifts may be a consequence of the fact that adolescence is an ambiguous status in American society. Stryker (1981) has defined a role as a set of social expectations associated with a status. Insofar as these expectations are shared by the individual and by other members of society, they make for self-concept stability. But if these expectations are not shared — if different people expect different things or if it is unclear what to expect — then self-concept variability is fostered by inconsistent reflected appraisals.

In American society adolescence is not a clearly defined status. There is no clear and publicly acknowledged entry point to the adolescent stage and no clear point of exit. Hence, some people treat the individual as a child, others as an adult, and still others are unsure about what stance to take. Given the varying attitudes and expectations that other people hold of him or her, and given the adolescent's sensitivity to these reflected appraisals, it is readily understandable that the adolescent should develop fluctuating attitudes toward the self.

We believe that it is meaningful to view the self-concept as a system of self-expectations. Such expectations apply to any and all features of the self — how competent one is in this or that regard, what one's personality qualities are, what one's characteristic internal feelings are, what one looks like, and so on. So long as these expectations are met, one's feeling of identity is secure. In adolescence, however, these expectations are grossly violated. Perhaps the most important assaults on the taken-for-granted system of self-expectations are the enormous physical changes that occur at this time. Tanner, Whitehouse, and Tokaishi (1966) report that the peak growth velocity for girls is between the ages of 12–14; for boys, it is between the ages of 14–16. That means that substantial and visible physical changes are occurring at a startling pace. Striking changes in the physical self arouse feelings of uncertainty about who one is. Expectations concerning internal physiological states are also grossly violated by the hormonal changes that accompany puberty. These totally unexpected changes, producing fluctuating and unpredictable feeling states, may contribute greatly to the self-concept volatility of adolescence.

In its nature, the abstract self-concept of adolescence tends to be more ambiguous than the concrete self-concept of childhood. This concrete self is objective and requires little interpretation. To a large extent the child's self-concept consists of clear and unambiguous elements: the self is 9 years old, has long brown hair, rides a bike, owns a dog, and has two brothers. There is nothing subtle, elusive, mysterious, or difficult to grasp about this self. There is no impetus to struggle with such questions as: Am I really 9 years old? Do I truly have long brown hair? Can I be sure that I genuinely own a bike? Do I deep down and at a fundamental level like grilled cheese sandwiches?

When, in adolescence, the self is conceptualized in abstract terms and comes to be viewed as a collection of traits, doubts and uncertainties are introduced. There are few objective and unambiguous facts about one's sensitivity, creativity, morality, dependability, and so on. These qualities are subject to varying judgments. People's assessments of their qualities may shift from one moment to the next, and stable generalizations may be difficult to attain. The shift in self-conceptualization from a focus on the overt and visible to the covert and invisible constitutes a movement from a realm of clarity and certainty to one of ambiguity and doubt.

The shift in the locus of self-knowledge from an external to an internal source introduces further uncertainty. So long as the young child can discover the final truth about the self from omniscient and omnipotent adults, all doubts are laid to rest. But when the locus of self-knowledge shifts inward, and adolescents must depend on autonomous judgment, reason, and insight to reach conclusions about the self, certainty is further undermined.

Another factor fostering uncertainty and variability of the self-concept is that, as Erikson (1959) pointed out, the adolescent must give consideration to future occupational and family roles. This means that the adolescent must make an effort to assess his or her potential. An assessment of one's potential, however, is based on a guess. Not only is the meaning of the current evidence about the self ambiguous, but the most critical information is inevitably lacking. To a large extent, people can only discover their potential by actually exercising their powers. Insofar as the adolescent's self-concept comes to focus on future possibility as well as present reality, it is inevitably cloaked in mystery, doubt, and uncertainty and is subject to swings and fluctuations.

In sum, if there is such a thing as an adolescent "identity crisis," it must certainly incorporate as a central feature the doubt, uncertainty, and volatility that appears so prominently in adolescence.

Gender.   Although the data are not abundant, they consistently indicate that girls' self-concepts are more volatile than boys'. In the Baltimore study (Simmons, Rosenberg, & Rosenberg, 1973), the differences are significant at each age level (8–11, 12–14, 15 and older). In a follow-up study of Milwaukee pupils (Simmons & Blyth, 1984), girls were significantly less stable at each of four grade levels: 6, 7, 9, and 10.

Thus, whereas girls' self-esteem probably differs little from that of boys, their self-concepts appear to be substantially more volatile. Indeed, this volatility appears to represent one of the major self-concept problems of girls. Precisely why this should be the case is not certain, but two factors may be suggested. The first is that girls may be more fully immersed in the role-taking stage, more sensitive to the internal thoughts and feelings of other people, and more concerned with others' attitudes toward them. For reasons noted, the stronger our efforts to learn what others think of us, and the more dependent we are on their judgments, the greater the likelihood that our self-feelings will fluctuate greatly. In addition, girls become greatly concerned with physical appearance at this age. The changes that accompany biological events carry corresponding changes in social events, thereby producing explorations with regard to dress, make-up, hair styling, and other artificial alterations of appearance. Adolescent girls are much more attuned to their changing physical appearance. The Baltimore data show that girls are more likely than boys to report that they have changed physically during the past year and that they have greater difficulty adjusting to these physical changes. Our data analyses indicate that the single strongest reason for the higher self-concept volatility among girls is their sense of change in physical characteristics.

What is true of barometric stability, however, is not necessarily true of baseline stability. Carlson (1965) studied subjects at the age of 11 and 17 and found no gender difference in the stability of the self-concept over this extended period. It is thus not so much low baseline self-esteem that disturbs adolescent girls as a fluctuating and variable barometric self-concept.

SUMMARY AND DISCUSSION

Although there are exceptions, the data suggest that, in general, self-concept disturbance tends to reach its peak in early adolescence, that is, about 12–13, or the early junior high school years. With regard to certain dimensions, such as self-esteem, matters improve in later years; in other cases, the disturbance continues at a steady level in the later years. Only rarely is there an increasing deterioration in the later years.

The available data also suggest that self-concept disturbance in adolescence is more severe among girls than boys. Although most attention has centered on self-esteem, it is probable that the gender differences in self-esteem, though significant, are rather small. But girls are clearly more likely to experience certain other self-concept difficulties in adolescence. For one thing, they are clearly more likely to have shaky or volatile self-concepts. In addition, adolescent girls are more likely to be characterized by high levels of public self-consciousness or social anxiety and to be inordinately sensitive to criticism or blame by people (Simmons & Rosenberg, 1975). In addition, we may note that, in adolescence, girls are more likely than boys to undergo the experience of "transient depersonalization" — a momentary loss of one's sense of identity, the experience of uncertainty about who and what one is (Elliott, Rosenberg, & Wagner, 1984). It is rather curious that the gender literature has overlooked a number of important differences in male and female self-concepts.

The features of the self-concept discussed in this chapter, of course, do not purport to exhaust the range of important self-concept dimensions. There is still much to be learned about change and development of the self-concept between middle childhood and adolescence. Such concepts as self-efficacy (Bandura, 1977, 1978; Franks & Marolla, 1976; Gecas & Schwalbe, 1983), self-monitoring (Snyder, 1974), self-schematization (Markus & Sentis, 1982), "impulsive" and "institutional" selves (Turner, 1976), individuation (Zimbardo, 1969), self-consistency (Gergen & Morse, 1967), self-presentation (Elliott, 1982; Goffman, 1956), internal and external locus of control (Lefcourt, 1982), learned helplessness (Abramson, Seligman, & Teasdale, 1978), "public" and "private" self-consciousness (Buss, 1980; Fenigstein, Scheier, & Buss, 1975), self-values or self-investment (Faunce, 1984; Rosenberg, 1965), have generally been neglected in developmental research. The most massive obstacle standing in the way of such research is the absence of measures that are equally reliable and valid for subjects across the age span. Hopefully, investigators will soon turn their attention to this thorny, though not insoluble, problem.

ACKNOWLEDGMENTS

The preparation of this paper was supported in part by Grant Number MH-39701 from the National Institute of Mental Health. We are grateful to Roberta G. Simmons, Anthony G. Greenwald, and Jerry Suls for their helpful comments.

REFERENCES

Abramson, L., Seligman, M., & Teasdale, J. (1978). Learned helplessness in humans: Critique and reformulation. *Journal of Abnormal Psychology, 87,* 49–74.

American Psychiatric Association. (1980). *Diagnostic and statistical manual of mental disorders* (3rd ed.). Washington, DC.

Bachman, J. G. (1970). *Youth in transition: The impact of family background and intelligence on tenth-grade boys* (Vol. 2). Ann Arbor, MI: Institute for Social Research.

Bachman, J. G., Kahn, R. L., Mednick, M. T., Davidson, T. N., & Johnston, L. D. (1967). *Youth in transition: Blueprint for a longitudinal study of adolescent boys* (Vol. 1). Ann Arbor, MI: Institute for Social Research.

Bachman, J. G., O'Malley, P., & Johnston, J. (1978). *Adolescence to adulthood: Change and stability in the lives of young men.* Ann Arbor, MI: Institute for Social Research.

Bandura, A. (1977). Self-efficacy: Toward a unifying theory of behavioral change. *Psychological Review, 84,* 191–215.

Bandura, A. (1978). The self in reciprocal determinism. *American Psychologist, 33,* 344–357.

Bannister, D., & Agnew, J. (1977). The child's construing of self. In J. Cole (Ed.), *Nebraska symposium on motivation.* Lincoln, NE: University of Nebraska.

Beck, A. T. (1967). *Depression: Clinical, experimental and theoretical aspects.* New York: Harper and Row.

Bernstein, R. M. (1980). The development of the self-system during adolescence. *Journal of Genetic Psychology, 136,* 231–245.

Blos, P. (1962). *On adolescence: A psychoanalytic interpretation.* New York: Free Press.

Bourne, L. E., & O'Banion, K. (1971). Conceptual rule learning and chronological age. *Developmental Psychology, 5,* 525–534.

Broughton, J. (1978). Development of concepts of self, mind, reality, and knowledge. *New Directions for Child Development, 1,* 75–100.

Burns, R. B. (1979). *The self-concept in theory, measurement, development, and behavior.* London: Longman.

Bush, D., Simmons, R., Hutchinson, B., & Blyth, D. (1977–1978). Adolescent perception of sex roles in 1968 and 1975. *Public Opinion Quarterly, 41,* 459–474.

Buss, A. H. (1980). *Self-consciousness and social anxiety.* San Francisco, CA: W. H. Freeman and Co.

Campbell, A. (1981). *The sense of well-being in America.* New York: McGraw-Hill.

Carlson, R. (1965). Stability and change in the adolescent's self-image. *Child Development, 36,* 659–666.

Damon, W., & Hart, D. (1982). The development of self-understanding from infancy through adolescence. *Child Development, 53,* 841–864.

Demo, D. H., & Savin-Williams, R. C. (1983). Early adolescent self-esteem as a function of social class: Rosenberg and Pearlin revisited. *American Journal of Sociology, 88,* 763–774.

Dipboye, R. L. (1977). A critical review of Korman's self-consistency theory of work motivation and occupational choice. *Organizational Behavior and Human Performance, 18,* 108–126.

Douvan, E., & Adelson, J. (1966). *The adolescent experience.* New York: Wiley.

Elkind, D., Medvene, L., & Rockway, A. S. (1970). Representational level and concept production in children and adolescents. *Developmental Psychology, 2,* 85–89.

Elliott, G., Rosenberg, M., & Wagner, M. (1984). Transient depersonalization in youth. *Social Psychology Quarterly, 47,* 115–129.

Elliott, G. C. (1982). Self-esteem and self-presentation among the young as a function of age and gender. *Journal of Youth and Adolescence, 11,* 135–155.

Engel, M. (1959). The stability of the self-concept in adolescence. *Journal of Abnormal and Social Psychology, 58,* 211–215.

Epstein, S. (1981). The ecological study of emotions in humans. In P. Pliner, K. R. Blankstein, & I. Spigel (Eds.), *Advances in the study of communication and affect: Vol. 5. Perceptions of emotions in self and others.* New York: Plenum Press.

Erikson, E. H. (1959). Identity and the life cycle: Selected papers. *Psychological Issues, 1,* 1–171.

Faunce, W. A. (1984). School achievement, social status, and self-esteem. *Social Psychology Quarterly, 47,* 3–14.

Fenigstein, A., Scheier, M., & Buss, A. (1975). Public and private self-consciousness: Assessment and theory. *Journal of Counseling and Clinical Psychology, 43,* 522–527.

Flavell, J. (1974). The development of inferences about others. In T. Mischel (Ed.), *Understanding other persons.* Oxford, England: Blackwell.

Flavell, J. H., Fry, C., Wright, J., & Jarvis, P. (1968). *The development of role-taking and communication skills in children.* New York: Wiley.

Franks, D. D., & Marolla, J. (1976). Efficacious action and social approval as interacting dimensions of self-esteem: Formulation through construct validation. *Sociometry, 39,* 324–341.

Franzoi, S. L., & Reddish, B. J. (1980). Factor analysis of the stability of self scale. *Psychological Reports, 47,* 1160–1162.

Gecas, V. (1972). Parental behavior and contextual variations in adolescent self-esteem. *Sociometry, 35,* 332–345.

Gecas, V., & Schwalbe, M. (1983). Beyond the looking-glass self: Social structure and efficacy-based self-esteem. *Social Psychology Quarterly, 46,* 77–88.

Gelman, R. (1978). Cognitive development. *Annual Review of Psychology, 29,* 297–332.

Gergen, K. J. (1972). Multiple identity: The healthy, happy human being wears many masks. *Psychology Today, 6,* 31–35, 64, 66.

Gergen, K. J. (1981). The functions and foibles of negotiating self-conception. In M. D. Lynch, A. A. Norem-Hebeisen, & K. Gergen (Eds.), *Self-concept: Advances in theory and research.* Cambridge, MA: Ballinger.

Gergen, K. J., & Morse, S. J. (1967). Self-consistency: Measurement and validation. *Proceedings of the 75th Annual Convention of the American Psychological Association, 2,* 207–08.

Goffman, E. (1955). On face-work: An analysis of ritual elements in social interaction. *Psychiatry: Journal for the Study of Interpersonal Processes, 18,* 218–231.

Goffman, E. (1956). *The presentation of self in everyday life.* Edinburgh: University of Edinburgh.

Harter, S. (1981). A model of intrinsic mastery motivation in children: Individual differences and developmental change. In W. A. Collins (Ed.), *Minnesota symposium on child psychology: Vol. 14.* Hillsdale, NJ: Lawrence Erlbaum Associates.

Harter, S. (1982). The perceived competence scale for children. *Child Development, 53,* 87–97.

Harter, S. (1983). Developmental perspectives on the self-system. In P. H. Mussen (Ed.), *Handbook of child psychology: Vol. 4. Socialization, personality, and social development.* (pp. 275–385). New York: Wiley.

Harter, S., & Connell, J. P. (1982). A comparison of alternative models of the relationships between academic achievement and children's perceptions of competence, control, and motivational orientation. In J. Nicholl (Ed.), *The development of achievement-related cognitions and behaviors.* Greenwich, CT: J.A.I. Press.

Harvey, O. J., Hunt, D. E., & Schroder, H. M. (1961). *Conceptual systems and personality organization.* New York: Wiley.

Heider, F. (1958). *The psychology of interpersonal relations.* New York: Wiley.

Hewitt, J. P., & Stokes, R. (1975). Disclaimers. *American Sociological Review, 40,* 1–11.

Horrocks, J. E. (1976). *The psychology of adolescence* (4th ed.). Boston, MA: Houghton Mifflin.

Inhelder, B., & Piaget, J. (1958). *The growth of logical thinking from childhood to adolescence.* New York: Basic Books.

Jackson, D. N., & Paunonen, S. V. (1980). Personality structure and assessment. In M. R. Rosenzweig & L. W. Porter (Eds.), *Annual review of psychology*. Palo Alto, CA: Annual Reviews.

James, W. (1950). *The principles of psychology*. New York: Dover. (Original work published 1890 by Henry Holt and Company).

Jersild, A. T., Brook, J. S., & Brook, D. W. (1978). *The psychology of adolescence* (3rd ed.). New York: Macmillan.

Jones, E. E., & Pittman, T. S. (1982). Toward a general theory of strategic self-presentation. In J. Suls (Ed.), *Psychological perspectives on the self: Vol. 1*. Hillsdale, NJ: Lawrence Erlbaum Associates.

Jones, S. C. (1973). Self and interpersonal evaluations: Esteem theories versus consistency theories. *Psychological Bulletin, 79*, 185-199.

Jourard, S. M. (1964). *The transparent self*. Princeton, NJ: Van Nostrand.

Kaplan, H. B. (1975). *Self-attitudes and deviant behavior*. Pacific Palisades, CA: Goodyear Publishing.

Kaplan, H. B. (1980). *Deviant behavior in defense of self*. New York: Academic Press.

Kaplan, H. B., & Pokorny, A. D. (1969). Self-derogation and psycho-social adjustment. *Journal of Nervous and Mental Disease, 149*, 421-434.

Keller, A., Ford, L. H., & Meacham, J. A. (1978). Dimensions of self-concept in preschool children. *Developmental Psychology, 14*, 483-489.

Korman, A. K. (1970). Toward a hypothesis of work behavior. *Journal of Applied Psychology, 54*, 31-41.

Lecky, P. (1945). *Self-consistency: A theory of personality*. New York: Island Press.

Lefcourt, H. M. (1982). *Locus of control: Current trends in theory and research*. 2nd. ed. Hillsdale, NJ: Lawrence Erlbaum Associates.

Lewis, M., & Brooks-Gunn, J. (1981). The self as social knowledge. In M. D. Lynch, A. A. Norem-Hebeisen, & K. Gergen (Eds.), *Self-concept: Advances in theory and research* (pp. 101-118). Cambridge, MA: Ballinger.

Livesley, W. J., & Bromley, D. B. (1973). *Person perception in childhood and adolescence*. London: Wiley.

Lowenthal, M. F., Thurner, M., & Chiriboga, D. (1975). *Four stages of life*. San Francisco, CA: Jossey-Bass.

Luck, P. W., & Heiss, J. (1972). Social determinants of self-esteem in adult males. *Sociology and Social Research, 57*, 69-84.

Lunzer, E. (1965). Problems of formal reasoning in test situations. In P. Mussen (Ed.), *European research in cognitive development. Monograph of the Society for Research in Child Development, 30*.

Maccoby, E. E., & Jacklin, C. N. (1974). *The psychology of sex differences*. Stanford, CA: Stanford University Press.

Markus, H., & Sentis, K. (1982). The self in social information processing. In J. L. Suls (Ed.), *Psychological perspectives on the self: Vol. 1* (pp. 41-70). Hillsdale, NJ: Lawrence Erlbaum Associates.

McCarthy, J., & Hoge, D. (1982). Analysis of age effects in longitudinal studies of adolescent self-esteem. *Developmental Psychology, 18*, 372-379.

McGuire, W. J., & McGuire, C. V. (1981). The spontaneous self-concept as affected by personal distinctiveness. In M. D. Lynch, A. A. Norem-Hebeisen, & K. Gergen (Eds.), *Self-concept: Advances in theory and research*. Cambridge, MA: Ballinger.

McGuire, W. J., & Padawer-Singer, A. (1976). Trait salience in the spontaneous self-concept. *Journal of Personality and Social Psychology, 33*, 743-754.

Mead, G. H. (1934). *Mind, self and society*. Chicago, IL: University of Chicago Press.

Merton, R. K. (1957). The role-set: Problems in sociological theory. *British Journal of Sociology, 8*, 106-120.

Montemayor, R., & Eisen, M. (1977). The development of self-conceptions from childhood to adolescence. *Developmental Psychology, 13,* 314–319.

Morse, S., & Gergen, K. J. (1970). Social comparison, self-consistency, and the concept of self. *Journal of Personality and Social Psychology, 16,* 148–156.

Mortimer, J. T., & Lorence, J. (1981). Self-concept stability and change from late adolescence to early adulthood. *Research in Community and Mental Health, 2,* 5–42.

Mortimer, J. T., Finch, M., & Kumka, D. (1982). Persistence and change in development: The multidimensional self-concept. In P. B. Baltes & O. G. Brim (Eds.), *Life-span development and behavior: Vol. 4* (pp. 263–313). New York: Academic Press.

Mullener, N., & Laird, J. D. (1971). Some developmental changes in the organization of self-evaluations. *Developmental Psychology, 5,* 233–236.

Murphy, G. (1947). *Personality.* New York: Harper.

Offer, D. (1969). *The psychological world of the teen-ager.* New York: Basic Books.

Offer, D., Ostrov, E., & Howard, K. I. (1981). *The adolescent: A psychological self-portrait.* New York: Basic Books.

O'Malley, P. M., & Bachman, J. G. (1979). Self-esteem and education: Sex and cohort comparisons among high school seniors. *Journal of Personality and Social Psychology, 37,* 1153–1159.

O'Malley, P., & Bachman, J. (1983). Self-esteem: Change and stability between ages 13 and 23. *Developmental Psychology, 19,* 257–268.

Peevers, B. H. (1984, July). *The self as observer of the self: A developmental analysis of the subjective self.* Paper presented at Conference on Self and Identity, Cardiff, Wales.

Penk, W. E. (1971). Developmental patterns of conceptual styles. *Psychological Reports, 29,* 635–649.

Piaget, J. (1951). *The child's conception of the world.* London: Routledge and Kegan Paul.

Piaget, J. (1976). *The child and reality.* New York: Penguin Books.

Pitts, R. A. (1978). The effects of exclusively French language schooling on self-esteem in Quebec. *The Canadian Modern Language Review, 34,* 372–380.

Radloff, L. S. (1977). The CES-D Scale: A self-report depression scale for research in the general population. *Applied Psychological Measurement, 1,* 385–401.

Rice, F. P. (1978). *The adolescent: Development, relationships and culture* (2nd Ed.). Boston, MA: Allyn and Bacon.

Rogers, C. M., Smith, M. D., & Coleman, J. M. (1978). Social comparison in the classroom: The relationship between academic achievement and self-concept. *Journal of Educational Psychology, 70,* 50–57.

Rosenberg, M. (1965). *Society and the adolescent self-image.* Princeton, NJ: Princeton University Press.

Rosenberg, M. (1975). The dissonant context and the adolescent self-concept. In S. Dragastin & G. Elder (Eds.), *Adolescence in the life cycle: Psychological change and social context* (pp. 97–116). Washington, DC: Hemisphere Publishing Company.

Rosenberg, M. (1977). Contextual dissonance effects: Nature and causes. *Psychiatry, 40,* 205–217.

Rosenberg, M. (1979). *Conceiving the self.* New York: Basic Books.

Rosenberg, M. (1985). Self-concept and psychological well-being in adolescence. In R. Leahy (Ed.), *The development of the self* (pp. 205–246). New York: Academic Press.

Rosenberg, M., & Rosenberg, F. (1981). The occupational self: A developmental study. In M. D. Lynch, A. A. Norem-Hebeisen, & K. J. Gergen (Eds.), *Self-concept: Advances in theory and research* (pp. 173–189). Cambridge, MA: Ballinger.

Rosenberg, M., & Pearlin, L. I. (1978). Social class and self-esteem among children and adults. *American Journal of Sociology, 84,* 53–77.

Rosenberg, M., & Simmons, R. G. (1972). *Black and white self-esteem: The urban school child.* Washington, DC: American Sociological Association.

Sarbin, T. R. (1962). A preface to a psychological analysis of the self. *Psychological Review, 59,* 11–22.

Savin-Williams, R. C., & Demo, D. H. (1983a). Conceiving or misconceiving the self: Issues in adolescent self-esteem. *Journal of Early Adolescence, 3,* 121–140.

Savin-Williams, R. C., & Demo, D. H. (1983b). Situational and transsituational determinants of adolescent self-feelings. *Journal of Personality and Social Psychology, 44,* 824–833.

Scarlett, H. H., Press, A. N., & Crockett, W. H. (1971). Children's descriptions of peers: A Wernerian developmental analysis. *Child Development, 42,* 439–453.

Schlenker, B. R. (1980). *Impression management.* Monterey, CA: Brooks/Cole.

Secord, P. F., & Peevers, B. H. (1974). The development and attribution of person concepts. In T. Mischel (Ed.), *Understanding other persons.* Oxford, England: Blackwell.

Selman, R. (1980). *The growth of interpersonal understanding.* New York: Academic Press.

Shantz, C. (1975). The development of social cognition. In E. M. Hetherington (Ed.), *Review of child development theory and research: Vol. 5* (pp. 257–323). Chicago: University of Chicago Press.

Simmons, R. G., & Blyth, D. (1984). *Moving into adolescence: The impact of pubertal change and school context.* Unpublished manuscript.

Simmons, R. G., & Rosenberg, F. (1975). Sex, sex roles, and self-image. *Journal of Youth and Adolescence, 4,* 229–258.

Simmons, R. G., Rosenberg, F., & Rosenberg, M. (1973). Disturbance in the self-image at adolescence. *American Sociological Review, 38,* 553–568.

Simmons, R., Blyth, D. A., Van Cleave, E. F., & Bush, D. M. (1979). Entry into early adolescence. *American Sociological Review, 44,* 948–967.

Snyder, M. (1974). Self-monitoring of expressive behavior. *Journal of Personality and Social Psychology, 30,* 526–537.

Stryker, S. (1980). *Symbolic interactionism.* Menlo Park, CA: Benjamin/Cummings.

Stryker, S. (1981). Symbolic interactionism: Themes and variations. In M. Rosenberg & R. H. Turner (Eds.), *Social psychology: Sociological perspectives.* New York: Basic Books.

Swann, W. B., Jr. (1983). Self-verification: Bringing social reality into harmony with the self. In J. Suls & A. G. Greenwald (Eds.), *Psychological perspectives on the self: Vol. 2* (pp. 33–66). Hillsdale, NJ: Lawrence Erlbaum Associates.

Tagiuri, R. (1968). Person perception. In G. Lindzey & E. Aronson (Eds.), *The handbook of social psychology: Vol. 3.* Reading, MA: Addison-Wesley.

Tanner, J. M., Whitehouse, R. H., & Takaishi, M. (1966). Standards from birth to maturity for height, weight, height velocity, weight velocity: British children, 1965. *Archives of Disease in Childhood, 41,* 613–635.

Turner, R. H. (1968). The self-conception in social interaction. In C. Gordon & K. Gergen (Eds.), *The self in social interaction* (pp. 93–106). New York: Wiley.

Turner, R. H. (1976). The real self: From institution to impulse. *American Journal of Sociology, 81,* 989–1016.

Werner, H. (1957). The concept of development from a comparative and organismic point of view. In D. B. Harris (Ed.), *The concept of development.* Minneapolis, MN: University of Minnesota.

Wylie, R. (1979). *The self-concept: Theory and research on selected topics* (Vol. 2) (rev. ed.). Lincoln: University of Nebraska Press.

Zimbardo, P. G. (1969). The human choice: Individuation, reason, and order versus deindividuation, impulse, and chaos. In W. J. Arnold & D. Levine (Eds.), *Nebraska symposium on motivation, 17.* Lincoln: University of Nebraska Press.

Processes Underlying the Construction, Maintenance, and Enhancement of the Self-Concept in Children

6

Susan Harter
University of Denver

The self-concept, like many such constructs, has waxed and waned in importance throughout the history of psychology. Although the self was a popular topic during earlier eras in which philosophical analysis and introspection dominated our thinking, we witnessed its demise during the hey-day of behaviorism and the more objectively based scientific pursuit of knowledge. However, the 1960s ushered in a resurgence of interest in the self-concept. In addition to its conceptual reentry into our formulations about the human organism, we observed a proliferation of affective education programs designed to enhance the self-images of our children. The idealistic goals of these Camelot-like ventures were never fully realized, however, and once again self-concept fell from grace. The majority of these efforts, both theoretical and applied, were plagued by problems of definition as well as measurement, resulting in a body of findings that were unconvincing, if not contradictory (see Wylie, 1974, 1979). As a result, educators returned to an emphasis on the traditional curriculum, and theorists redirected their attention to cognitive and behavioral constructs that seemed less elusive.

With the advent of the 1980s, the self has once again been resurrected as a legitimate psychological construct. Moreover, the resurgence of interest in the self has not been restricted to partisan subgroups within the field. On the contrary, the self has found advocates among developmentalists, social learning, theorists, cognitive–attributional theorists, educational psychologists, as well as those clinicians espousing cognitive–behavioral models of treatment. It would appear that theorists of many persuasions found the cognitive and behavioral models of the 1970s wanting. With the self excised, somehow these formultions did not seem to capture the essence of human experience. During the 1980s, therefore, many of us have sought to revive the self, as well as its affective correlates, giving them their rightful due.

This chapter focuses primarily on one programmatic effort to unravel some of the mysteries of the self that abound in the life of the developing child. Attention is directed to the following specific questions and concerns:

1. What are the prevailing models of self-concept? Is the self-concept best captured by a single score or do models that focus on domain-specific judgments provide a more accurate picture of the self-system? Are there developmental differences in the self-concept, particularly in its structure and content, and have these differences found their way into instruments designed to assess the self-concept? In addition to normative change, there are questions concerning the use of self-concept measures with special groups of children such as the learning disabled, the mentally retarded, and group with medical disorders, for example, the asthmatic.

2. Although certain models emphasize domain-specific judgments of competence and adequacy, others highlight the role of one's global sense of self-worth. At what ages are children capable of making such a judgment, and what processes do children employ to maintain or enhance their sense of self-worth, once it emerges? Moreover, what are the major determinants of self-worth? James' (1892) model would have us believe that adults engage in a cognitive appraisal of how successful they are in those areas of their life that are central or important to their sense of self. Cooley (1902), on the other hand, emphasized the role of significant others in the formation of the self, suggesting these others form the mirror, as it were, into which we gaze to garner information about our attributes. To what extent do we find these processes operative in children, and is one source of information more salient than the other?

3. What function does one's sense of global self-worth actually play, does it serve to mediate particular behaviors of interest? In our zeal for assessing the self-perceptions of children, have we given careful thought to what the concept of self-worth buys us in the market place, to what it predicts? Perhaps constructs such as self-worth are epiphenomenal, and we would do better to focus on more situation-specific indices in our predictions of a child's motivation, affect, and behavior.

4. How can we move beyond the rather static approach to the self and its assessment in order to investigate the dynamic interplay between the many facets of the self? For example, at what point in development do seemingly contradictory traits within one's self-concept — for example, smartness versus stupidity, kindness versus meanness — create tension or intrapsychic conflict within the self-system? Why should such conflict occur at certain stages of development, but not others?

MODELS AND MEASURES OF SELF-CONCEPT

There are a number of different conceptual models of the self-concept, each of which can be associated with a particular measurement strategy. Five approaches are briefly reviewed here; the interested reader is referred to a more complete discussion of these models (see Harter, 1983, 1985).

There are those, notably Coopersmith (1967), who have concluded that the self-concept is a unidimensional construct, best assessed by presenting the child subject with items tapping a range of content, for example, items dealing with school, friends, family, and self-confidence. In keeping with the unidimensional approach to the self-concept, one calculates a total score, summing across all items, giving them equal weight. This aggregate model, therefore, ignores the specific content of the items included under the assumption that one's total score will adequately reflect one's sense of self across the variety of domains in one's life.

This single-score approach has been challenged by those theorists and investigators who have argued that such a model may mask important distinctions that children make across the different domains in their lives. Thus, a multidimensional approach has been put forward as an alternative. In our own work, for example, we have employed factor-analytic procedures to document the fact that children, age 8 and older, make distinctions between five separate domains: scholastic competence, athletic competence, social acceptance, physical appearance, and behavior or conduct (Harter, 1982, 1984). Utilizing such an approach, the self is depicted as a profile of evaluative judgments across these domains. Mullener and Laird (1971) have adopted a similar approach, although the domains they have selected are somewhat different. They have identified intellectual skills, achievement traits, physical skills, interpersonal skills, and a sense of social responsibility.

The Piers–Harris self-concept scale (1969) falls somewhere between the unidimensional and multidimensional approaches. In their initial model, self-concept was viewed as unidimensional. However, subsequent factor-analytic studies have revealed the existence of several factors; because the scale was not designed with the intent of demonstrating the existence of separate domains, these factors do not point to a clear picture of differentiated dimensions that define the self. Low loadings, in certain cases, as well as cross-loadings, appear in this factor structure. However, on balance, the findings with this instrument suggest the utility of carefully constructing measures that, on an a priori basis, are designed to tap specific domains. If such an approach is adopted, findings indicate that the profile approach to an analysis of self-perceptions across domains is clearly justified (Harter, 1982, 1984).

A third approach to the self-concept can be found among those who espouse hierarchical models of the self. In these models, a construct such as self-concept or self-esteem represents a super-ordinate category under which other subcategories of the self are organized. For example, in Epstein's (1973) model, there are four second-order categories: competence, moral self-approval, power, and love worthiness. Further lower order categories may represent the types of competence, for example, mental and physical competence, and the lowest order categories would or could be defined in terms of specific abilities.

Other hierarchical models include those of Shavelson, Hubner, and Stanton (1976) and of L'Ecuyer (1981). Both models place self-concept at the apex and proceed to delineate the various levels within the hierarchy. For example, Shavelson et al. identify academic and differentiations within these general domains. Academic self-concept is further subdivided in a range of specific school subjects, for example, English, history, math, and science. The nonacademic domains included social self-concept, emotional self-concept, and physical self-concept. These domains undergo further subdivisions at lower levels of analysis.

The model proposed by L'Ecuyer (1981) provides an even more differentiated picture of the components of the self-concept. A number of self "structures" are identified, for example, the material self, the personal self, the adaptive self, and the social self. Each of these is further subdivided into a number of categories at the base of the hierarchy.

As has been noted previously (Harter, 1985a), these hierarchical models would appear to have considerable appeal and to advance our understanding of the organizational structure of the self, compared to those models that merely deal with the self-concept as a general aggregate of evaluations or those models that specify the various dimensions of the self-concept. However, upon closer examination, they present problems, particularly with regard to their operationalization. As has been discussed elsewhere in some detail (Harter, 1985), we need to be clear about what we hierarchizing, as well as what measurement strategy our conceptualization dictates. For example, do the lower level postulates in the self-system, such as the social, emotional, and physical self-concepts in the Shavelson et al. (1976) model, represent separate discrete factors? If so, in what sense do they combine to form the more general nonacademic self-concept? Is this to be thought of as a higher order factor? Moreover, does it reflect the phenomenological experience of the person, do we carry with us a nonacademic self-concept per se? Does the overall general self-concept at the apex represent yet an even higher order factor, and if so, how are the lower order postulates actually combined?

Such models are also problematic because certain domains may be more important to one's overall sense of self than others; yet, domains are not differentially weighted in terms of their importance to the self. On balance, as has been suggested earlier (Harter, 1985), it would seem that models of this type have heuristic value as an aid in organizing our thinking about the possible dimensions of the self-system. They may also allow us to test broad relationships among the constructs in the network. However, they appear to represent a conceptual model in the minds of the theorist, not the phenomenological network of constructs that defines the self-concept of individual subjects.

A fourth approach to the self-concept that emphasizes global self-worth can be found in the work of Rosenberg (1979), whose intellectual legacy can be traced directly to James (1892) and Cooley (1902). Both of these historical scholars of the self wrestled with the issue of whether individuals possessed a general sense of self-worth or self-esteem over and above the self-evaluative judgments one can make in the specific domains in one's life. They each concluded that this global evaluation of one's self is a phenomenological reality for adults. Rosenberg has made a similar argument, claiming that we should acknowledge the individual's general sense of self-worth, in addition to those evaluations of one's adequacy across the specific domains in one's life.

It is critical to realize that Rosenberg is not suggesting that one's sense of global self-worth is some simple additive combination of responses to the discrete items on a measure like the Coopersmith Self-Esteem Inventory (1967). Rosenberg (1979) has cogently argued that in all likelihood, the various discrete elements of the self are weighted, hierarchized, and combined according to an extremely complex equation of which the individual is probably unaware. For this reason, he has chosen not to empirically investigate the specific bases on which the global judgment of self-worth is constructed; rather, he has opted for the direct assessment of self-worth as an entity in and of itself. Thus, he has constructed a unidimensional measure that taps the degree to which one is satisfied with one's life, feels one has good qualities, has a positive attitude toward oneself, or, on the negative side, feels useless, desires more self-respect, or thinks one is a failure. This measure, he feels, assesses the phenomenological appraisal of global self-worth, although it finesses the complexities of the underlying hierarchy of discrete judgments that may be responsible for such an overall judgment about the self.

The fifth approach represents a combination of several of the themes already discussed. According to this approach, one needs to take into account the multidimensional nature of domain-specific judgments, as well as one's sense of global self-worth, assessing both. Moreover, it is critical to assess the importance of success for each domain, because a consideration of this importance hierarchy, in conjunction with our knowledge of the specific self-evaluative judgments in each domain, may well allow us to understand and predict self-worth. A similar argument has been made by Tesser and his colleagues who have demonstrated, with adult subjects, that if a dimension is highly relevant to one's own self-definition, performance judged to be inferior will threaten one's sense of self-esteem (Tesser, 1980; Tesser & Campbell, 1980; Tesser & Campbell, 1983).

In our own work with children, we have translated James' (1892) conceptual model, in which global self-worth or self-esteem reflects the ratio of one's successes to one's pretensions, into an empirical model that can be tested directly. In so doing, we are more optimistic than Rosenberg because we feel it may be possible to partially reconstruct the bases on which children are making their self-judgments, particularly their evaluation of global self-worth. Specifically, we have identified five domains in the lives of children, those named earlier under multidimensional approaches. Some of these are domains in which competence is clearly evident, for example, scholastic competence and athletic competence. The remaining three address adequacies that do not necessarily involve competence. These include social acceptance, physical appearance, and behavioral conduct. Scores across these discrete subscales provide a profile of one's competence/adequacy.

In addition, a separate subscale taps the child's general sense of self-worth. Although we formulated our own concept of self-worth in the lives of children independently of Rosenberg, the convergence is striking. Our general self-worth items tap the degree to which one likes oneself as a person, likes the way one is leading one's life, is happy with the way they are, feels good about oneself, and so on. Thus, we are in strong agreement with Rosenberg on the point that one does not assess this general attitude toward the self by adding up the evaluative responses to those items in the subscales tapping specific domains. Rather, one assesses global self-worth through a separate set of items that tap this construct directly.

In contrast to Rosenberg, however, we have sought to examine the relationship between global self-worth, so measured, and the discrete evaluations within each domain. More specifically, building upon James' contention, we have hypothesized that general self-worth among older children will be, in large part, based on the discrepancy between their domain-specific competence/adequacy evaluations and their attitudes concerning the importance of success in each of these domains. The viability of such an approach is examined later in the chapter. Before presenting these findings, we first deal with a number of issues relevant to the assessment of the various facets of the self-concept in children, with particular attention to developmental differences, as well as to the measurement of the self-concept in special groups of children with mental and physical disabilities.

ISSUES IN ASSESSMENT

Developmental Differences in the Content and Structure of the Self-Concept

In recent years there has been a renewed interest in how the self-concept may undergo developmental change. For the most part, these efforts are rooted in a cognitive–developmental perspective. The empirical findings (see Monte-

mayor & Eisen, 1977; Rosenberg, 1979), generally reveal that with development, children shift their focus from behavioral characteristics of the self in
the early years, to trait-like constructs during middle childhood, and then
to more abstract, psychological constructs during adolescence. Rosenberg
(1979) has aptly captured these shifting approaches to self-description by
noting that the young child functions like a behaviorist, whereas in middle
childhood the predominant orientation is that of a trait theorist; one sees yet
another shift in the adolescent, who appears in the guise of a Freudian
clinician.

There are those of us who have attempted to go beyond these accounts in
order to develop a more comprehensive model of the dimensions of developmental change. For example, in one such model (Harter, 1983) it has been
urged that we separate the structural dimensions of self-description from the
specific content domains to which these structures are applied. Structural dimensions here, refer, to simple descriptions of isolated attributes, to the subsequent organization of such attributes into trait-like constructs about the
self, as well as the later organization of trait labels into higher order abstractions. In addition to this structural developmental trajectory, developmental
differences can also be observed in the content categories to which structures
are applied, for example, descriptions of one's observable preference, abilities, and so on, followed by self-descriptions involving one's motives and
emotions, and finally one's inner thoughts.

Damon and Hart (1982) have recently proposed another model of the dimensions involved in self-description. In their formulation they build upon
James' distinction between the "Me" self and the "I" self. They identify four
conceptual components of the "Me" self: physical, active, social, and psychological self-constituents; as well as four dimensions of the "I" self: continuity,
distinctness, volition, and self-reflection. They propose that these can be
identified at four developmental levels during childhood and adolescence, infancy and early childhood, middle and late childhood, early adolescence, and
late adolescence.

Although models of this sort have obvious appeal, for the most part they
have not yet had a dramatic impact on our efforts to devise instruments that
are sensitive to both developmental as well as individual differences in self-
evaluation. All-encompassing conceptual frameworks of this sort are often
difficult to empirically examine. However, there are some specific steps we
might begin to take. For example, if spontaneous self-descriptions do show
predictable developmental shifts from the use of simple behavioral descriptors, to traits, to higher order abstractins, might we not want to capture these
shifts in our standardized instruments designed to tap the self-concept?

In our own efforts to construct instruments that tap individual differences
in self-evaluative judgments, there has been some attention to developmental
issues, although it has by no means been as systematic or as theory-based as
one might like. Nevertheless, four different developmental themes have

emerged in our attempts to devise such measures. The first involves the need to include different item content at different developmental levels (Harter & Pike, 1984). In the assessment of cognitive competence, for example, the pictorial items we have included in our instrument for the preschool and kindergarten level (ability to do puzzles, knowing one's letters, knowing one's numbers, etc.) are replaced, at the first and second grade levels, by more age-appropriate cognitive skills, for example, reading, spelling, ability to do simple arithmetic operations, and so on. Similar age-graded items were necessary in the athletic and social domains, as well.

A second developmental difference can be observed in the level of description captured by the language of our pictorial items for young children (4 to 7) compared to the manner in which items are worded on the questionnaire version appropriate for children ages 8 and older. At the younger ages, all of the items involve concrete descriptions of behaviors. However, on the older children's questionnaire, a number of the items are described in terms of trait labels, for example, smart, popular, kind, good-looking, although other items describe specific competencies more concretely. We have not yet attended to the implications of the fact that certain items are worded as trait labels, whereas other items retain a more behavioral flavor. Some recent intriguing findings with the learning disabled child, described in the next section, suggest that we might well explore this distinction.

A third developmental difference involves the number of factors that have emerged in our attempts to devise instruments for the 4- to 7-year-old age range compared to the 8- to 12-year-old range. We have found, for example, that among older children, cognitive and athletic skills define separate factors, whereas among the young children, these items define one single competence factor. The simpler factor pattern for the younger children, indicating that they make fewer distinction among domains, appears to be related to cognitive–developmental level. Furthermore, mental age appears to be a more powerful predictor than chronological age. In one study, with third to sixth grade educable retarded children whose mental ages were within the 4 to 7 year range, we found a similar factor pattern; these pupils, comparable in mental age to our young children of normal intelligence, did not make a distinction between cognitive and athletic skills. Although this pattern is readily interpretable, the findings have been somewhat serendipitous. Thus, in future research we would do well to incorporate this type of developmental thinking into the design of our instruments, making a priori predictions about the structure of the self-concept at different developmental levels.

Fourth, we need to adopt a developmental perspective with regard to the concept of global self-worth. It had been our conviction, derived from general developmental theory, that children would not be able to make meaningful judgments about their worth as a person until approximately the age of 8. The very concept of "personness," as a generalization about the self, is not yet firmly established among younger children. As a result, we reasoned, young children cannot make judgments of global self-worth, although they can evaluate their performance in the particular domains of their lives. Our findings with normal IQ children support this argument. Items tapping specific abilities, for example, doing well in sports or in one's schoolwork, have meaning, whereas items describing the degree to which one likes oneself as a person or is happy being he way they are do not have meaning for the young child. In fact, some even deny that they are a person, asserting that they are a boy or a girl. These observations converge with the findings of other investigators (see Ruble & Rholes, 1981; Suls & Sanders, 1982) who have placed the emergence of a number of generalized concepts about the self at around the age of 8.

The cognitive–developmental basis for the construction of such a global concept about the self was also brought home to us in our study with the mentally retarded. Although we gave these grade-school retarded children the questionnaire version of the scale designed for their normal IQ peers, we found that the self-worth subscale did not emerge as a separate factor as it did for the normal sample, nor did the self-worth items systematically or meaningfully load on any factor. Given that the mental ages of the retarded pupils approximated these of our young, normal IQ children, whom we predicted would not yet have developed a general sense of self, these findings were not surprising. In fact, they bolstered our conviction that global self-worth is a complex cognitive construction that does not emerge until approximately the mental age of 8.

Our own experiences, therefore, have lead us to appreciate the fact that developmentally appropriate self-concept measures may require differences in item content, in level of description, in factor structure, and in the inclusion or omission of particular self-constructs at different ages. For the most part, investigators have not given sufficiently thoughtful attention to these dimensions. Historically, the study of self-concept has been conducted by those interested in the psychometric demonstration of individual differences in how the self is evaluated. It has only been recently that developmental psychologists have begun to address the ontogenetic bases of self-description.

As mentioned earlier, some have proposed broad Piagetian-based models of self-description, where the implications of cognitive–developmental shifts are underscored (see Damon & Hart, 1982; Harter, 1983; Selman, 1980). For those at the interface of developmental and social psychology, some of these processes have been described more explicitly. For example, a number of investigators have now spoken to the developmental emergence of social comparison processes, and how these impact self-description (see Masters, 1971; Ruble & Rholes, 1981; Suls & Sanders, 1982). Others have adopted a more attributional framework, demonstrating that the young child does not differentiate between effort and ability in making attributions about the self (see

Dweck & Elliot, 1983; Kun, 1977; Nicholls, 1978). Certain investigators have also pointed out that not only are self-judgments in the young children absolute, rather than relative to others, but they tend to be relatively situation-specific and unstable. That is, young children do not think in terms of traits or dispositions that may endure across time as well as situations (see Dweck & Elliot, 1983; Ruble & Rholes, 1981; Suls & Sanders, 1982). Thus, there is a burgeoning literature on many of the developmental processes underlying self-description and self-evaluation, as well as the proliferation of models designed to capture the systematic nature of these changes (see Damon & Hart, 1982; Nicholls, 1983; Suls & Sanders, 1982).

Our goal, it would seem, is to integrate these findings into our psychometric assessments of the self-concept. In certain cases, such an integration may affect the nature of these measuring instruments, themselves. For example, items for young children should be couched in more concrete, behavioral terms, whereas items for older children should contain more trait-like descriptions as well as comparative references to others. Follow-up interviews could also illuminate the basis on which these self-judgments were made, including their attributional underpinnings as well as the degree to which they are considered to be stable. In this way, we should be able to capture the flavor of the processes underlying such judgments, rather than merely thinking of the self-concept as some standardized score or profile.

Differences Among Special Groups of Children

In recent years, considerable attention has been devoted to the assessment of the self-concept of children with a variety of intellectual, physical, or emotional deficits. The primary goal of such efforts is to determine whether or not the self-judgments of such children are more negative than those of children without handicaps. That is, the concern is with the level of the child's self-esteem. Typically, measures standardized for use with normal children are employed without questioning whether the scores derived from these instruments are reliable or meaningful. Our own work with special groups suggests considerable caution in this regard.

Our studies with the mentally retarded, for example, reveal that the psychometric properties of a number of our instruments are very different for this group (Silon & Harter, 1985). Findings with our Perceived Competence Scale for Children (Harter, 1982) provide a good example. Whereas the factor analysis for regular classroom children yields a clear 4-factor solution (scholastic competence, athletic competence, social acceptance, and global self-worth), we find a 2-factor solution for the mentally retarded. The scholastic and athletic competence subscale items did not define separate subscales, but combined to form one factor, suggesting that the retarded do not differentiate between different types of competencies. The social acceptance items, for the most part, defined the second factor.

Understandably, it is the more concretely worded items that load on these factors, not those couched in terms of trait labels. Thus, items tapping the degree to which one understands what they read, can remember things easily, and are good at outdoor sports, appear on these factors, whereas more general items, focusing on the degree to which one is smart, athletic, or popular, do not load on these factors. Moreover, as mentioned in the previous section, the global self-worth factor does not emerge at all. It should be emphasized that the resulting factor pattern is interpretable in that the structure is expectedly less differentiated, the items that define these factors are more concrete, and the relatively complex cognitive construction of the self as a global entity is not manifest. However, these findings have necessitated a special version of the scale for retarded children. The original version is not appropriate and will yield scores that are unreliable, if not meaningless, for the most part.

A quite different picture emerges when one administers the original instrument to children diagnosed as learning disabled (Renick & Harter, 1984). These are pupils within the normal range of intelligence who have circumscribed deficits in the areas of information processing, reading, writing, manipulation of symbols, and so on. With this group, we do obtain a 4-factor solution. However, the factor pattern for the learning disabled is somewhat different from the pattern we obtain normatively. Both the athletic competence and social acceptance factors emerge relatively unscathed. However, cognitive competence and self-worth do not emerge as discrete factors. Rather, we obtain two cognitive self-worth composite factors. The first such composite is largely made up of trait-like descriptions, for example, being smart, from the cognitive subscale, and being sure of yourself, or liking yourself as a person, from the general self-worth subscale. The second composite is defined by items that are much more concrete and behavioral, for example, feeling it is easy to understand what one reads (cognitive), thinking the way one does things is fine (general self-worth).

Several points are noteworthy in interpreting these findings. First, the pattern is just as differentiated in these learning disabled pupils as with regular classroom children in the sense that four factors are obtained. Unlike the retarded children, these average-IQ learning-disabled children are able to make as many distinctions as their regular classroom peers. However, two of the four factors are conceptually different. The fact that the learning disabled child's general sense of worth is intimately tied to his or her scholastic competence is certainly plausible, given that these cognitive deficits are central concerns in the child's life. What was initially puzzling, however, was why the factor pattern revealed two distinct cognitive self-worth combinations. Why is a trait composite somewhat separate from a behavioral composite?

It struck us that the messages that such pupils receive may facilitate such a distinction. That is, learning-disabled children are typically told by their teachers that they are not dumb or stupid; rather, there are some specific skills or behaviors that are hard for them to do. Thus, although reading or math may be difficult, this does not imply that they are stupid, and special-education teachers appear to reinforce this distinction. The fact that they score within the normal-IQ range, although they may have problems on certain subtests, is testimony to this observation. It would appear, therefore, that learning-disabled children are processing this message at some level, which, in turn, leads them to make a distinction between trait-like attributions and the more specific behaviors that are not necessarily manifestations of these traits. In normal children, without deficits, these traits and behaviors are psychologically linked.

We plan to pursue this finding more systematically because it represents an intriguing pattern of self-concept formation among the learning disabled. By dissociating, to some extent, one's trait-like capacities from performance at specific tasks, these pupils may be adopting a strategy, bolstered by their teachers, which allows them to protect the self. At a more procedural level, these findings have also necessitated a revision of our scale for the learning-disabled child to reflect this particular self-structure.

It is also interesting to contrast the findings for the mentally retarded and the learning-disabled children. Although our experience with both groups has dictated scale revisions, the outcomes are very different, indeed. The mentally retarded children require a scale structure that is simpler, items must be more concrete, and those tapping the self-worth construct must be eliminated altogether. The learning-disabled children, on the other hand, require a scale structure that takes into account the distinction they appear to be making between trait-like characteristics and behavioral attributes. The more general point to be underscored is that we simply cannot treat all children with intellectual deficits as a homogeneous group, because clearly, there are quite different processes influencing the structure and content of their self-perceptions. Moreover, children with physical handicaps would appear to require modifications in these same instrument. Not only do certain items need to be revised (Dalgin & Harter, 1984), but supplementary subscales tapping dimensions such as patience, effort, control of one's temper, and rule following may need to be added because these appear to be relevant to the self-concept of the handicapped child (Mayberry, 1985).

The Use of Social Comparison Among Special Groups

There is another sense in which the processes underlying self-evaluation differ in these special populations with deficits. Consider the following findings: The perceived cognitive competence of the mainstreamed learning-disabled child is significantly lower than the mean of regular classroom

represent a given child's profile. It had been our initial belief that childen age 8 and older, could make judgments of their self-worth, however, we found ourselves in the curious position of being able to reliabily measure an entity that we did not quite understand.

We returned to the font of wisdom on the subject of the self, William James, for theoretical guidance. James (1892) was quite explicit on the point that, as adults, we possess a global sense of self-worth or self-esteem in addition to self-judgments about our competencies within the specific domains of our lives. Moreover, James sought to formalize this relationship in his definition of the foundations upon which one's self-esteem rests. For James, self-esteem reflected the ratio of one's successes to one's pretensions. Thus, if one's successes were at a level equal to or greater than one's pretensions, high self-esteem would characterize the person's global judgment of self-esteem. Conversely, if one's pretensions toward success exceeded one's actual level of success, low self-esteem would result. One's pretensions may well change throughout one's life, however, at any point in time the relationship between one's hierarchy of pretensions and one's hierarchy of perceived competencies will determine or predict one's overall sense of worth.

In our own work, we have sought to operationalize the components of James' formula, and to put this model to an empirical test with children. Self-esteem, in our framework, is equivalent to self-worth, operationalized as responses to those general questions asking how much one likes the self as a person, likes the way one is leading one's life, is happy with oneself, and so on. We have translated the construct of success into competence or adequacy in the specific domains we have identified: scholastic competence, athletic competence, social acceptance, physical appearance, and behavioral conduct. As described earlier, our Self-Perception Profile for Children (Harter, 1984) provides a separate score for each domain.

Pretensions, in James' parlance, is operationalized as the importance of success in each of these discrete domains, with regard to how much one likes oneself as a person. Here, our formulation bears a close resemblance to that of Tesser and Campbell, who have adopted the term *relevannce* for a similar construct (Tesser & Campbell, 1980, 1983). Tesser and Campbell develop this construct within their model of the role of social comparison processes in the maintenance of self-esteem. If one compares oneself unfavorably on dimensions that are highly relevant to one's self-definition, low self-esteem will result. Favorable comparisons on highly relevant dimensions leads to high self-esteem. If the dimension is irrelevant, negative judgments will not threaten one's sense of esteem.

We have preferred to focus on importance or relevance as a translation of pretensions, rather than the ideal self (Rogers, 1950) as described in those models that have assessed the discrepancy between one's real and one's ideal self. As Rosenberg (1979) has cogently pointed out, there are different forms of one's ideal self ranging from one's committed ideal (I hope to make the varsity team), to one's fantasy ideal (I hope to quarterback for the Dallas Cowboys). Often it is difficult to ascertain what items such as "what would you like to be" or "what do you wish you were like" actually tap, and whether this represents a current aspiration that one feels one can reasonably achieve or a futuristic fantasy beyond one's capabilities. Thus, although the real— ideal discrepancy notion bears a strong conceptual resemblance to James' ratio of successes to pretentions, in our work with children we have sought to avoid some of the methodological and conceptual complexities of the real-ideal self construct.

In operationalizing importance, we present children with a separate rating scale in which they are asked to think about how important each of the five domains is to how they feel about themselves as a person. We employ the same question format as described for the competence items. Thus, a sample item reads: Some kids feel that how you do in school is important to how you feel about yourself as a person, but other kids do not feel that how you do at school is that important to how you feel about yourself as a person. Subjects pick which kids they are most like and then indicate whether that is just sort of true for them or really true for them. Both competence/adequacy judgments and importance ratings utilize a 4-point scale. Thus, we have five competence/adequacy judgments, five ratings as to the importance of success in each area, and our global self-worth score. The empirical question is whether the relationship between comptence/adequacy judgments and importance ratings predicts self-worth, and to what degree.

Empirical Evidence

To examine this question empirically, we translated James' notion of the ratio of successes to pretensions into the discrepancy between one's competence/adequacy judgments and the importance of success ratings. Because the essence of James' formulation is that one's self-esteem should primarily only be affected by domains that are important to the self, as captured by his term *pretensions,* we only examined the discrepancies for domains that are rated as a 4 (really important) or 3 (sort of important). Thus, for domains receiving such importance scores, we obtained a discrepancy score (competence minus importance), averaged over these domains. The bigger this discrepancy in the negative direction, that is, the more one's importance scores exceed one's competence/adequacy scores, the lower one's self-worth should be. High self-worth should be associated with scores close to zero, indicating that one's perceived competence and the importance of success are very congruent.

It should be noted that James' formula constitutes a ratio in which successes (competence) were to be divided by pretensions (importance). We opted to subtract these two scores from one another, rather than divide, because the former operation appeared to be a better analogue of the actual psychological processes involved. That is, a comparison of these two terms, resulting in the perception of either a discrepancy or congruence, seem to more naturally reflect how such parameters would be evaluated, rather than a model in which one term is divided into the other. In fact, we have calculated both the ratio score as well as the discrepancy score, and they yield almost identical correlations with self-worth. However, we prefer to report the discrepancy score for the reasons already outlined.

In our first investigation of this formulation we selected, from a larger sample of fifth and sixth grade pupils, three groups: high, medium, and low self-worth children. There were 30 children in each group. Strong support for our formulation was obtained with a $-.76$ correlation between the discrepancy score (competence minus importance across the five domains) and the self-worth score.

We inferred from this finding that children were weighing their competencies in relation to the importance of success in these domains, and that the outcome of this evaluative procedure, the product of this personal equation, provided the basis for their overall feelings of worth. For older children, therefore, it seemed that a model emphasizing this type of cognitive appraisal captures a sizeable portion of the variance associated with one's global self-worth. Thus, the Jamesian formulation would seem to be alive and well in the self-system of children at this age level.

These findings were replicated in a second sample of 30 high, 30 medium, and 30 low self-worth pupils in the fifth, sixth, and seventh grades. The discrepancy score for the high self-worth group was $-.27$, $-.62$ for the medium self-worth group, and -1.20 for the low self-group. The overall correlation between the discrepancy score and self-worth in this sample of 90 was .67.

There are several other statistical approaches that one can adopt to make the same point. For example, this formulation implies that the higher the self-worth, the greater the congruence between one's importance hierarchy and one's competence hierarchy. Correlational analyses reveal this to be true in that the correlation between one's importance scores and one's competence scores are highest for the high self-worth group, somewhat lower for the medium self-worth group, and lowest for the low self-worth group.

It should be noted that the competence scores in and of themselves are predictive of self-worth, largely because each of these domains in relatively important to children of this age. Thus, the large majority of importance scores are 4s and 3s. The average correlation between competence scores (combined across domains) and self-worth is typically around .55; correlations consistently are highest for the domains of scholastic performance, conduct, and appearance. However, if one takes into account the importance of domain, the correlation between competence and self-worth is highest for those domains rated as the most important, and systematically declines as important declines. Thus, there are converging findings attesting to the role of importance, and the overall pattern suggests that this type of discrepancy model accounts for certain processes involved in the self-worth judgments of children in the fifth to the eight grades, our target grades to date.

The Process of Discounting.

We next sought to illuminate the processes underlying this type of model. We hypothesized that in order to maintain a positive sense of self-worth, one must discount the importance of domains in which one is not performing competently, as well as endorse the importance of domains in which one is competent. This prediction is very similar to one advanced by Tesser and Campbell (1983) in their model of self-esteem maintenance. They postulated that if as a result of social comparison processes, one perceives oneself to be inadequate, one can remove this threat to one's esteem by decreasing the relevance of performance in that area, deeming it unimportant to one's self-definition, taking up another activity, and so on. Their findings with adults support this hypothesis.

In Fig. 6.1 we find strong evidence for such a phenomenon among children. There, for the purposes of demonstration, competence and importance scores have been plotted for children's two most competent and two least

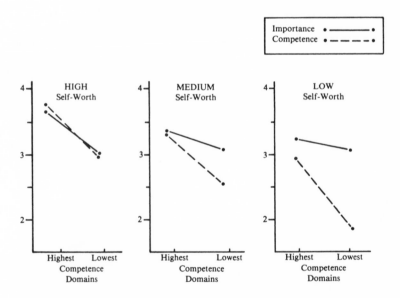

FIG. 6.1   Competence judgments and importance ratings for the highest and lowest competence domains of children with high, medium, and low self-worth.

competent domains. It can be seen that for the high self-worth group, the competence and importance scores are quite congruent. The highest competence scores are associated with high importance ratings, whereas the lowest competence scores are associated with comparably lower importance ratings. For the medium self-worth group, the slope of the importance rating curve is not as steep, indicating that such children continue to maintain the importance of areas in which they are least competent. The discrepancy between importance ratings and competence judgments for the least competent domain ratings is greatest for the low self-worth pupils. Although their competence scores are quite low, they seem unable to discount the importance of success at this activity. In fact, they consider it to be just as important as their most competent domain. It appears, therefore, that the ability to discount the importance of areas in which one is not competent is strongly associated with one's overall sense of self-worth. (This pattern of findings has now been replicated in several samples.)

Are their some domains that are easier to discount than others? When we examine the importance ratings of the three self-worth groups by domain we find that there are domain differences. Cognitive competence consistently yields the highest important scores ($M = 3.8$) and these values are virtually the same for the three self-worth groups (3.84, 3.78, and 3.82 for the high, medium, and low self-worth groups, respectively). Yet, the competence scores of these three groups show dramatic differences (3.24, 2.85, and 2.43). Thus, the lower the self-worth, the lower the cognitive competence, yet the medium and low self-worth groups continue to maintain the importance of success in this domain.

In two other domains, behavioral conduct and physical appearance, one finds a similar pattern. Conduct is judged to be the next most important domain after scholastic competence, and these importance ratings do not change as a function of self-worth group. Adequacy scores, however, do decline as a function of self-worth group, again indicating that the medium and low self-worth groups are not able to discount the importance of this domain, even though they consider their conduct to be less than admirable (3.31, 2.89, and 2.45 for high, low, and medium self-worth groups, respectively). In the domain of appearance, importance ratings are also similar across the three self-worth groups, although adequacy scores drop (3.39, 2.77, 2.11), indicating that the lower self-worth groups continue to endorse the importance of appearance, despite their judgments of their own appearance.

In the realm of athletic performance and social acceptance, there is evidence that both the medium and low self-worth subjects can, to some extent, discount the importance of these domains. As in all domains, competence or adequacy declines across the three self-worth groups, however, so does the rated importance of these two domains, somewhat. Thus, if one is not particularly athletic or popular, it appears that one can engage in at least mild to moderate discounting of the importance of these domains, in contrast to the areas of scholastic performance, conduct, and appearance.

A More Direct Test of the Discounting Hypothesis

From the pattern of scores reported earlier, we inferred that children in the three self-worth groups differed in their ability to discount the importance of areas in which they do not feel they are very competent. However, we were curious about whether children were aware of this process in themselves. Would they acknowledge that an area in which one is not very competent is actually less important? We sought to address this question with a new sample of high, medium, and low self-worth pupils, all sixth graders. For these children, we had both competence/adequacy judgments and importance ratings for each domain, as well as their overall self-worth scores.

Children were presented with vignettes, one for each of the five domains, in which a pupil (same gender as the subject) initially felt that skill at activities in the domain was very important, but later came to learn that he or she was not very competent or adequate. For example, for the domain of sports, the scenario is one of a child who feels that being on the soccer team is very important; however, as the season progresses, the child comes to realize that he or she isn't good at soccer. After the story is presented, the subject is asked to indicate which of two decisions the story child makes: (a) that the activity is not that important after all (one discounts the importance of this domain), or (b) that it is still important, even though he or she isn't very good at the activity (one continues to endorse the importance of this domain). The actual choices presented to the child subject describe the particular activity developed in the story.

The data that bore most directly on our hypothesis were those in which subjects made judgments about what a given story character would do (discount or continue to maintain the importance of the activity) for the subject's lowest competence domain. That is, we examined the percentage of discounting responses for the stories describing a situation that was most analogous to the real-life situation of the subject. The findings clearly indicated that there is a direct relationship between the percentage of discounting responses and children's level of self-worth, as presented in Fig. 6.2. We found that 80% of the high self-worth subjects indicated that the story character would decide that this domain was no longer important. Among the medium self-worth group, 45% supported the discounting decision, whereas the remaining 55% indicated that the story character would continue to feel that the activity was important. Among the low self-worth group, only 30% felt that the story character would discount the importance of the activity, whereas the majority of these pupils (70%) indicated that the story character

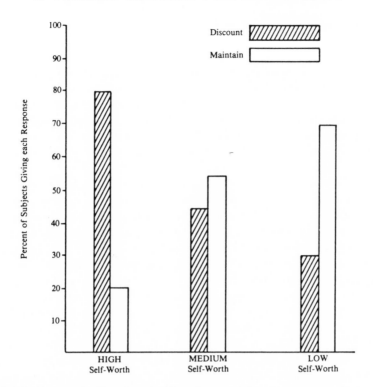

FIG. 6.2   Percent of subjects in each self-worth group giving each response to the story character's decision in the subject's least competent domain.

would continue to feel that the activity was important, despite the fact that his or her incompetence had been demonstrated.

The actual importance ratings subjects gave for their least competent domain are consistent with this pattern. The high self-worth pupils feel that their least competent domain is of only moderate importance ($\overline{X}$ = 2.6), the medium self-worth group claim that their least competent domain is somewhat more important ($\overline{X}$ = 3.3), and the low self-worth group report that their least competent domain is even more important, compared to the other two groups ($\overline{X}$ = 3.6).

This package of findings, across the three samples, provides considerable evidence that for this age level one's self-worth is highly related to the congruence or discrepancy between one's feelings of competence or adequacy and the importance of success in the domains we have tapped. The higher one's self-worth, the more one is able to discount the importance of domains in which one is not competent, while maintaining the importance of domains in which one is competent. This process can be inferred from the pattern of competence and importance scores. However, it can also be demonstrated more directly through the vignette procedure that allowed children to indicate whether or not a story character would decide that an activity, initially deemed important, loses its importance if the character learns that he or she is not very competent in that domain. Thus, it would appear that discounting the importance of activities in which one is not competent is an important process in maintaining one's self-worth for children in their middle school years (fifth through eight grades). We have yet to identify the youngest ages at which this process begins to operate, but plan to do so in future developmental studies.

It should be noted that although the greatest congruence between competence and important scores was manifest by the high self-worth group, their lowest competence scores, and, therefore, their lowest importance ratings, were not all that low. That is, these are pupils who perceive themselves to be relatively competent, even in their worst domain, and as a result, they do not have to discount the importance of their less competent domains to a very great degree.

The low self-worth pupils, in contrast, are among the least competent pupils. One may wonder why they do not discount the importance of the domains in which they are least competent, in order to protect their overall self-worth. We would submit as a reason the fact that the domains we have chosen are exceedingly difficult to discount. That is, we have selected domains that are highly valued among both the peer and adult culture, as well as society at large. Success at school and athletics, good conduct, social acceptance, and attractiveness are all values that are highly touted by our society. Thus, children may not have the luxury, as it were, of discounting success in these particular domains.

Nor does one have the choice to opt out of performing in these areas. Children are required by law to attend school, and within this milieu they are confronted with the need to achieve scholastically, gain social acceptance, demonstrate their physical prowess, behave themselves, and present a reasonable appearance. The child who does not feel adequate in one or more of these domains does not have the option of selecting another milieu more suited to his interests or abilities. Thus, the fact that the relatively incompetent child cannot readily discount the importance of these activities, coupled with the fact that he or she cannot avoid participating in situations where performance in these domains will be evaluated, combines to take its toll on one's overall sense of self-worth.

This analysis does not provide a very optimistic picture with regard to the likelihood that low self-worth pupils can better their opinion of themselves. One humane solution would be a more flexible social system in which accomplishments in a wide variety of areas are respected, rewarded, or deemed important. Mayberry (1985), for example, has hypothesized that among physically handicapped youngsters, self-worth may be maintained if other personal characteristics — for example, sense of responsibility, patience, effort, control of one's temper — are valued by significant others in the child's life. Nevertheless, given the particular hierarchy of contemporary societal values, with an emphasis on competition and social comparison, and the highly evaluative contexts in which children must perform, it may be exceedingly difficult for children with deficiencies in the primary domains we have identified to develop and maintain a positive sense of their worth as a person.

Additional Processes Associated with the Maintenance and Enhancement of Self-Worth

We have begun to examine the role of two other processes that appear to be associated with self-worth. The first involves the tendency to slightly inflate one's sense of competence. The second involves one sense of control over one's successes and failures.

With regard to the first issue, we were able, in one sample, to compare children's judgment of their competence with the teacher's evaluation, for the children's highest and lowest competence domains. These findings are presented in Fig. 6.3, for high, medium, and low self-worth groups. A comparison of these ratings reveals that the self-judgments of the high self-worth

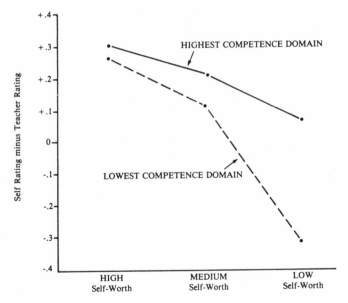

FIG. 6.3   Discrepancy between self- and teacher-ratings of competence. Plus values indicate that self-score is higher than the teacher's; minus values indicate that the self-score is lower than the teacher's.

group are approximately 0.3 (on a 4-point scale) higher than the teachers' ratings; that is, this group tends to see the self as slightly more competent than does the teacher, in both the highest and lowest domains. The medium self-worth group shows somewhat less of a tendency in this regard, particularly for their lowest competence domain where their scores are very similar to the teacher's rating. The low self-worth group shows virtually no tendency to inflate their feelings of competence; in fact, for their least competent domain, their judgments are somewhat lower than the teacher's. (High self-worth subjects are significantly different from low-self worth subjects, with the medium self-worth group falling in between.)

It would appear, therefore, that the high self-worth child has developed a positive attitude toward the self, one that just slightly exaggerates his or her competence or adequacy. It should be noted that this tendency is slight, and does not represent the type or degree of distortion that characterizes an unrealistic appraisal of one's abilities. In another series of studies (see Harter, 1985a), we have specifically identified children who over-rate and under-rate their cognitive competence, and have examined some of the maladaptive behavioral correlates of an inaccurate perception of one's abilities. In these studies we find that children who seriously distort their sense of competence (whose ratings are .8 or more discrepant from the teacher's ratings) avoid risk or challenge on problem-solving tasks, compared to children who are more accurate in their judgments of competence (ratings within .5 of the teacher's).

The magnitude of the discrepancies reported for the three self-worth groups, therefore, are not large. Nevertheless, the pattern is noteworthy, suggesting that there may be a slight, but systematic tendency for the high self-worth child to see the self as a bit more competent or adequate than one might actually be, as judged by teachers. Conversely, there is a tendency for the low self-worth child, in their least competent domain, to judge the self a bit more harshly than does the teacher. It would be interesting, as a follow-up, to obtain ratings from the parents. To the extent that they are a very important source of information or feedback concerning the child's self-perceptions (Davis & Harter, 1984), one may find more congruence between parent and child ratings than between teacher and child ratings.

With regard to the issue of the impact of one's sense of control on self-worth, Greenwald (1980) has cogently argued that among adults, one self-enhancement strategy involves the tendency to see the self as more responsible for one's successes than one's failures. He has coined the term "beneffectance" to describe this phenomenon. In our previous work we sought to determine whether this tendency was operative among children in the scholastic domain. Our findings (see Harter, 1985) revealed a clear developmental progression over grades 3–9. During the earlier grades, children tend to take almost as much internal responsibility for their scholastic successes as their failures. However, there is a systematic trend indicating that with development, children take less responsibility for their failures, although perceived internal control over successes remains high. Thus, it would appear that this is an enhancement strategy that children learn to acquire over the course of development.

In our previous studies, however, we did not directly relate individual differences in perceptions of control to self-worth. In our more recent work, we have begun to examine this issue. Thus, for high, medium, and low self-worth groups, we examined two types of control scores that were available for the scholastic domain. Given that this domain is judged to be important to one's sense of self by virtually all children, it seemed reasonable that perceptions of control over scholastic performance would be related to self-worth. The control scores we examined were obtained by administering Connell's (1980, in press) Perceptions of Control Scale for Children. This instrument assesses pereptions of control separately for successes and failures in each of the domains contained on our Self-Perception profile. Three sources of control are identified: Internal, Powerful Others (e.g., teachers in the cognitive domain), and Unknown (where the child has the option of indicating that he or she doesn't know who or what is responsible for his or her successes and failures).

Two contrast scores were derived for the present analysis. The first score was calculated as Internal responsibility for success minus Internal responsibility for failure, providing an index of the extent to which a child takes more personal responsibility for successes than failures. The second score was calculated as Internal responsibility for success minus External responsibility foor success (where External represented a combination of the two sources external to the child, Powerful Others, and Unknown). These scores, for the three self-worth groups, are presented in Fig. 6.4.

For the first score, it can be seen that high self-worth children take more responsibility for their successes than their failures. This tendency is less evident among the medium self-worth group, and is nonexistent for the low self-worth group where responsibility for successes and failures is identical. Thus, it would appear that the tendency to take more responsibility for one's success than one's failures is associated with higher self-worth.

The second score bears a similar, interpretable, relationship to self-worth. The degree to which children take more responsibility for their successes than they credit external sources is greatest for the high self-worth group, somewhat less for the medium self-worth group, and even smaller for the low self-worth group. (For both of these control scores, the high self-worth group was significantly different from the low self-worth group, with the medium self-worth group falling in between.)

Therefore, the pattern is relatively straightforward. In one domain, scholastic competence, which most children view as critical to their sense of self, their sense of personal or internal control over their successes, relative to

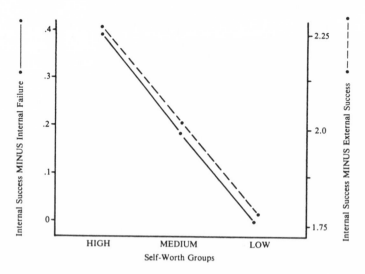

FIG. 6.4   Control contrast scores for each group: Internal Success minus Internal Failure and Internal Success minus External Success.

their control over their failures, as well as relative to external control over their successes, is systematically related to self-worth. Thus, a high sense of control for one's successes, in particular, is associated with high self-worth. The direction of cause and effect, however, remains to be explored. Do children with high self-worth come to adopt this type of attributional bias in order to maintain or enhance their self-worth? Alternatively, do children with this attributional bias come to see the self as more worthy? With one set of longitudinal data over grades 5, 6, and 7, during which we know these attributional styles change developmentally (Harter, 1985a), we hope to be able to examine these issues.

When one culls the findings for the several constructs we have now examined, one can present a cameo of the child with high self-worth. Such a child is relatively competent across the domains sampled (although there is also a profile or hierarchy of competence scores), he or she endorses the importance of one's most competent areas, while at the same time, discounts the importance of areas of less or least competence; thus, the competence and importance hierarchies are very congruent. The high self-worth child also tends to inflate his or her sense of competence slightly, relative to the judgment of the teacher. Moreover, the high self-worth child claims more responsibility for successes than failures.

The picture presented by the low self-worth child is just the opposite. The low self-worth child's competence scores are in the mid to low range yet he or she seems unable to discount the importance of success in those areas where he or she is not performing well. Thus, there is considerable discrepancy between competence and importance judgments. In addition, the low self-worth child tends to view the self as less competent than does the teacher, for the least competent domains. Finally, such children take equal responsibility for their successes and failures. Thus, it would appear that they have not developed adequate strategies for protecting and enhancing the self.

Our empirical exercise, in demonstrating the processes underlying one's judgment of self-worth, is important for theoretical as well as practical reasons. Theoretically, the findings indicate that James' formulation is very relevant, indeed, as are the types of self-enhancement attribution identified by Greenwald. Practically, these findings suggest strategies whereby one may alter one's sense of worth. James, himself, noted that self-esteem can be enhanced through one of two procedures: One can either lower one's pretensions or increase one's level of success, in order to bring the two more in line with each other. With regard to one's perceptions of control, increased responsibility for one's successes and decreased responsibility for one's failures, represent another strategy.

What should be emphasized is that these self-enhancement strategies must operate at the level of the specific domains. It is the congruence of importance and competence hierarchies across domains that is at issue here. One does not alter global self-worth directly. That is, general strategies designed to convince someone that he or she is a worthwhile person are not likely to be very successful, according to our analysis. Rather, one must make adjustments at the domain level, which, in turn, will influence self-worth. This point is critical because there are some who have misinterpreted our recent focus on the self-worth construct, inferring that we have abandoned our earlier emphasis on a domain-specific approach. Nothing could be further from the truth. Our position is that we need to assess domain-specific judgments, global self-worth, and their relationship, in order to best understand the self-system.

Self-Worth Among Depressed Children

Depressed children represent an interesting subgroup to examine with regard to feelings about the self. Low self-worth and self-deprecatory ideation have long been accepted as part of the diagnostic picture of adults, although there has been less consensus on this issue in our diagnostic systems for children. Weinberg, Rutman, Sullivan, Penick, and Dietz (1973), for example, consider low self-worth to be one of the cardinal or primary symptoms of childhood depression, whereas the Diagnostic and Statistical Manual of Mental Disorders considers low self-worth to be one of the secondary symptoms; depressed affect and lack of interest are the two primary manifestations.

According to our developmental findings, self-worth, as a global judgment about the self, cannot be a symptom of depression until approximately third grade, the age at which this concept of self emerges. In the later elementary grades, however, one can examine the degree to which this type of judgment is associated with depression. We have addressed this question is one study with fifth and sixth graders that involved approximately 1000 pupils. We enlisted the aid of teachers, asking them to identify children who manifest the affective and motivational symptoms of depression, that is, sadness or depressed mood, despondency, and/or lack of energy and interest in age-appropriate activities. (We specifically did not ask teachers to select children based on their own perceptions of the child's attitudes toward the self.) Forty-four children were identified.

The pattern for this group of depressed children was as follows: First of all, their self-worth scores (2.3) were extremely low, compared to the norm (3.0) for this age. Secondly, scores were low in at least one (and often two) of the three specific competence domains tapped, cognitive, social, and physical competence. The average score for their lowest domain was 1.75. Thirdly, these children reported that success in their lowest competence domain was just as important to them as success in their highest domain. That is, they showed no indication of discounting the importance of domains in which they were not performing well. Finally, when we examined the congruence of child and teachers ratings with regard to judgments of competence in the specific domains, we found that there was considerable agreement. We have interpreted this to mean that these depressed children were quite realistic in their assessment of their strengths and weaknesses. These findings are consistent with recent studies that have demonstrated that adult depressives are quite accurate in making judgments about the relationship between their abilities and performance outcomes (see Alloy, 1982).

Taken together, these findings suggest a constellation of self-attitudes or self-statements that characterize the depressed child at this age: "I am not very competent in certain areas, I am right about these judgments of incompetence, yet success in these areas is still extremely important to me, and, as a result, I feel terrible about myself as a person." Given that these children were selected on the basis of depressed affect and low energy or interest, it would appear that these self-attitudes are intimately related to mood and motivation.

More recently, we have sought to examine these relationships more directly through the construction of a self-report measure in which we have identified four possible components of depression: (a) mood or affect, (b) energy/pleasure, (c) self-worth, and (d) self-blame (Harter & Polesovsky, 1984). We have administered this scale to normative samples of third through eighth graders. Each of these four subscales demonstrates good internal consistency. Interestingly, factor analyses reveal a 3-factor solution for ths 4-subscale instrument among both elementary and junior high school pupils.

The first factor is defined by all items on both the self-worth and the affect subscales. The self-blame subscale as well as the energy/pleasure subscale each define a separate factor, although these factors are all correlated with one another.

We had not predicted that self-worth and affect would be so highly correlated that they would define one factor. These findings suggest that the degree to which one is sad or depressed versus happy or cheerful is highly related to one's general attitude of self—how much one likes oneself as a person. Moreover, they raise the issue of causality: Does one develop an attitude about the self that, in turn, influences ones' mood? Coversely, do certain events influence one's mood in a positive or negative direction, which, in turn, leads one to have related feelings about one's self-worth? Alternatively, do both affect and feelings about the self develop in syncrony? We pursue these issues in the next section on the larger theoretical model.

DETERMINANTS AND FUNCTIONS OF SELF-WORTH: THE LARGER THEORETICAL MODEL

In preceding sections, we have reported on our examination of one possible determinant of self-worth, derived from James' (1892) formulation, the congruence or discrepancy between one's competence and the importance of success in various domains. The findings indicated that older elementary school children appear to be enaged in a cognitive appraisal of these factors, weighing and comparing both their competence and the importance of success. The outcome of such an appraisal appears to strongly influence the child's overall feelings of worth as a person.

In contrast to this type of cognitive–analytical model, Cooley (1902) postulated that the origins of our sense of self lie in our perceptions of what significant others think of us. According to Cooley therefore, the self is a social construction, based on our reading of others' opinions toward the self. Mead (1934) developed a similar theme in his notion of the "generalized other," which represents the pooled or collective judgments of the significant others in one's life. Implicit in these formulations is a modeling process wherein we imitate the attitudes that these others' hold of us, and these reflected appraisals come to define what Cooley termed the "looking glass self."

These two positions, the cognitive–analytical model derived from James (1892), and the looking glass self model postulated by Cooley (1902), are not necessarily antithetical. Both types of processes may well be operative, and each may account for a significant portion of our sense of self. Recently, we have sought to examine this contention empirically among middle school children. That is, we have compared the contribution of the competence—importance discrepancy with the contribution of the perceived opinions of others toward the self. To what degree do each of these sources of information about the self influence one's sense of global self-worth? The operationalization of the competence — importance discrepancy construct has been described in detail in an earlir section of this chapter.

In discussing Cooley's formulation, Rosenberg (1979) has cogently argued that it is our perception of what significant others think of us that is critical, what we imagine their appraisal to be. Thus, we defined the construct of others' opinion as the degree to which children felt that significant others acknowledged their worth, for example, treated them as a person, listened to their ideas, felt that they were important, and so on. Two types of significant others were identified: parents and peers. Our self-report scale, therefore, taps a combination of social support and positive regard from these two sources. With such a measure we can examine the hypothesis that regard for the self represents an internalization of the perceived regard that significant others have for the self.

A major goal in testing the larger theoretical model was to compare the contribution of the competence — importance discrepancy with that of social support/positive regard, as determinants of global self-worth. Thus, we sought to examine the extent to which the original formulations of James (1892) and Cooley (1902) aid us in understanding the antecedents of self-worth among older children.

A second major purpose was to determine the degree to which self-worth, in turn, influences other systems within the individual. Specifically, we have identified two general systems: affect (happy vs. sad) and motivation (energy and interest vs. its absence). Our initial interest in these two constructs was sparked by our efforts to devise an instrument sensitive to a variety of components that have been implicated in the study of depression (Harter & Polesovsky, 1984). The affect subscale of this instrument provides a general index of self-reported happiness or cheerfulness versus sadness or depression. The motivation subscale provides an index of the degree to which children have the energy, interest, or desire to engage in age-appropriate activities or behaviors. Thus, these judgments were not domain-specific, but required our subjects to provide a general assessment of their affect, as well as level of motivation, just as they were required on the self-worth subscale to make a relatively global judgment about their worth as a person.

Within the past decade a number of theorists have introduced models in which self-judgments elicit an affective reaction that, in turn, mediates behavior (e.g., Bandura, 1978; Kanfer, 1980; Wicklund, 1975). Within the domain of scholastic performance, our own research (Harter & Connell, 1984) reveals that perceived competence mediates both affect about one's competence, as well as one's motivational orientation toward schoolwork. Our present effort is an attempt to determine whether this same type of model is applicable at the level of more global constructs about one's self-worth and its role as a mediator of one's general affective and motivational states.

Our intent here is to determine whether self-worth, as we have defined it, is an important mediator of other systems that we deemed critical, or whether it is best viewed as epiphenomenal. As we noted at the outset of this chapter, the self has been resurrected as a legitimate psychological construct and is now finding its way into numerous formulations. Thus, it behooves us to determine whether this construct has utility as a predictor or mediator of behavior. That is, what precise function does self-worth play in the larger network of constructs? If it does not mediate other systems of importance, if we find that it is more epiphenomenal in nature, we may do well to check the enthusiasm of the many investigators from a variety of disciplines who are clamoring for measures of self-concept.

The larger theoretical model, then, includes the two determinants described, the competence — importance discrepancy and social support/ positive regard. Self-worth is placed in the middle of the model and there are two systems that we feel it might well mediate: general affect and motivation (see Fig. 6.5). Specifically, we predicted that both the Jamesian competence — importance discrepancy score, and the social support/positive regard component derived from Cooley's formulation would contribute heavily to self-worth. Based on previous findings within the domain of scholastic performance, we predicted that there would be a strong path from self-worth to affect that, in turn, would have a strong influence on one's motivation. Self-worth may also impact motivation directly, although its primary influence should be mediated by the affective component. We compared this model to two alternative models (see Fig. 6.5), employing path-analytic or causal modeling techniques to determine how adequately each of the three models fit the data (Harter & Hogan, 1985).

Model B represents an attempt to determine the degree to which we need the construct of self-worth at all. That is, if our interest is in predicting the affective and motivational responses of children, might it not be possible that our two determinants, the discrepancy construct and the social support/ positive regard construct, directly impact one's affect and motivation? To what extent do we need to invoke self-worth as a mediator? Model B, then, was an attempt to determine whether self-worth is best viewed as epiphenomenal. Specifically, this model retains the paths from the discrepancy score and the social support/positive regard score to self-worth, since these determinants continue to be critical. However, we removed (or set to zero) the two paths from self-worth to both affect and motivation. Its parenthetical status in Fig. 6.5 denotes the fact that it can no longer act as a mediator. Rather, the initial determinants in the model, the discrepancy construct and social feedback are depicted as having a direct impact on both mood and motivation.

The third model examines the role of affect as a mediator. During the 1980s emotion or affect has returned to the fold of constructs that enjoy the favor of theorists (e.g., Izard, 1978; Leventhal, 1980; Zajonc, 1980). More-

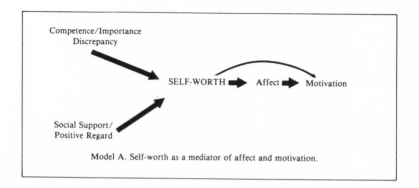

Model A. Self-worth as a mediator of affect and motivation.

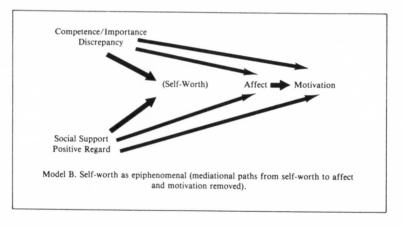

Model B. Self-worth as epiphenomenal (mediational paths from self-worth to affect and motivation removed).

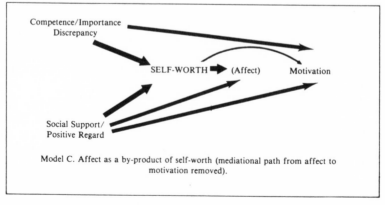

Model C. Affect as a by-product of self-worth (mediational path from affect to motivation removed).

FIG. 6.5   Three alternative models tested.

over, for many, affect is conceptualized as central, as the organizer of behavior, as it were. Specifically, in Model C we sought to assess whether it was a critical determinant or mediator of motivation. Thus, we retained the paths from discrepancy and social support to self-worth, as well as the path from self-worth to affect. However, we deleted the path from affect to motivation, that is, removed its potential mediating effect on motivation. Affect, in this model, is viewed primarily as a by-product of one's sense of self-worth, but plays no role in influencing one's motivation.

The findings overwhelmingly support Model A, which provides a vastly better fit than either B or C (see Harter & Hogan, 1985, for details). However, there were several refinements, several small, additional paths that improved the fit even more. This best-fitting model is presented in Fig. 6.6. There it can be seen that the major paths predicted for Model A are indeed present. Interestingly, the path coefficients from the discrepancy score and the social support score to a self-worth were identical, suggesting that each of these sources of self-worth are important and comparable in magnitude. However, they are not strongly correlated with each other. It would appear, therefore, that James and Cooley identified critical determinants of self-worth or self-esteem, although these sources are relatively independent of each other.

On the question of whether self-worth has a mediating function, the answer is a resounding yes. The path from self-worth to affect is the largest in the model. Although self-worth has a small effect on motivation, directly, its influence is primarily mediated through affect which is represented by a strong path from affect to motivation. The importance of self-worth as a mediator was also seen in our comparison of Model A and Model B. When the mediational paths from self-worth were removed in Model B, the fit was drastically worse ($\chi^2 = 3.08$ for Model A compared to 148.67 for Model B, where in these tests of fit, the smaller the chi-square, the better the fit).

In addition to the major paths predicted in Model A, Fig. 6.6 also depicts three additional paths that improve the overall fit, although their contribution is much smaller. The social support/positive regard construct has a small, but direct impact on both affect and motivation. Moreover, the discrepancy between one's competence and the importance of success has a small, direct effect on motivation.

On the mediational role of affect, as tested by a comparison with Model C, the relatively poor fit of Model C attests to the importance of affect as a mediator of one's general level of motivation. Thus, although the primary intent of our modeling was to assess the role of self-worth, a secondary goal was to determine whether affect is also critical to this network of constructs. The findings indicate that it definitively is critical, in terms of its impact on motivation, which we assume, in turn, woulld impact behavior. In future studies,

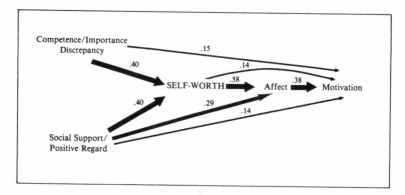

FIG. 6.6   Best-fitting model: Model A with refinements.

we plan to include behavioral variables in the model in order to test this hypothesis directly.[1]

In summary, these modeling efforts lead to several conclusions. With regard to the determinants of self-worth, there is strong support for both James' and Cooley's formulations. Older children appear to be weighing their competencies against the importance of success in the domains we have tapped; in addition, their perceptions of the regard by significant others, namely, parents and peers, also directly impacts their sense of self-worth. Whether the magnitude of the impact of these two sources of information regarding the self varies with one's developmental level is a question we are currently exploring. It may well be that the positive regard by significant others, particularly parents, is a more potent force during the early years. The Jamesian model may be less applicable among younger children because they may not have the cognitive skills to simultaneously compare hierarchies of perceived competence and importance of success, a comparison that in turn would result in a judgment impacting self-worth.[2]

---

[1]There are obviously other models that could have been tested with the network of variables we now have. For example, given the high correlation between competence and self-worth, a model with such a direct path, circumventing the discrepancy score, may well provide a good fit. On another point regarding the looking-glass self construct, one's perceived sense of support or regard from others may reflect the projection of one's sense of worth, such that a model in which self-worth leads to regard/support may provide a better fit. In our explorations with these alternatives, we have determined that they do not yield a fit superior to Model A with refinements. However, it was beyond the scope of this chapter to explore these alternatives in detail.

[2]It should be noted that both James and Cooley intended to enlighten our understanding of the adult self. We have extended the Jamesian analysis to adults, utilizing the same approach. Employing our Adult Self-Perception Profile (Messer & Harter, 1984), which taps 11 specific domains plus self-worth, we have found that the discrepancy score is a strong predictor of self-worth. We have yet to examine the role of positive regard and social support.

A second conclusion is that we cannot treat the construct of global self-worth as epiphenomenal. It clearly has a function within the network of constructs we examined, the most important of which is its direct impact on the general affect or mood of the individual. Middle school children who like themselves as people are the happiest, whereas those who have a more negative sense of their overall worth as a person are more apt to feel sad and depressed. The particular affective state of the individual, in turn, has a powerful influence on one's general motivation. The child who tends toward sadness or depression has little energy or desire to engage in age-appropriate activities, whereas the child reporting happiness or cheerfulness is highly motivated to engage in such activities.

The third conclusion is embedded in this last observation. Although self-worth bears some relationship to one's general level of motivation, the mediating role of affect is critical. This particular finding is a welcome one, given our tendency in past years to focus primarily on the role of cognitions within the self-system, to the exclusion of affective constructs. Thus, for those of us interested in motivational and behavioral consequences it is imperative that we give more credance to the mediational role of self-judgments, as well as their affective consequences. They are far from epiphenomenal.

THE EFFECT OF EDUCATIONAL TRANSITIONS ON SELF-WORTH

The studies presented in earlier sections of this chapter have dealt with the child's self-worth at one point in time. We have also been interested in whether self-worth changes, particularly as a function of changes in educational environment. We have some evidence concerning the role of transitions among children who make the educational shift from sixth grade within an elementary school to seventh grade in a seventh, eighth, and ninth grade junior high school. Among the many developmental changes occurring at this point in one's life, for example, cognitive and pubertal advances, there are shifts in one's social status as one moves from being the oldest in elementary school to being the youngest in junior high, lowest on the totem pole, as it were. Increasing academic demands may present additional forms of challenge or stress. A number of investigators have documented the effects of such changes on te self-system of adolescents, for example, Simmons, Rosenberg, and Rosenberg (1973), and Rosenberg (this volume).

In a dissertation by Riddle (1985), we investigated the effects of the shift to junior high school on various facets of the self-concept. The findings revealed that this transition does not have a unilaterally devastating effect on all students. For some, perceived academic and social competence decline markedly, whereas many show virtually no such negative reaction. Moreover, there is a subgroup who actually seem to flourish in this new environment, as reflected by increases in their academic and social competence scores.

Of particular interest within the context of this chapter, however, are changes in self-worth. Here, as in the specific domains, Riddle was able to identify three groups: those whose self-worth scores increased between sixth and seventh grades (20%), those whose self-worth scores decreased over this period (19%), and those whose scores remained the same (61%). The self-worth scores of these three groups were not significantly different in the sixth grade, however, the longitudinal changes in self-worth across the grade shift resulted in significant group differences in self-worth durng the seventh grade.

When we examined the discrepancy scores of these three groups, we discovered what one might expect (see Fig. 6.7). For those whose self-worth increased, the discrepancy between competence judgments and importance ratings decreased; for those whose self-worth decreased, their discrepancy scores increased. These changes were statistically significant, as were group differences in the fall, after the change in schools. Thus, it would appear that those students whose self-worth is enhanced across this transition are able to make their competence and importance hierarchies more congruent, whereas for those whose self-worth suffers, the discrepancies between competence

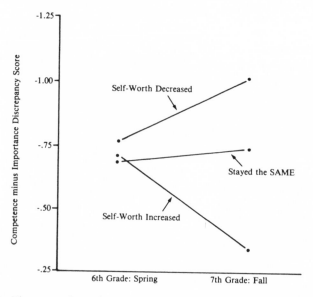

FIG. 6.7   Discrepancy Score changes in groups that increased in self-worth, decreased, and remained the same.

and importance hierarchies are made larger. In our future research, we plan to turn our attention to various other groups undergoing transitions in their lives, in order to examine the processes responsible for changes in self-worth.

STATIC VERSUS DYNAMIC APPROACHES TO THE SELF-CONCEPT

In the preceding section, we described one empirical effort to examine possible changes in the self-system over time. This type of endeavor reflects our conviction that constructs such as perceived competence and self-worth are not static or trait-like in nature. We have yet to catalogue the variety of events that may be responsible for changes in the self-system; however, we feel strongly that investigators interested in constructs involving self-perceptions should remain sensitive to the potential for genuine shifts in judgments concerning the self.

There is another sense in which our approach to the study of the self must allow for an appreciation of the dynamics underlying such appraisals. We have touted a domain-specific approach, given findings that indicate that elementary school children and adults make distinctions between their competencies in the different areas of their lives. However, we have assessed each of these self-perceptions separately. That is, our questionnaire procedures have not allowed us to examine the manner in which these various characteristics might be integrated. Nor have they been sensitive to the fact that particular aspects of the self may be perceived as contradictory or in conflict.

Recently, in a dissertation by Monsour (1985), we have begun to address these issues among adolescents, in grades 7, 9, and 11. We devised a procedure in which we first asked subjects to write down characteristics of the self within four different contexts or roles: what they are like with their family, their friends, in romantic relationships, and at school. We then asked subjects to literally create a picture or puzzle of the self by transferring these descriptors to round gummed labels and then spatially arranging them within a large circle. The circle has a smaller core circle for the characteristics that are the most important attributes of the self, then a concentric circle for aspects of the self that are less important, and an outer ring for descriptors that are the least important aspects of the self.

Interestingly, we find that the majority of attributes in the center ring, at the core of the self, are one's positive characteristics. Adolescents tend to locate their less admirable characteristics in the outer ring of the self-picture. Negative attributes that do find their way into the center of the self are described as aspects of the self tha the subject is trying to change. This pattern is illuminating in that it represents another manifestation of how one tries to protect or enhance the self. To the extent that our most positive characteristics are viewed as central to the self, one may maintain a relatively positive self-image. By relegating one's negative characteristics to the outer ring, one denies their importance or centrality to the self.

Perhaps the most fascinating finding, from a developmental perspective, involves the degree to which adolescents at these ages experience conflict within the self-system. To assess intrapsychic conflict, we first asked subjects to indicate whether any of the attributes he or she had identified constituted opposites, for example, friendly versus mean, cooperative versus obnoxious, smart versus dumb, self-conscious versus relaxed. Of those opposites that the subject identifies, we next ask whether or not these opposites appear to be clashing, fighting, struggling, "at war," or in conflict with each other. That is, does the subject perceive these opposites as provoking intrapsychic conflict within the self, or can such opposites happily coexist without causing the experience of such tension?

The findings indicate that among seventh graders, although opposites are identified, only a minority of these opposites are viewed as clashing within the self. That is, they do not appear to cause much conflict. There is a dramatic shift at ninth grade where virtually all subjects report that a number of the opposites within the self are in conflict, struggling against one another. Moreover, they describe this phenomenological experience of intrapsychic conflict very convincingly. By eleventh grade, however, the incidence of these struggles declines somewhat. On several converging measures we find the same peak at ninth grade. For example, subjects were also asked to select, from a list of emotion terms, the feelings that accompany their perceptions of the opposites and clashes in their personality. The acknowledgement of the emotions "mixed up" and "confused" also peaks in the ninth grade. Thus, the general picture is one of maximum susceptibility at ninth grade to conflict, concern, and confusion surrounding the fact that there are contradictions within the self-system (see also Rosenberg this volume). Why should this peak occur around ninth grade? An application of cognitive–developmental principles to our understanding of the nature of self-theory provides some clues. Numerous theorists of the self have likened the self-concept to a theory that one constructs about the self (see Harter, 1983). Epstein (1973) has been most explicit in delineating the criteria that define any good theory, for example, parsimony, testability, external validity, and internal consistency. Just as any scientific theory must meet these criteria in order to be acceptable, so, reasons Epstein by analogy, must a theory of the self.

Although Epstein's general point is well taken, from a developmental perspective we must ask at what age or stage is one capable of constructing such a theory, be it of the world or of the self. A Piagetian analysis would place this cognitive advance at the stage of formal operations when the adolescent becomes capable of hypothetico-deductive reasoning, the hallmark of the logic of science. Given that it may be somewhat more difficult to apply such reasoning to the psychological realm of self-judgments, compared to the realm of chemical and physical properties investigated by Piaget, one may well expect a lag or decalage with regard to the application of hypothetico-deductive reasoning to one's self-theory.

Putting these arguments together, it becomes plausible why in middle adolescence intrapsychic conflict of the type we have documented should come to be experienced. At this point in development, the adolescent, with his or her newfound cognitive abilities, is capable of constructing a theory of self that meets the formal criteria outlined by Epstein. Moreover, as Piagetians have demonstrated, with newly developed cognitive capacities comes a penchant for exercising these structures. The criterion of internal consistency appears particularly relevant to our own findings. The very young adolescent has the ability to detect opposties, but presumably they are not that bothersome because he or she is not yet trying to fit them into a comprehensive self-theory. By the ninth grade, however, the adolescent, in his or her formal contruction of a self-theory, has the ability to evaluate this system of postulates about the self from the standpoint of whether they are internally consistent or contradictory. The fact that opposites within the self are not only acknowledged, but become conflictual, confusing, and bothersome is understandable because they violate the criterion of internal consistency and put one's self-theory in jeopardy. These findings, therefore, highlight the need to adopt a cognitive–developmental perspective, particularly with regard to the dynamic interplay among the characterisitics that comprise the self.

SUMMARY AND CONCLUSION

In our treatment of processes underlying self-concept formation in children, it is essential that whatever model we adopt be examined through the use of measures that are sufficiently sensitive and psychometrically sound. A particular weakness of past studies of self-concept has been the failure to utilize adequate measuring instruments, a point that Wylie (1979) underscores relentlessly. Two specific themes involving assessment were emphasized in this chapter. The first highlighted several developmental considerations concerning the content and structure of the self that have implications for how we should best assess the self-concept at different ages or stages. The second theme concerned the measurement of the self-concept among special groups of children with intellectual and/or physical limitations. The evidence presented indicates that our standardized measures are not appropriate in their original form with such groups. Adaptations of these instruments are necessary in order to adequately assess the self-judgments of these children. Moreover, additional procedures may be required in order to illuminate the meaning of the responses to items designed to tap various facets of the self-concept.

The general approach we have urged is one in which domain-specific judgments, as well as global self-worth, are assessed. Chilcren clearly make distinctions between their competencies in different domains and, thus, a profile approach best portrays the complexity of these self-perceptions. The separate assessment of global self-worth provides an independent index of the degree to which one likes oneself as a person, a judgment that can then be related to self-perceptions in specific domains.

Our findings provide support for James' notion that our global sense of self-worth, in part, reflects the degree to which we are successful in those domains that we deem important. Children with high self-worth are those whose competence and importance hierarchies are quite congruent. That is, areas of high competence are, indeed, very important, whereas the importance of domains in which one is not so successful is discounted. Through this process, the self is enhanced. In contrast, children with low self-worth manifest large discrepancies between their domain-specific competence judgments and ratings of the importance of success in these areas. They seem unable to discount the importance of domains in which their competence is low. Children judged to be depressed on the basis of their affect, as well as lack of motivation and energy, represent one specific group of children with low self-worth. Not only do they seem unable to discount the importance of areas in which they perceive themselves to be incompetent, but their competence judgments appear to be relatively accurate.

In our larger model of self-worth, we sought to test the theoretical formulations of both James (1892) and Cooley (1902). Cooley focuses on the self as a social construction, claiming that our sense of self was derived from the reflected appraisals of others, what we imagine them to think of us. The findings support this claim in that our construct of social support/positive regard was also strongly predictive of self-worth. In fact, it appears to be just as critical a determinant of self-worth as the discrepancy construct, at least for middle-school children, aged 11 to 14.

A major goal of our statistical modeling procedures was to determine what function self-worth serves as a mediator of both affect and motivation. The findings revealed that self-worth should not be relegated to the realm of the epiphenomenal, but that it serves an important role in mediating the extent to which one is happy versus sad, which in turn influences the amount of energy and interest one has available. Thus, both self-worth and affect were demonstrated to be critical to the prediction of one's motivational level.

Finally, it was urged that we not treat the self-concept as a static, trait-like construct. Not only is it susceptible to change, but there are other dynamic considerations with regard to how well the constituent parts of the self-concept are integrated. Middle adolescence appears to be a particularly vulnerable period, during which inconsistency within the self provokes considerable intrapsychic conflict. This phenomenon was interpreted in terms of cognitive–developmental advances that have specific implications for the nature of adolescents' self-theory.

There is much more to be investigated, both from a developmental perspective, as well as from an individual-differences approach. Historically, theorists and investigators have tended to adopt only one these frameworks. Future progress, however, will depend on an integration of approaches in order to more fully illuminate the processes underlying the construction, maintenance, and enhancement of the self.

ACKNOWLEDGMENT

Preparation of this chapter was facilitated by N.I.C.H.D. Grant HD 09613.

REFERENCES

Alloy, L. B. (1982). The role of perceptions and attributions for response-outcome non-contingency in learned helplessness. *Journal of Personality, 50*, 443–479.

Bandura, A. (1978). The self-system in reciprocal determinism. *American Psychologist, 33*, 344–358.

Connell, J. P. (1980). *A multidimensional measure of children's perceptions of control.* Unpublished master's thesis, University of Denver.

Connell, J. P. (in press). A model of the relationships among children's self-related cognitions, affects and academic achievement. *Child Development.*

Cooley, C. H. (1902). *Human nature and the social order.* New York: Charles Scribner's Sons.

Coopersmith, S. (1967). *The antecedents of self-esteem.* San Francisco, CA: Freeman.

Dalgin, F., & Harter, S. (1984). *Determinants of the self-concept in the physically handicapped child.* Unpublished manuscript, University of Denver, CO.

Damon, W., & Hart, D. (1982). The development of self-understanding from infancy through adolescence. *Child Development, 53*, 841–864.

Davis, J., & Harter, S. (1984). *Social comparison and other's opinion as determinants of self-perceptions of one's intelligence and kindness.* Unpublished manuscript, University of Denver, CO.

Dweck, C., & Elliot, E. S. (1983). Achievement motivation. In E. M. Hetherington (Ed.), *Handbook of child psychology: Socialization, personality, and social development* (Vol. 4). New York: Wiley.

Epstein, S. (1973). The self-concept revisited or a theory of a theory. *American Psychologist, 28*, 405–416.

Greenwald, A. G. (1980). The totalitarian ego: Fabrication and revision of personal history. *American Psychologist, 7*, 603–618.

Harter, S. (1982). The perceived competence scale for children. *Child Development, 53*, 87–97.

Harter, S. (1983). Developmental perspectives on the self-system. In M. Hetherington (Ed.), *Handbook of child psychology: Social and personality development* (Vol. 4). New York: Wiley.

Harter, S. (1984). *The Self-Perception Profile for Children: Revision of the Perceived Competence Scale for Children.* Unpublished manuscript, University of Denver, CO.

Harter, S. (1985). Competence as a dimension of self-evaluation: Toward a comprehensive model of self-worth. In R. Leahy (Ed.), *The development of the self*. New York: Academic Press.

Harter, S., & Connell, J. P. (1984). A comparison of alternative models of the relationships between academic achievement and children's perceptions of competence, control, and motivational orientation. In J. Nicholls (Ed.), *The development of achievement-related cognitions and behaviors*. Greenwich, CT: J. A. I. Press.

Harter, S., & Hogan, A. (1985). *A causal model of the determinants of self-worth and the affective and motivational systems which it mediates*. Paper presented at the meeting of the Society for Research in Child Development, Toronto, Canada.

Harter, S., & Pike, R. (1984). The pictorial perceived competence scale for young children. *Child Development, 55,* 1962–1982.

Harter, S., & Polesovsky, M. (1984). *Components and correlates of childhood depression*. Unpublished manuscript, University of Denver, CO.

Izard, C. (1978). Emotions and motivations: An evolutionary developmental perspective. *Nebraska Symposium on Motivation*. Lincoln, NE: University of Nebraska Press.

James, W. (1892). *Psychology: The briefer course*. New York: Holt, Rinehart & Winston.

Kanfer, F. H. (1980). Self-management methods. In F. H. Kanfer & A. P. Goldstein (Eds.), *Helping people change: A textbook of methods* (2nd ed.). New York: Pergamon Press.

Kun, A. (1977). Development of the magnitude-covariation and compensation schemata in ability and effort attributions of performance. *Child Development, 48,* 862–872.

L'Ecuyer, R. (1981). The development of the self-concept through the life span. In M. D. Lynch, A. A. Norem-Hebeison, & K. Gergen (Eds.), *Self concept: Advances in theory and research*. Cambridge, MA: Ballinger.

Leventhal, H. (1980). Toward a comprehensive theory of emotion. In L. Berkowitz (Ed.), *Advances in experimental social psychology* (Vol. 13). New York: Academic Press.

Masters, J. (1971). Social comparison by young children. *Young Children, 27,* 37–60.

Mayberry, W. (1985). *A domain-specific approach to the Self-concept in the handicapped: Traditional versus non-traditional domains*. Unpublished Master's thesis, University of Denver, CO.

Mead, G. H. (1934). *Mind, self, and society*. Chicago, IL: University of Chicago Press.

Messer, B., & Harter, S. (1984). *The Self-Perception Scale for Adults*. Unpublished manuscript, University of Denver, CO.

Monsour, A. (1985). *The structure and dynamics of the adolescent self-concept*. Unpublished doctoral dissertation, University of Denver, CO.

Montemayor, R., & Eisen, M. (1977). The development of self-conceptions from childhood to adolescence. *Developmental Psychology, 13* 314–319.

Mullener, N., & Laird, J. D. (1971). Some developmental changes in the organization of self-evaluations. *Developmental Psychology, 5,* 233–236.

Nicholls, J. G. (1978). The development of the concepts of effort and ability, perception of academic attainment, and the understanding that difficult tasks require more ability. *Child Development, 49,* 800–814.

Nicholls, J. G. (1983). *The differentiation of ability*. Paper presented at the meeting of the Society for Research in Child Development, Detroit, MI.

Piers, E., & Harris, D. (1969). *The Piers–Harris children's self-concept scale*. Nashville, TN: Counselor Recordings and Tests.

Pike, R. (1985). *Dimensions of the self-system within severely asthmatic children*. Unpublished doctoral dissertation, University of Denver, CO.

Renick, M. J., & Harter, S. (1984). *A developmental study of the perceived competence of learning and disabled children*. Unpublished manuscript, University of Denver, CO.

Riddle, M. (1985). *Changes in perceived scholastic competence, social acceptance, and self-worth as a function of the transition to 7th grade in junior high school*. Unpublished doctoral dissertation, University of Denver, CO.

Rogers, C. M., Smith, M. D., & Coleman, J. M. (1978). Social comparison in the classroom: The relationship between academic achievement and self-concept. *Journal of Educational Psychology, 70,* 50-57.

Rogers, C. R. (1950). The significance of the self-regarding attitudes and perceptions. In M. L. Reymert, (Ed.), *Feelings and emotions: The Mooseheart symposium.* New York: McGraw-Hill.

Rosenberg, M. (1979). *Conceiving the self.* New York: Basic Books.

Ruble, D., Boggiano, A. K., Feldman, N. S., & Loebl, J. H. (1980). Developmental analysis of the role of social comparison in self-evaluation. *Developmental Psychology, 16,* 105-115.

Ruble, D. N., Feldman, N. S., & Boggiano, A. G. (1976). Social comparison between young children in achievement situations. *Developmental psychology, 12,* 192-197.

Ruble, D., & Rholes, W. (1981). The development of children's perceptions and attributions about their social world. In J. Harvey, W. Ickes, & R. Kidd (Eds.), *New directions in attribution research* (Vol. 3). Hillsdale, NJ: Lawrence Erlbaum Associates.

Selman, R. (1980). *The growth of interpersonal understanding.* New York: Academic Press.

Shavelson, R. J., Hubner, J. J., & Stanton, G. C. (1976). Self-concept: Validation of construct interpretations. *Review of Educational Research, 46,* 407-441.

Silon, E., & Harter, S. (1985). Perceived competence, motivational orientation, and anxiety in mainstreamed and self-contained educable mentally retarded children. *Journal of Educational Psychology, 77,* 217-230.

Simmons, R., Rosenberg, F., & Rosenberg, M. (1973). Disturbance in the self-image in adolescence. *American Journal of Sociology, 38,* 553-568.

Suls, J., & Sanders, G. (1982). Self-evaluation via social comparison: A developmental analysis. In L. Wheeler (Ed.), *Review of personality and social psychology* (Vol. 3). Beverly Hills, CA: Sage.

Tesser, A. (1980). Self-esteem maintenance in family dynamics. *Journal of Personality and Social Psychology, 39,* 77-91.

Tesser, A., & Campbell, J. (1980). Self-definition: The impact of the relative performance and similarity of others. *Social Psychology Quarterly, 43,* 341-347.

Tesser, A., & Campbell, J. (1983). Self-definition and self-evaluation maintenance. In J. Suls & A. G. Greenwald (Eds.), *Psychological perspectives on the self* (Vol. 2). Hillsdale, NJ: Lawrence Erlbaum Associates.

Weinberg, W. A., Rutman, J., Sullivan, L., Penick, E. C., & Dietz, S. G. (1973). *Journal of Pediatrics, 83,* 1065-1072.

Wicklund, R. A. (1975). Objective self-awareness. In L. Berkowitz (Ed.), *Advances in experimental social psychology* (Vol. 8). New York: Academic Press.

Wylie, R. (1974). *The self-concept: A review of methodological considerations and measuring instruments* (Rev. ed. Vol. 1). Lincoln, NE: University of Nebraska Press.

Wylie, R. (1979). *The self-concept: Vol. 2. Theory and research on selected topics.* Lincoln, NE: University of Nebraska Press.

Zajonc, R. (1980). Feeling and thinking: Preferences need no inferences. American Psychologist, 35, 151-175.

7

How Adolescence Became the Struggle for Self: A Historical Transformation of Psychological Development

Roy F. Baumeister and Dianne M. Tice
Case Western Reserve University

The majority of our knowledge about adolescence is based on studies of modern American adolescents. To what extent is this knowledge universally applicable? The purpose of this chapter is to give an account of how the modern Western version of adolescence evolved historically. Historians disagree as to whether the late 19th century saw the "discovery of adolescence" (Gillis, 1974), the "invention of the adolescent," (Kett, 1977), or neither (Stone, 1977). In order to evaluate these arguments it is necessary, first, to step outside our own cultural history and consider adolescence from a cross-cultural perspective.

A CROSS-CULTURAL VIEW OF ADOLESCENCE

It is probably safe to say that very few generalizations apply to people of all different cultures. Those few may pertain mainly to such banal physical facts as the need for food, sleep, and oxygen. For present purposes, the important physical fact is puberty, that is, a characteristic set of bodily changes occurring between childhood and adulthood and signifying the body's readiness for sexual reproduction.

Cultures do vary in the timing of puberty (e.g., Fried & Fried, 1980). Thus, for example, whereas the age of menarche in today's America is under 13, in Norway in 1850 the average age was over 17 (Laslett, 1971). The differences (which some scholars dispute) may be due to variations in nutrition and body weight. Still, the variations appear to be mainly a matter of timing; the physical changes do occur at some point.

It seems reasonable to add that in most cases the physical changes of puberty have some impact on the person's emotional life. Bodily changes may alter the physical self-concept (Stevens-Long & Cobb, 1983). Whether the increase in self-consciousness that we associate with early adolescence (e.g., Simmons, Rosenberg, & Rosenberg, 1973; Tice, Buder, & Baumeister, in press) varies cross-culturally with age of puberty is an important question for further study. The sexual changes probably alter or increase sexual feelings, creating new motivations and altering relationship patterns (e.g., Sullivan, 1953). In particular, long-standing emotional attachments may be altered or broken by the pubescent sexuality (e.g., Blos, 1962; Cohen, 1964). The peculiar emotional patterns that attend puberty probably vary greatly across cultures, and even across individuals within a culture. We are suggesting only that puberty commonly affects emotional life, without arguing for any universality in the precise type of effect it has (see also Cohen, 1964).

Furthermore, in most cultures the individual undergoes some transition in identity between childhood and adulthood (LeVine & LeVine, 1966; Monroe & Monroe, 1955; see also Fried & Fried, 1980). This transition generally involves taking on the role (or one of the possible roles) of an adult member of that society (Brown, 1963; LeVine & LeVine, 1966; Monroe & Monroe, 1955). In most cultures, this transition in identity coincides — very approximately — with physical puberty (e.g., Cohen, 1964; Lincoln, 1981).

Initiation rites of adolescence have received a fair amount of study. Two common features of such rites stand out. First, the initiation involves teaching the adolescent the traditional knowledge and world-view of the society (e.g., Keesing, 1982; see, however, Bettelheim, 1954; Loeb, 1929). Although children inevitably absorb some part of that knowledge simply by living in the society, other features or elements of it are imparted specifically at the transition to adulthood. Second, the most common focus of initiation rites appears to be gender identity (e.g., Keesing, 1982; LeVine & LeVine, 1966; Lincoln, 1981; see also Poole, 1982). Many practices indicate a belief that adult maleness must be created ritualistically (e.g., Keesing, 1982; Poole, 1982). Interestingly, the ritual creation of manhood often appears to involve symbolic femininity, even to the point where some initiations involve explicit sexual behavior (e.g., Bettelheim, 1954; Keesing, 1982; Poole, 1982).

In most cases the transition from childhood to adulthood is brief (e.g., Cohen, 1964). The transition period lasts a few days or weeks (e.g., LeVine & LeVine, 1966). In a few cases the transitional status lasts more than a year, but even in those it is common for there to be a specific brief period within the longer period, in which the transition is enacted (Hopkins, 1983; see also Keesing, 1982). The modern American pattern — in which adolescence lasts for many years, is not epitomized by a single ritual event, and has poorly defined beginning and endpoints (cf. Elder, 1980) — is highly exceptional (e.g., Eichorn, 1975; Fried & Fried, 1980; Goodman, 1967; Hopkins, 1983).

SUMMARY

We have examined anthropological studies of adolescence in the effort to create a fundamental picture of adolescence that transcends our present historical and cultural context. Adolescence can be considered a time of transition in identity from child to adult. The timing coincides approximately with puberty, and adolescence may, therefore, be characterized by some emotional instabilities. Adolescence is commonly used as a time to initiate the young person into the traditions, knowledge, and world-view of the culture. Initiation into adult gender roles is a common theme, although adolescent initiations may address other issues too.

ADOLESCENCE: A VICTORIAN INNOVATION?

Various historians have argued that adolescence first appeared in our society during the late 1800s. Demos and Demos (1969) say adolescence "did not exist before the last two decades of the nineteenth century" and say adolescence was "on the whole an American discovery" (p. 632). Gillis (1974) speaks of the "discovery of adolescence" between 1870 and 1900. Clearly, these historians are not contending that puberty originated in Victorian America. Rather, their arguments must be understood to mean that adolescence was first recognized late in the 19th century as a concept of a certain stage of life, and as a problem. The emergence of this cultural conception grew out of a number of developments, rather than out of sudden and honest awareness of teenage behavior. For that reason, Kett (1977) explicitly prefers to describe the late Victorian development as an "invention of the adolescent," rather than as a discovery, for in his view the cultural conceptions were largely imposed by society on the actual teenagers.

There is some literary evidence in support of the view that adolescence became a new concept and problem at the end of the 19th century. Kiell's (1959) extensive review of adolescent characters in literature acknowledges that the problems of adolescence were not unknown to earlier writers (e.g., Goethe), but he insists that the novel of adolescence is mainly a phenomenon of the 20th century. Putz (1979) agrees with Kiell that it was around the turn of the century that literature began to emphasize the problems and struggles of adolescence.

In contrast, the eminent historian L. Stone (1977) says, "The idea that adolescence, as a distinctive age-group with its distinctive problems, was a development of the 19th century is entirely without historical foundation," and later he labels that idea "sheer historical fantasy" (p. 377). He quotes Shakespeare, one of whose characters bemoans the ages 16–23 as a time of "getting wenches with child, wronging the ancientry, stealing, fighting." Stone says that in the 16th and 17th centuries, Londoners experienced "constant anxiety" about the dangers resulting from the large number of unmarried apprentices. He gives evidence that such anxieties would have been well-founded, for the apprentices were a troublesome lot who periodically went so far as to riot.

We suggest the following resolution to that controversy about whether adolescence emerged late in the 19th century. Adolescence has, indeed, existed prior to the 1800s as a concept of a particular and problematic stage of life. Later in the 19th century, however, the problem of adolescence changed fundamentally, and a new concept of adolescence became more salient to society.

Our task for the remainder of this chapter is to explain the transformation of adolescence during the late 19th century. It was that transformation that resulted in the form of adolescence in modern Western society. Put another way, late in the Victorian era there occurred a fundamental change in the identity transition associated with puberty. Our explanation has two parts: First, we attempt to describe precisely what the change was. Second, we discuss its causes.

HOW ADOLESCENCE CHANGED

Thus far, we have argued that adolescence has long had some degree of recognition as a distinct and troublesome stage in life, but that adolescence changed fundamentally into its modern form during the Victorian era. We shall characterize the change in four ways: first, according to the prevailing cultural conceptions of adolescents; second, according to the social and economic status of adolescents; third, according to the task or occupation of the adolescent; and finally, according to the developmental process associated with adolescence.

Conception.   Kett (1977) provides a clear discussion of the change in American concepts about teenagers. Pre-Victorian American concepts of "young people" were fuzzy. In that agricultural society, knowledge of one's own precise age was often unreliable and was not very important, for farm tasks were assigned more on that basis of physical size and development than chronological age. For present purposes, Kett's most important observation is that in 1800, Americans did not think of youth as a period of personal indecision, awkwardness and uncertainty, or passive and helpless vulnerability. Rather, the general attitude was that puberty meant the young person was ready and able to do an adult's share (or almost) of work around the farm, shop, or house.

At the end of the 19th century, however, the new conception of adolescence characterized the young person as prone to conformity, anti-intellectual, and passive, (Kett, 1977, p. 243). In contrast to earlier practices, it was felt that adolescents needed extensive or even constant supervision by adults. This need was extended to leisure activities, resulting in Victorian innovations such as the Boy Scouts and the YMCA (see also Gillis, 1974). Kett adds that this passive, vulnerable, and awkward phase of life was considered normal and desirable. He says society came to believe that everyone should experience adolescence (see also Modell, Furstenberg, & Hershberg, 1976).

Socioeconomic Status.   Prior to 1800, the status of teenagers is best characterized as "semidependent" (Gillis, 1974; Kett, 1977). Although legally they had few autonomous rights, in daily life they were neither supported nor supervised by their parents. For centuries, the practice of fostering out was predominant: Around age 7 or 8, children were sent away by their parents to live in other households where they were, in a sense, unpaid employees (see also Aries, 1962; Stone, 1977). Traditionally, in Europe, the children were treated almost as part of the family by the foster household in which they were placed, but during the 18th century that arrangement deteriorated (Gillis, 1974). As industrialization began and fostering out declined, people tended instead to send their children away to work in factories. Then, as urbanization progressed urban families of the working classes increasingly tended to have their children living in the parental home while working in factories.

For children beyond the age of puberty, their traditional socioeconomic status had also been semidependent, although there were wide variations (of semidependency) according to birth order and social class. The young person was busy being trained or otherwise prepared for a specific adult role. The parents arranged the apprenticeship, military commission, or whatever situation for the young person; but, again, the young person's dependency did not extend far beyond arranging the situation. (An exception is the case of the oldest son, whose situation typically led to taking over the parental farm, estate, or shop.) Parents determined the career of the child, but once situated the young person was not substantially dependent on them.

Although the history of marriage is complex, it is fair to say that the picture resembles that of occupation. Parents arranged the marriage, sometimes taking the young person's preferences into account. Marriage normally marked the end of the semidependent period—but that entailed that marriage often had to be deferred until the man was independently established, such as when the parents died and bequeathed the estate. During the 19th century, the young person became the primary decision-maker in choice of spouse, although parents retained veto power.

Thus, the social and economic status of youth prior to the Victorian period was as follows: semidependent on parents; having some responsibilities; generally lacking power to choose spouse or vocation, but able to govern one's daily life to some extent; committed by parents to a particular (future) adult role; and supporting oneself economically by work, but without having much control or money.

In contrast, the new socioeconomic status of young people by the turn of the 20th century was as follows: The person lived with parents, except in the case of boarding school (including college), and, either way, was economically dependent on the parents. Other than schoolwork, a young person had few or no responsibilities (see Bronfenbrenner, 1974, for detailed analysis of the decline of giving responsibilities to young people). The adolescent had the eventual power of choosing one's own occupation and spouse, and, typically, there were multiple options. Commitments to adult roles were either provisional (easily revoked and altered), or lacking. Erikson (1950, 1968) coined the term *psychosocial moratorium* to describe this uncommitted, dependent, and isolated status of youth. These descriptions are still applicable to adolescence today.

The change in socioeconomic status is, thus, from semidependent to dependent; from committed to uncommitted; from responsible to irresponsible; from lacking options to having multiple options for adult identity.

Task.   In past centuries, the labor of children has been far too valuable for nonwealthy parents to permit the children to spend much time in school, except for irregular intervals or seasons when the farm required little work (Gillis, 1974). Industrialization did not change matters much, for children could earn money to contribute to meager family incomes. Gillis records how bitterly the working class opposed attempts to enforce compulsory education laws late in the 19th century. Gillis points out, however, that the labor of teenagers was not always so valuable. The small farms of poor families did not require so much labor, teenagers eat a lot, and besides there were always more younger children. Therefore, says Gillis, even when children were kept at home for the preteen years, the teenager's place was never in the parental home. The younger sons of the lower classes were apprenticed, sent away for work as laborers, or enlisted in the military. Daughters worked as domestic servants in the households of the well-to-do. The oldest son was also sent away for work, although he would eventually return; his younger brothers generally had to seek their own fortunes if the apprenticeships did not lead to lifelong careers. Among the upper classes, teenage children were sent away to schools, travels, and elsewhere. "Elsewhere" varied depending on circumstances: younger sons were again superfluous so parents steered them into military or clerical careers, and superfluous daughters became nuns.

The point of the preceding discussion is that teenagers of past centuries were generally occupied with preparations for fixed, particular adult roles that had been chosen for them. Their developmental task involved finishing the highly specific training for the allotted adult role, and otherwise just passing the time until the adult role would become available — such as by an offer of marriage, successful graduation from apprentice to master, or inheritance. If the person was dissatisfied with his or her lot, the developmental task required either learning to accept it or possibly discovering that one had a religious "calling" to devote one's life to God. (Kett, 1977, records that such religious awakenings were especially common among young men who were discontent with their occupational prospects.)

In contrast, the developmental task of the modern adolescent is to get a nonspecific liberal arts education that is presumed to be a prerequisite for all sorts of jobs, even housewifery. The precise adult role is often not marked out for the teenager. Although many teenagers can articulate specific occupational ambitions, these are simply preferences and are subject to revision or alteration. Indeed, the second developmental task of modern adolescence is to make choices regarding adult roles: to choose a specific job and begin working toward it, and to choose a spouse.

Developmental Process.   In part, the developmental task of adolescence (described in the previous section) determines the process. Still, the developmental process deserves some attention in its own right. By process, we mean the way personality and character evolve through adolescence.

In past centuries, the developmental process of the teen years was focused on religious and moral character development. Religious conversion experiences were associated with youth for centuries. Young Puritan males rebelled against their stifling, strict upbringing, but typically a powerful experience led one to regret these "sins of youth" and to become a committed Puritan adult (Greven, 1977). The early 19th century was the era of the mass revival meetings, at which many young people had powerful religious reawakenings (Kett, 1977).

As for moral development, it was around the 17th century that society developed a strong concern over instilling characterological virtue in the young (Aries, 1962; Stone, 1977). One of the pervasive fears about urbanization was that city life exposed gullible youth to corrupting influences. At the start of the 19th century, the concept of "decision of character" was the paradigm for adolescent development (Kett, 1977). Decision of character entailed personal exertion by the adolescent, especially the male adolescent, in order to become a virtuous adult.

The developmental process of the modern adolescent is concerned with personal values, just like that of the pre-Victorian adolescent, but the modern adolescent is permitted or required to choose and develop his or her own values. Identity crisis has replaced decision of character. Erickson (1968) has held that all modern adolescents undergo identity crises, although in many cases the crisis may be unconscious. Marcia (1966, 1967) operationalized identity crisis as a period of struggle to adopt a religious and political ideology and to choose an occupation. Subsequent research has indicated that many, but not all, adolescents undergo identity crises, and that such crises appear to be beneficial for the individual's adult personality (for review and discussion, see Baumeister, Shapiro, & Tice, 1985; Bernard, 1981; Bourne, 1978; Waterman, 1982).

CAUSES OF THE TRANSFORMATION OF ADOLESCENCE

The changes in the nature of adolescence were the result of a complex set of social trends and developments. Our discussion of these causes is organized around the following themes: change in locus of self-definition: changes in family relations; the social creation of the "moratorium" status of teenagers; and society's loss of ideological consensus.

Locus of Self-Definition.   Perhaps the most important factor in the creation of the modern form of adolescence was the shift in the locus and burden of self-definition. In previous eras, society had defined the adult identity for the individual. Rather abruptly, however, the adult identity was left mostly up to the adolescent to choose and define.

We focus on marriage and career. These define the adult's role in society, and the adolescent process of crystallizing adult identity may be regarded as complete once the person is married and has an (adult) job (Elder, 1980).

The choice of one's spouse had for centuries resided with one's parents, but the parental role declined through a series of stages (see Smith, 1973; Stone, 1977). By the early 19th century, the person was free to choose his or her own spouse, subject only to parental consultation and veto. By the end of the 19th century, even the parental veto power was in jeopardy. Thus, with regard to marriage, the adolescent had assumed the opportunity and burden of determining his or her own adult identity.

With regard to occupation, the picture is more complex than with marriage, but the outcome is the same. Traditionally, most people have been farmers, and there was little option of becoming anything else. As manufacturing and trade led to the rise of the middle class, a variety of jobs came to exist, but it was the parents who determined the child's future occupation, by arranging apprenticeships, placing the young person in a trade or profession, and so forth. Fass (1977) emphasizes that the family's vital connection to society has for centuries been, in part, a matter of placing the offspring in particular adult roles. It is only during the past century that this system has collapsed, in effect severing the family's relation to society at large. Beginning late in the Victorian era, the young person's occupation follows from his or her education. The industrial, urban society that grew up in the 19th century offers the individual a wide range of career options, and parental influence is at best an ancillary or occasional factor in securing the job.

Thus, with occupation, as with marriage, the actual adult identity came to be chosen by the adolescent, rather than determined by parental decision and influence in a context of limited opportunity. The modern system has one advantage over the traditional one in that the modern individual has much greater freedom and opportunity. On the other hand, the determination of adult identity requires the adolescent to make a series of difficult and complex choices, under highly uncertain conditions. One may doubt whether the inner resources of the average adolescent are capable of making effective choices of such great importance. It may be no coincidence that the field of vocational counseling expanded rapidly at the end of the 19th century (Kett, 1977), for adolescents may feel a need for expert advice to help face the difficult choice of occupation.

As the adolescent adopted the burden of determining his or her own adult identity, adolescence came to be a time of difficult, important, and far-reaching decisions. Until those decisions are made and implemented – at which point adolescence ends – the condition of the adolescent is one of being uncommitted, transitional, inchoate, and needing to find inside oneself (a.k.a. "finding oneself") criteria for making those decisions.

Family Relations.   The family has undergone major and fundamental changes in the past 2 centuries, and these have affected the lives of the offspring. Before discussing the specific changes in the treatment of young people, it is important to mention two basic changes regarding the family itself. First, the importance of family life for individual fulfillment escalated enormously throughout the 19th century. During the 18th century, "private" life of home and family was regarded as secondary to "public" life in the civilized society at large. By 1900, however, the value hierarchy had reversed, such that home and family life was considered of primary importance (see especially Sennett, 1974, for detailed description and analysis of this reversal).

Second, the function of the family changed in a fundamental way. We have already described how the family's connection to society at large deteriorated (Fass, 1977). This was part of a more general trend in which the family was converted from an economic unit into a network of primarily emotional relationships (Burgess & Locke, 1945). The traditional farming family was, in a sense, a small corporation whose main occupation was the production of goods, both for its own consumption and for sale or exchange. In contrast, few 20th century Western families are engaged in joint productive labor by all members; instead, the primary function of the family is as a locus for intimate relationships, ideally characterized by warmth, mutual support, nurturance, and affective exchanges.

Family historians of previous centuries typically emphasize the consequences of high child mortality (e.g., Aries, 1962; Gillis, 1974; Hunt, 1970; Stone, 1977). A newborn baby's chances of surviving to age 20 were probably no better than 50%, and it was not uncommon for a couple to lose all their children to disease. As a result, it was risky for parents to love any given child very much, because the risk of heartbreak was so great. It was not until the 18th or 19th centuries that parents dared form strong emotional bonds to each child.

The lasting decrease of child mortality rates, beginning around 1800, had another effect besides strengthening the affective bonds between parent and child, and this was the need for birth control. Simply put, it was no longer necessary for a couple to have as many babies as possible. At first, family planning was typically done by spacing the births at long intervals. By the end of the 19th century, however, family planning had arrived at the modern practice of having all the children within a few years of each other and then no more (Kett, 1977). As these children grew up, society encountered a novel circumstance: large numbers of families in which all the offspring were teenagers simultaneously. This undoubtedly contributed to the salience of adolescence and adolescent problems.

Even more important was the fact that adolescent children were now living with their parents. As the practices of fostering out and apprenticeship training disappeared, children remained in the parental home until marriage. Katz and Davey (1978) noted the common belief that industrialization weakened the family, but their (and other) data emphatically contradict that belief. Industrialization raised the average home-leaving age significantly (see also Modell et al., 1976).

We suggest three consequences of the shift toward having children remain in the parental home until they marry. First, again, the salience of adolescence and adolescent problems probably increased. To be sure, the adolescent penchants for mischief and masturbation may have been deplored by earlier periods, but these are more likely to worry parents than to worry an apprentice's master. (This may be especially true because of the increased emotional investment by 19th century parents in their children.) Fear of sexuality, including masturbation, reached remarkable peaks during the Victorian era, and the adolescent male was the focus and symbol of that threat (Smith-Rosenberg, 1978).

The second consequence of having children remain in the parental home concerns their emotional development. Blos (1962), building on Freud's work, characterizes adolescence as a revival of Oedipal conflicts. The teenager is physically ready for adult sexual behavior, but is emotionally still tied to the parents. If the psychodynamic hypothesis is correct, then the day-to-day emotional turmoil of adolescence would presumably be made more acute by constant exposure to the parents, in contrast to the historically earlier practices under which teenage children saw their parents only seldom. The third consequence is that the likelihood of intergenerational conflict would be increased by living together. There is one further trend that also may have contributed to increasing generational conflict. We have said that during the 19th century adolescents acquired the power of determining their own adult identities. A corollary is that the parents lost corresponding power (see also Smith, 1973). Once the young person stopped needing the parent to arrange a suitable marriage or career, the parent has lost the most potent means of forcing his or her will on the offspring. The parents' main weapons in the struggle are only emotional rejection and disinheritance. These may not be enough to subdue an angry adolescent, especially a male one who can easily become self-supporting. (Because of job discrimination, a female's opportunity to reject parental demands would not have been as large as a male's, perhaps until quite recently. Late in the 19th century, a female adolescent could probably defy her parents with reasonable impunity only if she were about to marry someone to support her.)

The combination of increased importance of family life, increased contact with children, and disruption of the traditional balance of power, thus, could quite plausibly increase conflict between parents and children. There is some historical evidence that such conflict (especially father–son) was particularly high late in the 19th century (e.g., Smith-Rosenberg, 1978; also see Anderson, 1971.)

Thus, changes in family relations toward the end of the 19th century probably increased the salience and the intensity of adolescent problems. For the adolescents themselves, emotional conflicts with parents may have increased, the emotional maturation associated with the sexual changes of puberty may have become more difficult, and the emotional demands on them may have increased. For the parents, concern over their young may have intensified, conflict with adolescents may have increased, their power to resolve disputes by authoritarian fiat was undermined, and teenage misbehavior may have become more salient and threatening.

Creation of Moratorium.   The "psychosocial moratorium," by which Erickson (1950, 1968) has characterized modern adolescence, has two essential features: transitional status and lack of commitment. A third feature, nonessential but still very important, is the condition of being physically and meaningfully isolated from society's mainstream.

Transitional status is associated with adolescence in most cultures, as we have said. The transitional status lasts longer in modern Western societies than in most others, but this has been the pattern for centuries.

The uncommitted status of adolescents, however, became a common feature of adolescence during the 19th century. The separation of adolescents from the rest of society also occurred then, and it is a feature that is quite rare (except for brief ritual isolations) in Western history and in other cultures. Both of these developments were shaped by the new educational practices of the 19th century, and we turn now to examine these.

The extreme degree of age segregation that defines the daily lives of modern Western adolescents is almost unknown in other cultures (e.g., Fried & Fried, 1980). Today's teenagers typically spend most of the day in the exclusive company of people born in the same year as they themselves, although they are often under adult supervision. This age segregation is not without its critics. Bronfenbrenner (1974) has argued forcefully that isolating schools and teenagers from the rest of society contributes to alienation among the young. In the cynical view of Larkin (1979), compulsory education is simply a means of "warehousing" teenagers to keep them out of the labor force, lest they compete for adult jobs and depress wage structures. Other, more benign motives for requiring education could be cited. These include the desire to help lower class children find opportunities to improve their lot and the desire to combat the exploitation of child labor in factories.

Regardless of what the motives were, it is hard to deny that compulsory schooling for teenagers, graded by age, defines the daily lives and environments of today's teenagers. Some historians go so far as to say that the educational practices were the main cause of the Victorian invention or discovery of adolescence (e.g., Gillis, 1974, p. 105).

Age segregation has two sides. In addition to isolating the adolescent from most of society, it increases the importance of the other teenagers. The peer group becomes the most important and interesting feature of adolescent social life, or, indeed, of adolescent life altogether. Kett (1977) notes that youth groups had existed prior to the 1880s, but any given group might include ages from preteen to 35. In contrast, 20th century peer groups are much more homogeneous by age. The escalating importance and homogeneity of adolescent peer groups may explain several features of 20th century adolescence, including conformity, susceptibility to fads, and preoccupation with intergroup competition (Fass, 1977).

Age segregation is not the only consequence of the spread of compulsory, universal schooling. It helped bring about the uncommitted status of youth. Because the same liberal education was the prerequisite for a large number (and variety) of jobs, the job did not have to be chosen in advance—in sharp contrast to the apprenticeship system. Victorian society believed that liberal education would generally improve the career prospects for boys and the marriage prospects for girls. Thus, the choice of adult identity could be postponed until nearly the end of schooling.

A corollary of the preceding point is that the stress on liberal, nonspecific education actually did expand the adolescent's career (and perhaps marriage) options, so the choice of adult identity was made more difficult. At age 19, today's typical college sophomore has an educational background that is — so far, at least — suitable for dozens (perhaps hundreds) of occupations. In contrast, the 19-year-old mechanic's apprentice of 1720 was not prepared for much at all, except being a mechanic.[1]

Loss of Ideological Consensus.   By the Victorian era, people were aware that society as a whole no longer believed in the Christian creed (e.g., Howe, 1976) and they feared that the loss of the Christian foundation threatened the moral system too (Meyer, 1976).

The effects of fundamental, ideological uncertainty on the emotional life of adolescents should not be ignored. We have suggested, on the basis of cross-cultural evidence, that the acceptance of society's traditional values and knowledge is a general feature of the adolescent transition. When a society abandons or even questions these basic beliefs and values, then that important feature of adolescence becomes highly problematic. Moreover, the lack of firm, ultimate beliefs and values changes the nature of adolescent misbehavior from merely troublesome or rebellious mischief to either alienation, the search for firm foundations for choice and action, or identity crisis.

The religious conversion experiences of pre-Victorian youth were, perhaps, the immediate predecessor of the adolescent identity crisis. Often they followed a period of youthful indulgence, rebellion, or misbehavior (cf. Greven, 1977). After the conversion experience, the young person returned to being a model person or citizen, living within the values and standards of the community. Of course, for some people, several such religious conversion experiences were necessary! (cf. Kett, 1977, p. 82).

Following Blos (1962), we may analyze such events in this way. The onset of puberty gives rise to desires and feelings that are stronger than the young person has had, and he or she finds it difficult to manage them. A period of indulgence and misbehavior follows, ending when the person finds mature and socially acceptable patterns for those energies (see also Sullivan, 1953, on intrapsychic "collisions" of adolescent needs). At this point, the adolescent is likely to have guilt over the recent period of misbehavior. A religious context, however can enable the adolescent to interpret his or her own personal experience in terms of religious symbols, such as the struggle against temptation

---

[1]The 19th century apparently was a transitional period during which there was a wide variety of jobs but few entry requirements. Thus, whereas today becoming a physician takes years of study, passage of difficult examinations, and state licensing, in the 19th century one could decide to become a physician and start seeing patients almost overnight, in extreme cases.

and toward redemption. The religious framework also provides a clear model of how to resolve the period of adolescent turmoil, by furnishing a model of the proper Christian life. For these adolescents, then, this period was one of sins of youth, but not identity crisis. Fundamental values and beliefs were available to shape the adolescent crisis, interpret it, and show how to resolve it.

Without a firm religious faith, the 20th century adolescent has a much more difficult time than his predecessor. In order to resolve the emotional turmoil of adolescence, the individual must actively choose his fundamental beliefs and values, because society as a whole does not hold to one single set. Perhaps, for that reason, the modern adolescent is prey to eccentric religious cults and political activist groups, who offer firm consensual interpretatons of life. Even if today's adolescent ends up with a personal affirmation of Christianity, it is the result of a difficult search and choice, not the natural or inevitable outcome.

CONCLUSION: WHY THE STRUGGLE FOR SELF?

Our purpose has been to explain why adolescence in modern Western society has become a phase of soul-searching, identity crisis, and struggle for self. This pattern appears to have evolved late in the 19th century. Our answers may be summarized and integrated as follows

Adolescence is innately a time of transition of self, as can be inferred by comparing different cultures and different historical periods. The transition of self has two parts, the bodily maturation and the change in social identity. The bodily changes have certain direct effects, including effects on the emotional life of the person. However, it is the transition of social identity that varies most across cultures, and the modern adolescent's struggle for self must be explained primarily in terms of how society and culture shape that transition. In other cultures, the transition in social identity from child to adult is carried off without anything like the difficulties of identity crisis (e.g., Fried & Fried, 1980; Goodman, 1967; Mead, 1928/1950).

Several social developments of the late 19th century transformed adolescence into a period of struggle for self. The most important of these were the developments that placed the burden of self-definition onto the young person himself or herself. Previously (and in other cultures too), the adult identity had been mostly determined by the social environment, and the young person simply had to accept or earn it. Instead, the modern Western adolescent must choose and construct the adult identity out of a myriad of options. Requiring the self to create itself is a large and somewhat paradoxical demand, and it alone may be sufficient to explain why adolescence became a time of identity crisis. Nonetheless, there were other factors too.

General, liberal education was one major development that helped transfer the burden of self-definition onto the adolescent, for its nonspecificity and universality entailed that the teenager had a full spectrum of career options available to choose from after high school. (In contrast, the previous system trained the apprentice for one specific occupation.) An important side effect of the Victorian educational practices was the creation of moratorium status for the teenager. The adolescent moratorium is a protracted, uncommitted condition that isolates young people from the rest of society. In consequence, the adolescent peer group takes on power and influence as the defining feature of the daily lives of adolescents. Membership in the peer group, then, serves as a transitional identity that may last for years (cf. Demos & Demos, 1969). This may, in turn, further prolong adolescence, if the adolescent prefers the transitional identity and the peer group activities over the struggle to make the hard choices necessary to create adult identity.

Social identities do not exist in atomistic isolation, but rather draw meaning and substance from a larger cultural context. Initiation into a mature, reasonably complete understanding of this context is a common feature of adolescence in various cultures (e.g., Cohen, 1964). Consequently, Western society's loss of ideological consensus regarding fundamental religious, moral, and political truths (a loss that became acutely and widely felt during the 19th century) made the adolescent construction of adult identity immeasurably harder. In an important sense, while society was offering adolescents an increasing range of choices for identity, it was simultaneously depriving them of unequivocal bases for interpreting and making those decisions. As a result, the adolescent's task is not merely to define an identity within a given context, but, to some extent, to choose and create the context as well.

Finally, a series of changes in family life have increased the salience and vividness of adolescent problems and have probably intensified the problems. Drastic increases in the frequency of contact between adolescents and their parents have likely increased the emotional turmoil of adolescence. This turmoil, while not necessarily a part of the struggle for self, undoubtedly gets mixed up in it as it pervades the ongoing experience of adolescence. Economic dependency increased parents' immediate power over their adolescent offspring, but other changes reduced the parents' power to determine the adult identity of their young. These contrasting developments of parental power further accentuated the gulf between the daily condition of the adolescent and the adult self that the adolescent's task is to create.

Some Implications

In closing, we have some observations about the relevance of historical perspectives (such as this chapter) for current research on psychological development.

A first and obvious point is that one must be extremely cautious in generalizing across cultural and historical boundaries from research findings about adolescence. Modern adolescence may have a higher level of historical relativity than most other developmental phenomena under study. One of the major contributions of Erikson's work was that cultural factors affect human development, and it is probably no mere coincidence that he specialized in the study of adolescence. It is important to keep the implication in mind that cultural change is likely to entail alteration in adolescent development patterns.

We discussed a particular transformation of adolescence late in the 19th century. It must be acknowledged that adolescence has continued to change and evolve during the 20th century (e.g., Elder, 1980; Kett, 1977). Although the basic pattern established late in the 19th century is still applicable, there have been numerous fluctuations and refinements. Entry into the adolescent moratorium has moved to younger ages (Kett, 1977). Indeed, it is now possible to distinguish effectively between early and late adolescent stages. Late adolescence, which culminates in the transition to adulthood, has changed in several contradictory ways during this century. Age of final departure from school has gone up, but age of marriage and of establishing an independent household has gone down (Modell et al., 1976). Additionally, the late adolescent issues of sex roles and gender relations have altered substantially in recent decades. Whitbourne and Waterman (1979), in a methodologically commendable attempt to distinguish between patterns that reflect ontogenetic processes and patterns that reflect social change, emphasize the importance of the latter in recent evidence about female adolescent development. Our general point is this: Not only is adolescence historically and culturally relative, it may be changing from decade to decade in our society in at least some important respects. This could be regarded as discouraging, for the conclusions a researcher draws early in one's career may be obsolete or inapplicable by the end of one's career. On the other hand, the changing nature of adolescence itself potentially provides a rare and valuable opportunity to study the effects of social change on individual development. Longitudinal studies with cohort comparisons of adolescents would avoid numerous difficulties that plague cross-cultural methods of studying how culture affects personality and development, such as the problem of translating a measure into foreign languages and, thereby, altering its psychometric properties.

It seems worth adding that the issue of cross-cultural generalizability extends beyond developmental studies. In particular, much research in personality and social psychology, including most of our own, uses late adolescents (college students) as experimental subjects. Conclusions based on such studies may, again, be prone to historical relativity, because of the historical relativity of adolescence itself. It is, therefore, helpful to take into account the current status and patterns of adolescence in considering research findings.

For example, adolescence is currently a time of moratorium and identity choice that entails some variation and exploration in the adolescent's behavior patterns, as we have discussed. Modern adolescents therefore may be unusually low in their stability of behavior patterns. Studies of cross-situational consistency in personality (see West, 1982, for overview of recent controversy), if they are based on late adolescent subjects, may persistently underestimate the degree to which personality is stable and consistent among humanity in general.

A last point is that the psychological study of adolescence is, itself, a historical development. The transformation of adolescence we have described coincided with G. Stanley Hall's massive seminal treatise on adolescence, and adolescence has been a topic of study ever since. Thus, part of the transformation of adolescence involved creating a conception of adolescence as a phenomenon deserving and requiring scientific study. Undoubtedly, the psychological study of adolescence has been shaped by cultural norms and expectations as to what a teenager ought to be like and to be doing, for such norms and expectations affect researchers' preconceptions. We hope that awareness of such preconceptions can be stimulated by studies such as ours, leading ultimately to improved scientific clarity.

This chapter began with our attempt to separate adolescence, per se, from its current historical and cultural form. We end with the comment that this distinction is, itself, in need of further empirical evidence. Our depiction of modern adolescence suggests several directions for such study. For example, one could compare typical modern American adolescents with other adolescents who have few or no self-defining choices to make, or with those who live in an environment permeated with firm ideological consensus, or with those who are radically separated from their parents for the entire adolescent phase. We hasten to add that both similarities and differences between such groups are of interest. Ultimately, it is desirable to know what features of adolescence are culturally durable and universal, as well as to know what ones are relative and mutable.

ACKNOWLEDGMENTS

We thank M. Stern, B. Levy, and J. Korbin for their suggestions. Parts of this work are based on a forthcoming book *Identity* by R. Baumeister, to be published by Oxford University Press, 1986.

REFERENCES

Anderson, Q. (1971). *The imperial self.* New York: Knopf.
Aries, P. (1962). *Centuries of childhood: A social history of family life* (R. Baldick, Trans.). New York: Random House.

Baumeister, R. F., Shapiro, J., & Tice, D. M. (1985). Two kinds of identity crisis. *Journal of Personality, 53.*

Bernard, H. S. (1981). Identity formation during late adolescence: A review of some empirical findings. *Adolescence, 16,* 349–357.

Bettelheim, B. (1954). *Symbolic wounds: Puberty rites and the envious male.* Glencoe, IL: The Free Press.

Blos, P. (1962). *On adolescence.* New York: The Free Press.

Bourne, E. (1978). The state of research on ego identity: A review and appraisal (Pt.2). *Journal of Youth and Adolescence, 1,* 371–392.

Bronfenbrenner, U. (1974). The origins of alienation. *Scientific American, 231*(2), 53–61.

Brown, J. K. (1963). A cross-cultural study of female initiation rites. *American Anthropologist, 65,* 837–853.

Burgess, E. W., & Locke, H. J. (1945). *The family: From institution to companionship.* New York: American Book.

Cohen, Y. A. (1964). *The transition from childhood to adolescence.* Chicago, IL: Aldine University Press.

Demos, J., & Demos, V. (1969). Adolescence in historical perspective. *Journal of Marriage and the Family, 31,* 632–638.

Eichorn, D. H. (1975). Asynchronizations in adolescent development. In S. E. Dragastin & G. H. Elder (Eds.), *Adolescence in the life cycle.* New York: Wiley.

Elder, G. H. (1980). Adolescence in historical perspective. In J. Adelson (Ed.), *Handbook of adolescent psychology.* New York: Wiley.

Erickson, E. H. (1950). *Childhood and society.* New York: Norton.

Erickson, E. H. (1968). *Identity: Youth and crisis.* New York: Norton.

Fass, P. (1977). *The damned and the beautiful: American youth in the 1920's.* New York: Oxford University Press.

Fried, M. N., & Fried, M. H. (1980). *Transitions: Four rituals in eight cultures.* New York: Norton.

Gillis, J. R. (1974). *Youth and history: Tradition and change in European age relations, 1770–present.* New York: Academic Press.

Goodman, M. E. (1967). *The individual and culture.* Homewood, IL: Dorsey Press.

Greven, P. (1977). *The Protestant temperament.* New York: Knopf.

Hopkins, J. R. (1983). *Adolescence.* New York: Academic Press.

Howe, D. W. (1976). Victorian culture in America. In D. Howe (Ed.), *Victorian America.* University of Pennsylvania Press.

Hunt, D. (1970). *Parents and children in history.* New York: Harper & Row.

Katz, M. B., & Davey, I. E. (1978). Youth and early industrialization in a Canadian city. In J. Demos & S. S. Boocock (Eds.), *Turning points: Historical and sociological essays on the family.* Chicago, IL: University of Chicago Press.

Keesing, R. M. (1982). Introduction: Toward a multidimensional understanding of male initiation. In G. H. Herdt (Ed.), *Rituals of manhood: Male initiation in Papua, New Guinea* (pp. 1–43). Berkeley, CA: University of California Press.

Kett, J. F. (1977). *Rites of passage: Adolescence in America 1790 to the present.* New York: Basic Books.

Kiell, N. (1959). *The adolescent through fiction: A psychological approach.* New York: International Universities Press.

Larkin, R. W. (1979). *Suburban youth in cultural crisis.* New York: Oxford University Press.

Laslett, P. (1971). Age of menarche in Europe since the 18th century. *Journal of Interdisciplinary History, 2,* 221–236.

LeVine, R. A., & LeVine, B. B. (1966). *Nyansongo: A Gusii community in Kenyo.* New York: Wiley.

Lincoln, B. (1981). *Emerging from the chrysalis: Studies in women's initiation*. Cambridge, MA: Harvard University Press.

Loeb, E. M. (1929). Tribal initiations and secret societies. *University of California Publications in American Archeology and Ethnologies XXV*, 249–250.

Marcia, J. E. (1966). Development and validation of ego-identity status. *Journal of Personality and Social Psychology, 3*, 551–558.

Marcia, J. E. (1967). Ego identity status: Relationship to change in self-esteem, "general maladjustment" and authoritarianism. *Journal of Personality, 38*, 118–133.

Mead, M. (1928/1950). *Coming of age in Samoa*. New York: New American Library.

Meyer, D. H. (1976). American intellectuals and the Victorian crisis of faith. In D. Howe (Ed.), *Victorian America* (pp. 59–80). University of Pennsylvania Press.

Modell, J., Furstenberg, F. F., & Hershberg, T. (1976). Social change and the transition to adulthood in historical perspective. *Journal of Family History, 1*, 7–32.

Monroe, R. L., & Monroe, R. H. (1955). *Cross-cultural human development*. Monterey, CA: Brooks/Cole.

Poole, F. J. P. (1982). The ritual forging of identity: Aspects of person and self in Bimin-Kuslusmin male initiation. In G. H. Herdt (Ed.), *Rituals of manhood: Male initiation in Papua, New Guinea* (pp. 99–154). Berkeley, CA: University of California Press.

Putz, M. (1979). *The story of identity: American fiction of the sixties*. Stuttgart, W. Germany: Metzler.

Simmons, R., Rosenberg, F., & Rosenberg, M. (1973). Disturbances in the self-image at adolescence. *American Sociological Review, 38*, 553–568.

Smith, D. S. (1973). Parental power and marriage patterns: An analysis of historical trends in Hingham, Massachusetts. *Journal of Marriage and the Family, 35*, 419–428.

Smith-Rosenberg, L. (1978). Sex as symbol in Victorian purity: An ethnohistorical analysis of Jacksonian America. In J. Demos & S. S. Boocock (Eds.), *Turning points*. Chicago, IL: University of Chicago Press.

Stevens-Long, J., & Cobb, N. J. (1983). *Adolescence and early adulthood*. Palo Alto, CA: Mayfield Publishing.

Stone, L. (1977). *The family, sex and marriage in England 1500–1800*. New York: Harper & Row.

Sullivan, H. S. (1953). *The interpersonal theory of psychiatry*. New York: Norton.

Tice, D. M., Buder, J., & Baumeister, R. F. (in press). Development of self-consciousness: At what age does audience pressure disrupt performance? *Adolescence*.

Waterman, A. S. (1982). Identity development from adolescence to adulthood: An extension of theory and review of research. *Developmental Psychology, 18*, 341–358.

West, S. (Ed.) (1982). Personality and prediction: Nomothetic and idiographic approaches [Special issue]. *Journal of Personality, 51*.

Whitbourne, S., & Waterman, A. (1979). Psychosocial development during the adult years: Age and cohort comparisons. *Developmental Psychology, 15*, 373–378.

Author Index

Italics denote pages with bibliographic information.

Subject Index

DATE DUE

OCT 1 9 1989			
NOV 1 5 1989			
OCT 0 8 1990			
NOV 0 5 1990			
2-23-91			
APR 0 3 1991			
4-1-94			
APR 1 7 1997			
GAYLORD			PRINTED IN U.S.A.